THE BOC
REVELA
and the Work
of the Priest

Eighteen lectures, conversations
and question-and-answer sessions
in Dornach from 5 to 22 September 1924,
reconstructed from notes taken by the
participants

RUDOLF STEINER

Translated by J. Collis

RUDOLF STEINER PRESS
LONDON

Rudolf Steiner Press
51 Queen Caroline Street
London W6 9QL

First published 1998

Originally published in German under the title *Vorträge und Kurse über christlich-religiöses Wirken, V. Apokalypse und Priesterwirken*, volume 346 in the Rudolf Steiner *Gesamtausgabe* or collected works, by Rudolf Steiner Verlag, Dornach, Switzerland. This authorized translation published by kind permission of the Rudolf Steiner Nachlassverwaltung, Dornach

A catalogue record for this book is available from the British Library

ISBN 1 85584 052 9

Cover by Trisha Connolly, incorporating artwork by Anne Stockton
Typeset by DP Photosetting, Aylesbury, Bucks
Printed and bound in Great Britain by Cromwell Press Limited, Trowbridge, Wiltshire

CONTENTS

Publisher's Foreword   1
Introduction *by René Querido*   5
Greeting *by Johannes Werner Klein*   9

LECTURE ONE, Dornach, 5 September 1924   11
The Act of Consecration of Man and the Book of
Revelation. Meaning of the word 'apocalypse'. The four
ages of the Mysteries and of the Transubstantiation. The
Cabeiri in the third age.

LECTURE TWO, Dornach, 6 September 1924   22
Changes in experiencing the Transubstantiation in the
different Mystery ages.

LECTURE THREE, Dornach, 7 September 1924   37
Future experiences of the Transubstantiation will be in
the 'I'-organization. The validity of anthroposophical
truths. Alpha and Omega. Earlier and future conditions
of consciousness. First words of the Book of Revelation.

LECTURE FOUR, Dornach, 8 September 1924   52
The letters to the Angels of the congregations at Ephesus
and Sardis. Understanding the numbers in the Book of
Revelation: twelve, seven, twenty-four.

LECTURE FIVE, Dornach, 9 September 1924   67
During the fifth post-Atlantean age human beings will
increasingly develop an awareness of death as a
companion. To read the Book of Revelation one must
apply one's will.

LECTURE SIX, Dornach, 10 September 1924   82
Number secrets in the Book of Revelation. Humanity
formerly encompassed by the cosmic number secrets; in
today's stage of the earth's evolution humanity is
extricating itself from the laws of number.

LECTURE SEVEN, Dornach, 11 September 1924   95
The year 333. The apocalyptist's prophetic vision of a
possible departure from the Christ Principle and return to
the Father Principle. Mohammedan teachings. 666—the
number of the Beast. Transubstantiation and karma.

LECTURE EIGHT, Dornach, 12 September 1924   109
Christ's connection with the sun. The Genius and the
Demon of the Sun. Sorat and the number 666. The
necessity to strive for spirituality. Michael mystery, Christ
mystery, Sorat mystery.

LECTURE NINE, Dornach, 13 September 1924   122
The Book of Revelation as a prophetic picture showing
the development of Christianity after the Mystery of
Golgotha. The essential difference between Christianity
and other religious creeds. Building the Old and the New
Jerusalem.

LECTURE TEN, Dornach, 14 September 1924   136
Various pictures from the nineteenth chapter of the Book
of Revelation. The work of the priest today.

LECTURE ELEVEN, Dornach, 15 September 1924   149
The three stages in the fall of the powers opposing the
Christ-Impulse: the fall of Babylon, the fall of the Beast
and the False Prophet, the fall of the divine adversaries
(Satan).

LECTURE TWELVE, Dornach, 16 September 1924   163
Transition from the fourth to the fifth post-Atlantean age.
Coming age in which human beings will have conscious
visions. The woman clothed with the sun.

LECTURE THIRTEEN, Dornach,
17 September 1924   176
The principle of numbers. The age of the trumpets.
Human beings with no 'I'. The evolution of races and
development of individuals.

PARTICIPANTS' QUESTIONS, 18 September 1924   190

LECTURE FOURTEEN, Dornach,
18 September 1924   193
Threefold human being and threefold humanity: cloud
people, rainbow people and people with fiery feet.
Humanity split into races and nations. Examples: Russia
(Bolshevism), Czechs and Slovaks.

LECTURE FIFTEEN, Dornach, 19 September 1924   205
Events in nature and history. The sea of glass. Love and
light. Pouring out of the phials of wrath. Answers to
participants' questions.

PRELIMINARY TALK, 20 September 1924   218

LECTURE SIXTEEN, Dornach, 20 September 1924   224
The unity of starry world and earthly world. Fixed stars,
planets, comets. The seven-headed and the two-horned
beast. The nature of comets; Biela's comet.

LECTURE SEVENTEEN, Dornach,
21 September 1924   234
   The Book of Revelation as a book of initiation. The
   letters, seals, trumpets, divine love and divine wrath in
   their relation to physical world, soul world and spiritland.
   Perceiving the hierarchies and how they work. Religion
   and knowledge.

LECTURE EIGHTEEN, Dornach,
22 September 1924   247
   The development of the consciousness soul.
   Intellectuality and Satan. The danger of forming new
   group souls: Gog and Magog. Impulses from the Book of
   Revelation in the work of the priest.

Appendix, 'To the Members' *by Rudolf Steiner*   260

A Note From the Editors of the German Edition   264

Notes   268

Index of Names   281

Colour Plates   *between pages*   154 and 155

PUBLISHER'S FOREWORD

These lectures on the biblical Book of Revelation comprise the fifth and last course given by Rudolf Steiner for priests, or those moving towards the priesthood, in the 'movement for religious renewal'—The Christian Community. They were attended by 57 priests and also members of the Executive of the Anthroposophical Society. In an article in the Newsletter for members of the Anthroposophical Society (see Appendix), Rudolf Steiner confirmed that attendance at the lectures was 'strictly limited', and that he could not report on 'what by its very nature can only be intended for the circle of priests'.

Although no official stenographer was present at the lectures, notes taken by a number of participants were gathered together at the end of the course and given to a group of them who had the responsibility of compiling a single copy. The texts created in this way were immediately duplicated. It is not known what became of the original notes.

Since 1924, this text (in a somewhat revised form) has been in private circulation among the priests of The Christian Community. For many years the Rudolf Steiner *Nachlass-verwaltung*, the literary estate of Rudolf Steiner—a fully independent organization which holds the literary copyright to his work—has not ventured to publish its copy of the notes, respecting Steiner's original intention that they were intended only for the circle of priests. In 1995, however, the decision was taken—without the support of The Christian Community—to publish a version of the texts. This publication appeared through the estate's publishing arm, Rudolf Steiner Verlag, as volume 346 in Rudolf Steiner's collected works in the original German.

Since the publication of volume 346, *Apokalypse und Priesterwirken*, Vol. 5 in the series *Vorträge und Kurse über christlich-religiöses Wirken*, the contents of this course have been in the public domain. Unauthorized English translations appeared almost immediately, often of very poor quality, and have been in wide circulation. The book is quoted freely in German, and extensive quotations have also appeared in English publications. In this context, Rudolf Steiner Press decided that it would be sensible to publish an official, authorized translation. This, we felt, would be the only practical response to the given situation.

It should be noted, however, that despite the excellent editorial work on the part of the Swiss publishers, the text is still something of a compromise, and cannot necessarily be regarded as an authentic record of the lectures. (Readers are directed to the full report by the editors of the original German edition on p.264.)

*

During September 1925—the last month of his lecturing work—Rudolf Steiner was giving four to six lectures daily, with several courses running concurrently. The course of lectures on drama was the central event at Dornach at the time. It had been intended for actors and speech artists, but so many people wished to attend that the restriction had to be waived, and the lectures were heard by an audience of over 700. From 8 to 18 September Steiner lectured to physicians and priests on pastoral medicine, and to members of the Anthroposophical Society on the karmic relationships between individuals. The sessions for members of the First Class of the School of Spiritual Science—an esoteric school within the Society, open to members who feel a full commitment to the spiritual stream of Anthroposophy—continued, and Steiner also spoke separately to the workers at the Goetheanum.

Marie Steiner later wrote of this period—September 1924—as 'a final glorious blaze of his spirit ... An unimaginable abundance of spiritual gifts was lavished upon us. It was like a confluence, a concentration of all he had done over four decades to bring an awakening to humanity: a ripe fruit and a concentrated seed force for the future that will provide spiritual fruition for ages yet to come.'

The present lectures began in the lecture room of the carpentry workshop next to the remains of the first Goetheanum (burnt down by suspected arson on New Year's Eve 1922) in Dornach, Switzerland. They continued in Haus Brodbeck, now Rudolf-Steiner-Halde, and were finally moved to a larger room in the building office housed near the carpentry shop in a wooden building that no longer exists.

*

The Christian Community was established in 1922 through the 'mediation' of Rudolf Steiner.[1] Although Steiner cooperated fully with its founding (undertaken principally by the respected Lutheran preacher Friedrich Rittelmeyer)[2] and, significantly, conveyed 'the cultus and the teachings on which the cultus is based', nevertheless he was emphatic that the movement was 'entirely independent' of the Anthroposophical Society. In his anthroposophical work Rudolf Steiner sought to found a modern science of the spirit. The Christian Community, on the other hand, has the task of 'religious renewal'.[3] However, Anthroposophy could fully support this movement, 'even though the anthroposophical movement had to regard its own task as lying in the cultivation of spiritual life from other angles'.

*

A note on the translation:
In The Christian Community, the communion service is known as 'the Act of Consecration of Man', in German *die*

Menschenweihehandlung. In the lectures contained in the present volume, Rudolf Steiner used this term both when speaking about the service of The Christian Community and when describing religious rites throughout the ages that involved the mystery of the Transubstantiation. For the purposes of this translation the term is used with upper case initials to denote the service of The Christian Community and with lower case initials when the lecturer was obviously speaking about past ages. He occasionally used the term *Weihehandlung*, which has been rendered 'act of consecration'.

The hierarchy of The Christian Community consists of an *Erzoberlenker*, two *Oberlenkers*, and four *Lenkers*. Together they constitute the Circle of Seven. There are also additional *Lenkers* with responsibility for particular countries or regions of a country. Priests in individual communities are responsible to their appointed *Lenker*. Although comparisons could be drawn with the positions of archbishop, bishop etc., the fact remains that The Christian Community is a unique church and the above terms are not adequately translatable into English.

A note on the illustrations:
The original blackboard illustrations are extant as they were drawn on black paper pinned to the board. All of them are reproduced in this volume either in the section of colour plates or as separate (black and white) illustrations within the text.

SG, London, July 1998

INTRODUCTION[1]

It is interesting to note that Rudolf Steiner spoke repeatedly about the Apocalypse, the Book of Revelation, over a period of more than twenty-one years, stretching from 1904 to 1924, including four major cycles of lectures on this topic in 1904, 1907, 1908 and 1909.[2]

The course of lectures he gave to the priests of The Christian Community in September 1924 contains some remarkable revelations, quite apart from what was specifically addressed to the priesthood. It should also be noted that the eighteen lectures came to an end on 22 September, just a week before Steiner had to relinquish speaking to audiences, and was forced to take to his sick bed for the six months until he died in March 1925. This very fact gives what he revealed and prophesied out of the Book of Revelation a very special meaning.

It may be helpful to consider briefly the life of John the Evangelist, the author of the Book of Revelation. Who was this remarkable individuality? In the lecture course *The Gospel of St John and its Relation to the Other Gospels*, Steiner stated that Lazarus, who was brought back to life by the Christ (see John 11), was none other than John, the Disciple whom the Lord loved.[3] He was present with the Apostles at the Last Supper and was the author of the John Gospel, the three epistles of John, and the Book of Revelation.

Before his initiation Lazarus was a rich man, brother of Mary and Martha, who owned considerable tracts of land in Galilee. They also had a house in Bethany that Christ Jesus visited on a number of occasions, and where he stayed at night during Holy Week.

John-Lazarus can be considered not only as the most intimate disciple of Christ Jesus, but also as one of the greatest Christian initiates. While all the disciples fled before the Crucifixion, John-Lazarus, together with Mary the Mother of Jesus, Mary the wife of Cleophas and Mary Magdalene, stood beneath the Cross. We recall that some of the last words spoken from the Cross were addressed to Mary the Mother and to John: 'When Jesus therefore saw his mother, and the disciple whom he loved standing by he saith unto his mother, "Woman behold thy son!" Then saith he to the disciple, "Behold thy mother!" And from that hour that disciple took her unto his own home.' (John 19, 26–27) This relationship is deeply significant for it existed not through the kinship of blood but through the living word of Christ. It is something that points to the future.

Legend tells us that after the Resurrection John-Lazarus travelled for some time before returning to the Holy Land. Then, together with Mary the Mother, he settled in Ephesus, one of the principle Mystery Centres of the ancient world, dedicated to the Goddess Artemis (Diana), the place of the living Word.

It would appear that Mary the Mother dwelt in a small house at the top of the mountain overlooking the Mystery Centre, while John lived close to the sea below.

Titus Flavius Domitianus (AD 51–96) succeeded his brother as Roman emperor in AD 81. Initially, his reign appears to have been benevolent, but later he was given to ordering the most atrocious cruelties, especially against the Christians. John-Lazarus, already in his eighties, was dragged in chains to Rome and subjected to a terrible series of tortures. Legend tells us how he survived these ordeals in a most amazing way. Not having been able to kill him, the emperor ordered John-Lazarus to be exiled to Patmos, a small mountainous island of great beauty close to the Turkish coast and not far from Ephesus. It was there, in a cave half-way up the mountain, that John resided, and dictated the Book of Revelation to Prochoros, his companion and secretary. This work, the last book of the Bible, has often been characterized as a book with seven seals. It is perhaps the most profound of all Christian esoteric writings. After the death of Domitianus in AD 96, John was able to return to Ephesus, where he lived for several more years, writing the Gospel of John. He died when he was over one hundred years old.

The first chapter of the Book of Revelation begins as follows: 'The Revelation of Jesus Christ, which God gave unto him, to show unto his servants things which must shortly come to pass; and he sent and signified it by his angel unto his servant John: Who bare record of the word of God, and of the testimony of Jesus Christ, and of all things that he saw. Blessed is he that readeth, and they that hear the words of this prophecy, and keep those things which are written therein, for the time is at hand.'

We can readily see that John, the Christian initiate whom the Lord loved, received by the grace of Christ Jesus a prophetic revelation that he felt urged to impart to the world. The style is imaginative throughout, and highly dramatic. Aspects of the spiritual past of humanity, going back to the beginning of the post-Atlantean period, are revealed, and we are taken through the future ordeals that human beings will have to face.

Towards the middle of this remarkable work we hear of 'a great wonder in heaven; a woman clothed with the sun, and the moon under her feet, and upon her head a crown of twelve stars. And she being with child cried, travailing in birth, and pained to be delivered. And there appeared another wonder in heaven; and behold a great red dragon...' (Rev. 12, 1–3)

We then hear how the Archangel Michael intervened and how the great dragon was cast out. In the next chapter, however, two more beasts appear on the earth: one rises out of the sea, and the other out of the earth. This second beast has two horns like a lamb, but speaks like a dragon. 'And he exerciseth all the power of the first beast before him, and causeth the earth and them which dwell therein to worship the first beast, whose deadly wound was healed. And he doeth great wonders, so that he maketh fire come down from heaven on the earth in the sight of men. And deceiveth them that dwell on the earth, by the means of those miracles which he had power to do in the sight of the beast; saying to them that dwell on the earth, that they should make an image to the beast, which had the wound by a sword, and did live ... And that no man might buy or sell, save he that had the mark, or the name of the beast, or the number of a man; and his number is Six hundred threescore and six.' (Rev. 13, 12–14 and 17–18)

This being is known as Sorat, the Sun Demon and the most powerful opponent to Christ Jesus in the universe. Sorat rises every 666 years to deceive humanity. Now that in 1998 three times 666 years have run their course since the birth of Christ, it will aim its wrath at humanity again.[4] Sorat will do everything in its power to obliterate humanity's connection with the spiritual world and tempt humanity to deny the Christ.

At the end of Lecture Eight Rudolf Steiner urged his listeners most earnestly to consider the three mysteries of our time: the mystery of Michael (who according to Steiner became regent in 1897), the mystery of the appearance of Christ in the etheric realm (from the beginning of the twentieth century), and the mystery of Sorat the Sun Demon (that is rearing its head at the end of the twentieth century). One can truly say, 'The time is at hand!' and we are faced all over the world with tremendous challenges. Will the call of Revelation be heard?

René Querido, Boulder, Colorado

GREETING *by Johannes Werner Klein*[1]

Dornach, 5 September 1924

As Dr Rittelmeyer is unwell and therefore unable to be here, it has fallen to me to speak a few words on behalf of our circle and express our gratitude to the destiny that has made it possible for us to come to you once again. We feel like a little band of travellers clinging together in a boat tossed by the stormy waves of our time, constantly faced with the danger of drowning and unable to turn either to any representative of external culture or to anyone who stands for what passes as the culture of the spirit in these times. We cannot but feel blessed by being able to come to you, and grateful that you have called us and will speak to us here.

Two years have passed since we stood here before you as a group in that powerful moment when our life's task descended upon us. For most of us this is the first time we have returned to this place, and we now look with deep dismay at the physical remains of the Goetheanum and cannot help returning in memory to the White Hall where the destiny of our life spoke to us so powerfully; it is the spot where the earth out there is now most deeply torn.

Most strongly in our awareness there lives the reflection of what has taken place here since then; the message of the Christmas Foundation Conference echoes on. The joy we were given at that time lives on in us, for there is once more a Mystery Centre on the earth. Coming to you once again in this circle, we therefore first and foremost want to express how profoundly we wish to join and enter as intensively and strongly as possible into the impulses that have gone forth from this place since that time. Without exception all the friends have by now personally applied for membership in the School of Spiritual Science.[2] As a circle we want to express by this that we intend to belong to the work going on here at Dornach in the most intimate and profound way imaginable.

We have now been working in the world for a further year. Our work has remained within the boundaries of Germany, but as a circle we have gained considerably in numbers and I would now like to introduce to you the new friends in our circle. [Eleven individuals were introduced who had joined the circle of priests of The Christian Community since the autumn of 1922.[3]]

We do not consider the meetings we have had together over the past year to be our most important achievement. Nevertheless they have become for us the clearest sign that the spiritual world has gained an interest in our work and that we have been accorded a place in the spiritual worlds which allows us to receive guidance. Our awareness of this can provide the starting point from which our confidence in what we are doing can germinate more and more from our thinking down into the real depths of our being. With this growing confidence in what we are doing we come to you who are for us the voice of the true revelation of the spiritual world. We ask you to give us whatever it is that can enable us to continue finding our way as time goes on.

LECTURE ONE

Dornach, 5 September 1924

My dear friends, to begin by replying to your kind words, I would like to say that it is fully justifiable that you should have spoken them just now in the name of the circle of priests. One cannot always call something spoken with the best intentions by human beings fully justifiable, but in this instance one can do so. I say this because the inner spiritual impulse that is intended to flow from the Goetheanum through the anthroposophical movement always contains an aspect that goes far beyond any theoretical understanding, indeed beyond any understanding altogether. A way of expressing approximately what is meant would be to say: The tasks human beings must undertake today are growing great again. They are growing great because the forces once available in the times when humanity was able to turn away more or less from the impulses of the ancient Mysteries are now exhausted.

The ancient Mysteries unfolded actual divine substances and divine forces on the earth in full reality. Humanity had to develop sufficiently for there to be a time when people were left more or less to their own devices, a time when the divine substances and forces were unable to work directly on the earth through human beings. The forces that held sway in earthly humanity during that intermediate period of human evolution are now exhausted. Though not the most lofty, it is perhaps a significant, important and far-reaching occult truth that the forces which were able to become effective in human evolution without the help of the Mysteries are now exhausted, so that human evolution cannot proceed further unless forces from the Mysteries enter into evolution once again.

Under the influence of this truth it must be sensed that today something other than understanding alone is necessary for someone who wants to work out of genuine spirituality in any branch of the anthroposophical movement. Something must come about anew that resembles the working of the old Mysteries, something that is described as an offering and devotion of the whole human being, an opening out of the whole human being within his or her task.

The words you have spoken would not be profoundly true if it were not entirely obvious—and it *is* entirely obvious— that in your circle of priests this impulse is at work in pure inwardness, the impulse to give one's whole humanity as an offering to the work that you have recognized as being holy. Before all the divine powers who shine their light to lead our work I am able to say: The words you have said about your enthusiasm and devotion to the task express the truth fully, genuinely and honestly. It has been abundantly obvious that the whole circle of priests is filled with the most noble and inward effort—with all the inner spirituality human beings have—to render the sacrifices that need to be made today fully fruitful. Even now it is possible to say that what you have done is the beginning of something that can bring satisfaction to the divine being of the cosmos. By saying this I am making an important statement.

Your work has remained within Germany, certainly. But the reasons for this will in all probability be overcome in the not too distant future. Interest in the religious renewal that was burning in your hearts when you came to me here for the founding of your priestly work is taking hold of souls in widespread regions outside Germany. How far it will be possible to go beyond Germany's borders will depend on the inner strength you can have within you.

We cannot help being deeply moved in our hearts when we

think of how your movement was inaugurated and initiated here two years ago with the holy Act of Consecration of Man in the very hall where the flames were first seen which then destroyed our beloved Goetheanum.[1] As you see, that is the spot where the earth is now most deeply scarred. But through your fine devotion a beginning has been made towards transforming what took place in that room—the first to be devoured by the flames—into what is surely a holy deed for the earth. If you continue with the sacred zeal that first took hold of you, the impulses within your circle of priests will continue to develop in the right way.

Having gathered once again at this place, we shall have important matters to address in the light and in the warmth that have come to us through the Christmas Foundation Conference like a kind of compensation for our earthly losses. We shall consider what could be a genuine help to you in taking further your impulses of soul.

This time we shall endeavour to allow ourselves to be approached by the profound content of the Book of Revelation. Taking the Book of Revelation as our point of departure, we shall endeavour to bring before our souls all that at this moment in time is especially important for your priesthood. By looking at the Book of Revelation in particular, we shall be able to centre all our work here on the Act of Consecration of Man, which is what gives your priestly work its meaning and purpose. We shall have before us on the one hand the Act of Consecration of Man and on the other the Book of Revelation.

Today already we shall give a brief hint about how we want to inaugurate this, how we want to inaugurate the work of your priestly movement. We shall save what arises in direct connection with the needs of your work as priests, what needs to be said about the practicalities of your priestly work, or about a review of the past and a prospect for the future—we shall save all these things for moments when they fit naturally with the inner aspect of our considerations. Today I will begin by telling you how we shall take our work forward over the next few days.

Let me first greet all of you wholeheartedly in the name of all those powers who have brought you together here who, as you know, are the multitudes of powers who follow Christ. May they give the right religious impulses, the right theological insight and the right impulses for today in working with a cultus that you want to adopt religiously, theologically and ceremonially in the deepest Christian sense. This is the sense in which we want to be together and this is the sense in which the work we are about to undertake together is to be shaped.

We begin by pointing out something great in our time, something great that consists in an entirely new attitude of the human soul towards that which comes about through a priestly action. What is present in the action of the priest when the Act of Consecration of Man is celebrated is something that human beings have always sought, for as long as there has been a humanity on the earth.

If we want to understand the light in which the Act of Consecration of Man must appear today for the priest celebrating it and for the layperson receiving it, we must first consider what the Act of Consecration of Man has meant, means now and will mean in human evolution on earth as time moves on. But if there is to be an understanding of what the Act of Consecration of Man is today while it is being celebrated, we must, from another angle, also be filled with the true content of what John, initiated by Christ himself, wanted to give to Christian posterity through his Book of Revelation. Strictly speaking the two belong together—a fitting frame of mind in celebrating the Act of Consecration of Man, and a fitting frame of mind in imbuing oneself with the substance of the Book of Revelation.

For the moment, let us set aside the specific form of

apocalypse or revelation given to Christians in John's Book of Revelation. Let us use the term 'apocalypse' to mean all occult truths bestowed on humanity in order to give it a genuinely priestly impulse for its further evolution. A great deal can be encompassed by the concept of apocalypse which appears in a concentrated summary in John's Book of Revelation in a form that is attuned to the Christ. Whenever apocalypse or revelation has been sought it has always been understood that comprehending apocalypse profoundly and fully was only possible when one was standing entirely within the act of consecration of man.

Much will become clearer if we begin by stating that there were, in the past, Mysteries which I shall call the ancient Mysteries. Rather than going into the matter of specific dates, I want in this introduction simply to describe the four successive stages of the Mysteries. There were ancient Mysteries, there were semi-ancient Mysteries, there were semi-new Mysteries and we are now at the point at which new Mysteries will begin. We thus have four stages of evolution in the understanding human beings have for apocalypse or revelation and for an act of consecration of man.

Looking at the ancient Mysteries which existed amongst human beings in the distant dawn of human evolution on the earth and which had the task of bringing to human beings everything that was holy, true and beautiful, we can say: The essential aspect of the ancient Mysteries was the way the gods descended from their divine thrones and came down to human beings, and the way those human beings who bore the priestly office within the Mysteries associated face to face, being to being, with the gods. Just as human beings today associate with one another being to being, so in the Mysteries of those ancient times did the gods associate with human beings and human beings with the gods.

As there are natural laws that are valid in time, so are there also primeval, eternal laws that do not, however, infringe human freedom. Among these primeval, eternal laws there are some that relate to how the gods associate with human beings. These primeval, eternal laws came into play when in the ancient Mysteries of earliest human existence the gods themselves associated with human beings, and when all teachings received by human beings came about between the divine teachers and the human beings themselves. When the cultus brought the supersensibly powerful gods to be there amid the celebrants, this was when something was attained in the ancient Mysteries that has always given meaning to an act of consecration of man, namely the Transubstantiation. What, though, was Transubstantiation in the ancient Mysteries?

In the ancient Mysteries, Transubstantiation was what the gods regarded as the ultimate through which they entered into association with human beings. The ceremonies were determined in accordance with the primeval, eternal laws I mentioned just now. Out of certain stellar constellations that were known to genuine ancient astrology, and out of the coincidence of these constellations with conditions that can be determined by human beings, the way was opened from the gods to human beings and from human beings to the gods.

If you can get an overview of ancient chronology you will find that there are various chronologies, some, for example, that reckon with 354 days and others that reckon with 365 days. Leap days and leap weeks were inserted into these chronologies to compensate for the non-compatibility of human calculations with the progress of the cosmos. What human beings were able to calculate never quite conformed with the actual progress of the cosmos. Somewhere or other there was always a small remainder. The priests of the ancient Mysteries paid particular attention to those small remainders that occurred where human chronology did not conform to the progress of the cosmos. By dividing the year into months and weeks, they laid down certain periods when this non-conformity was particularly conspicuous, so that after several lunar months there were always a few days left before the new year began.

Someone who wants to gain an understanding of the progress of human evolution would do well to look closely at those periods when human beings, by inserting days or weeks like this, used this to express the non-conformity of human calculations with the progress of the cosmos—those periods which the priests then regarded as holy weeks. In those holy weeks which used to make it obvious that the thinking of the gods is different from the thinking of human beings, in those times that used to make this non-conformity obvious, it is possible, if the heart of the gods is in harmony with the heart of human beings, for the path to be found that leads from the gods to human beings and from human beings to the gods.

The moment when the gods entered into the Mysteries—this was something people were able to observe through the ancient astrology which enabled them to understand it in the right way. At the end of each year, or at the end of a moon cycle of 18 years, or at the end of other periods, there were always holy times that signified the non-conformity, the borderline, between human intelligence and divine intelligence, holy times when the priests in the Mysteries were able to recognize that the gods could find their way to them and that human beings could find their way to the gods.

It was in such times that the priests of old sought to preserve the effective forces of sun and moon in the substances with which they celebrated the act of consecration of man, so that what they had received in the holy times could be spread out over all the other parts of the year when they would need to celebrate. They also preserved what the gods had made out of the earth's substances and forces during the holy times. They kept the water from those times, the mercurial element, so that at other times of the year they would be able to celebrate the act of consecration of man in such a way that it would contain the Transubstantiation in the way the gods themselves had done it in those acts of consecration of man that had taken place in the 'dead times', as they called them, the times that were holy.

Thus in those ancient Mysteries, in times when the cosmic language, not the human language, was current amongst human beings, people sought to make contact with the gods who then descended into the Mysteries and who on each occasion made holy once more the act of consecration of man. On each occasion, too, an understanding of apocalyptic things was bestowed upon the human beings who celebrated the act of consecration of man. This is how the great truths were taught in those ancient times when being in the midst of the act of consecration of man meant being filled with apocalyptic substance. The act of consecration of man is the path of knowledge; apocalypse, revelation, is the content of the holy knowledge.

Now we come to the semi-ancient Mysteries, those Mysteries of which at least a faint shimmer remained in historical times. (Of those that I have described as the ancient Mysteries nothing historical remains; they can be researched only by spiritual science.) The time had come when the gods withdrew from human beings and no longer descended into the Mysteries with their own being; but they continued to send down their forces. It was the time when the act of consecration of man was to receive through the Transubstantiation that shining light of the divine that was intended always to illumine the act of consecration of man.

The Transubstantiation was now no longer accomplished through learning from astrological observation of cosmic processes about which substances and forces should flow into the celebration of the Transubstantiation. Now the secret was sought in a different way. The inner nature especially of what the old alchemists called 'leavens' was taken up. A leavening agent is a substance that has reached a specific age while having gone through various stages of bringing about transformations in other substances without changing its own substance. To make an everyday comparison we need only think of how bread is baked. The principle is the same. You save a small piece of your previous batch of dough and add it to the new batch as a leavening agent. Imagine how in the semi-ancient Mysteries age-old substances, having retained their own inner substantiality through the ages while other substances were undergoing transformation, were stored in holy vessels that were themselves ancient and holy objects, venerable objects in the Mysteries.

From these ancient vessels were taken the substances that were the leavening agents with which the Transubstantiation of the old, still holy alchemy was performed. People in those days knew: The initiated priest understands the transformation, the Transubstantiation taking place through the forces preserved in the substances; he knows that they send forth sun-radiance in the holy quartz-crystal vessels. What was looked for in them, the reason they were needed, was that they were seen to be the celebrant's organ of perception for apocalypse, for revelation.

The following was something that took place in those semi-ancient Mysteries: The priest was tested at the moment when he approached the holy place and the ancient leavening agents began to transform the substances in the holy quartz-crystal vessels in such a way that he could see in those vessels how the substances sent forth sun-radiance. The vessel containing the little sun was a monstrance. It was a Host such as can only be recreated in imitation nowadays. The moment when he saw the sun-radiance of the Host was the moment in which he became a priest in his inner being. (Plate 1)

Nowadays in the Catholic church, everyone going to church sees the consecrated Host, for now it is no more than a symbol for what it once was. In those days, however, only those individuals were genuine priests who beheld the consecrated Host in that they saw a sun-radiance in the substances that had been preserved. At such a moment their knowing was open to receive that which is apocalyptic.

Next came those Mysteries of which the Mass of more recent times is a reflection. The Catholic Mass, the Armenian Mass and other Masses have developed in a very complicated way out of the semi-new Mysteries. Although they have now become external, these Masses still bear within them the full principle of initiation. In the ancient Mysteries the gods were present; in the semi-ancient Mysteries the forces of the gods were present. In place of these there came into the semi-new Mysteries what human beings can perceive when the Word awakens in them, the magical Word, the Word in which inwardness resounds, the Word that penetrates into the depths of understanding concerning the inner being of the sounds of speech. For in the age of the semi-new Mysteries human speech was juxtaposed with the speech of the cultus, that cultic speech of which a last remnant remains in the different religious creeds. In it, everything depends on rhythm, on the inner understanding of the sounds of speech, on the understanding of how the sounds of speech emanating from the mouth of the priest enter inwardly into human hearts. The magical Word, the cultic Word spoken in the holy place was the first way upwards to the gods or, initially, to the forces of the gods.

Thus:

First age of humanity:
ancient Mysteries—the gods descend.

Second age of humanity:
semi-ancient Mysteries—the gods send down their forces.

Third age of humanity:
semi-new Mysteries; the human being learns the magical speech and in intoning the magical speech begins to ascend to the forces of the divine world.

That was the meaning of all that was intoned in the act of consecration of man during the third age of the Mysteries. It was the time when the element of the Cabeiri provided the contemporary religious cultus living in the Mysteries. The services, the sacrifices of the Cabeiri, which were celebrated at Samothrace, are a part of all that is ceremonial in the semi-new Mysteries, a part of all the ceremonies the priest had to perform.

Imagine the altar of the Cabeiri at Samothrace. The Cabeiri standing on it as external reminders were offering vessels, jars in which were contained, not leavening agents now, but substances which human understanding could find if it was able to delve into the inner spiritual nature of the substance. The sacrificial substances in the jars were set alight, the smoke rose up, and in the ascending smoke the magical speech made visible the Imagination of that which the Word intoned. Thus the path upwards to the divine powers became externally visible in the sacrificial smoke.[2] That was the third stage in the evolution of the Mysteries and in what is contained for human beings in the act of consecration of man.

Although these first stages have become decadent, a good many of their external aspects have been preserved. In that moment over there in the now burnt-down Goetheanum when you inaugurated a new priesthood in the movement for a Christian renewal, in that moment a new age of the Mysteries began, a new age for the Act of Consecration of Man and for an understanding of apocalypse, of revelation. Tomorrow we shall begin to speak about what must now stream through your hearts in order to fulfil properly the fourth stage of the Mysteries.

LECTURE TWO

Dornach, 6 September 1924

We shall first look more closely at the connection between the Act of Consecration of Man and what is meant by apocalypse, or revelation, before considering John's Book of Revelation itself, and its significance for the present and future work of the priest.

Yesterday it was our task to point to three past ages in the Mysteries in so far as they sought to use what took place within the priest in order to transport him into an apocalyptic mood. We spoke of very ancient Mysteries in which the gods themselves descended in order to work in the Mysteries together with human beings. We also spoke of semi-ancient Mysteries in which the gods sent down their forces, so that by living in these divine forces human beings became able to work together with the gods in the cosmos.

I pointed out that the path began to lead in the opposite direction in the third age, that of the semi-new Mysteries. Here the human being shaped the forces, which he first had to develop himself, in such a way that they could lead up to the gods. We see how by intoning the magical Word in the ceremonial of the cultus—whether by speaking the magical Word into the smoke as mentioned yesterday, causing the Imagination to appear in the smoke through the Word, or whether the Word itself lived directly in the human being's whole mood of soul—the human being sought the path to the divine, spiritual forces of the cosmos in such a way that it was in the Word that one saw the working of the divine spiritual world.

This developing of a specific religious sense by human

beings—something that can only be described separately—was always paralleled by the necessary precondition for it: a particular form of Transubstantiation that was the focal point of the holy act of consecration of man. Priests today and in the near future are called upon to experience this Transubstantiation, and with it everything truly belonging to the work of the priest, in a new form. This will not easily be possible without a thorough understanding of what Transubstantiation and apocalypse consist of in real life in the four successive ages of human evolution.

We have seen the one aspect: The Act of Consecration of Man—including the Transubstantiation—is a deed conducted by a human being in collaboration with the divine, spiritual world. To work as a priest is impossible if there is no awareness of the fact that a human being can act in consort with the gods.

Let us look again at the oldest form of the act of consecration of man and the oldest form of bringing about the Transubstantiation. We see that the times when the gods find their way to human beings are those that represent the difference between what human beings can calculate as the sequence of the seasons in the course of the year and what takes place in the cosmos. The gods descended in those periods of time that were as though set aside, those holy periods into which human beings had to insert something because the course of the cosmos did not conform with their calculations. During those periods when human beings had to place themselves directly under the influence of the cosmos in order to carry out the Transubstantiation, they preserved something of the substances that were then transformed by the cosmos so that they would be able to use them to bring about the Transubstantiation in subsequent seasons.

The appropriate place for the priests and laypeople to be when the Transubstantiation was to be brought about was under the ground, in caves in the cliffs. In the times of the ancient Mysteries when full consciousness of the presence of the gods and the meaning of the Transubstantiation was developed, we see everywhere that people endeavoured to hold the holy ceremony in rock temples, in subterranean temples.

The fact that they endeavoured to do this is connected with the experiences the priests had during the Transubstantiation. In Transubstantiation the substantiality of earthly matter is transformed. Indeed, the overall process includes that of taking into one's own body the substance that has undergone Transubstantiation, so that in this sense the last two main parts of the Act of Consecration of Man—the Transubstantiation and the Communion—form a unit, with the Gospel Reading and the Offertory being the preparation. If we regard the Transubstantiation and the Communion as a single priestly act in this way, a single act within the ceremonial of the cultus, we can point to the interpretation adopted by those in the most ancient Mysteries who were known as the 'Fathers'. This was a degree attained in initiation, the degree of 'Father'. This designation, 'Father', remains to this day the name of the priests in many confessions.

When celebrating the Transubstantiation in the subterranean temple, the rock temple, the priest experienced how his physical organism became one with the whole earth. That is why temples in the rocks, subterranean temples, were used. Even when we live between birth and death in our ordinary earthly consciousness we must, after all, in reality feel ourselves to be one with the cosmos all around us. This is how it has been throughout the whole earthly evolution of humanity.

The air you now have inside your body was a moment ago outside it, and in another short moment it will be outside it again. The air inside your body forms a totality with the air outside your body. The whole phenomenon goes like this:

There is an ocean of air, and when you breathe in, a part of this ocean of air is transformed into you. The air is inhaled, it seeps into every last cranny, entirely filling you and becoming a human form. This human form dissolves once more into the ocean of air when you breathe out. The aeriform human being constantly comes into being and dies away again, only we are unaware that this is happening.

When ancient Indian yogis did their breathing exercises consciously they were aware of what was happening. They did not feel separate from the earth's ocean of air; they felt at one with it; in every systole and diastole they felt a continuous coming into being and dying away of the aeriform human being. This can be felt quite easily merely by carrying out breathing exercises, only it is no longer an appropriate thing for people to do these days. *21ˢᵗ April 2016*

The human being in the physical world is not solely an earthly human being. He is an earthly human being when what we call the physical body is mainly at work in him, but he is also a fluid human being. The whole human being is filled with circulating fluid, so the earthly human being and the fluid human being work on each other and influence one another mutually. The fluid human being is mainly dependent on the ether body, for the forces of the ether body work less in what is solid and more in what is fluid.

In addition we also have within us the aeriform human being and the warmth human being. The aeriform human being who takes care of breathing is under the influences of the astral body, and the warmth human being is chiefly influenced by the working of the 'I'-organization. You need only consider the different degrees of heat you find when you take the temperature of different parts of your body, externally or internally. Even this rather coarse method of measuring temperature shows the human being to be a differentiated warmth organism.

So we find all four elements in the human being: earth

influenced by the physical body, water influenced by the ether body, air influenced by the astral body, and heat, fire, influenced by the 'I'-organization.

What happened with the ancient 'Fathers' through the Transubstantiation combined with the Communion was that they felt their physical organization in its links with the earth when they went down into the rock or subterranean temple in order to become one with this earthly evolution.

Everything people today think about the nature of their own being—they think 'scientifically', so they say—is in fact entirely wrong, or indeed nonsense, for actually we have to have quite different inner pictures of the human being. These inner pictures are what arose for the ancient 'Fathers' from the holy sacrifice for the consecration of man through a direct vision brought about by the Transubstantiation. They knew that we not only breathe air through our respiratory organs, but also ceaselessly take in all kinds of substances from the cosmos through our sense organs; through our hair, through our skin all kinds of substances are ceaselessly absorbed from the cosmos. Just as someone breathing consciously feels the air being sucked into his respiratory organs, so did the priest in ancient times feel the substances from the silica-environment, in which he found himself in the subterranean temple of consecration, entering and filling his organization of nerves and senses. Just as the aeriform human being feels the air moving on when he breathes consciously, so do these substances fill the whole organism. The priests in ancient times knew that our system of metabolism and limbs receives nothing into its make-up from what we eat. Nothing of what we eat goes into our system of limbs and metabolism.

Substances are absorbed out of the cosmos. Today's whole theory of nutrition is untrue. The 'Father', as he celebrated, felt what is eaten and transformed by the digestive system moving up from the metabolic human being into the human being of nerves and senses, especially the head. He knew:

What I eat is transformed in me into the substance of my head and all that is connected with it; what builds the organs in me that take care of metabolism is absorbed from the cosmos through a more subtle form of breathing. He felt the substances of the cosmos being taken in from all sides through senses and nerves and then going on to constitute his system of metabolism and limbs. He felt the downward streaming flow that originates from all the directions of the cosmos and streams into his organism from above downwards. And he felt how what we take in directly in the form of food is first transformed within our body before turning in the opposite direction and going to constitute our upper human being. 28ᵗ Apnl 2016.

As he celebrated the Transubstantiation, the 'Father' had two streams within him, one flowing upwards, the other downwards. When he then proceeded to the Communion he knew, through having become conscious of his physical body in these streams, that he was linked to the cosmos. What he had just received through celebrating at the altar he incorporated into the downward and upward flowing streams within him; having become one with the earth, he incorporated what he had prepared on the altar into the streams which belonged both to the earth and to his body, he incorporated it into the divine on earth, which is a mirror of the universe. He knew himself to be at one with the universe, with that which was outside of him. He knew that this Meal, of which he had partaken in this way, was a Meal being solemnized by his cosmic human being. Through what was flowing into the upward and the downward streams he felt burgeoning within himself the divine human being who was permitted to be a companion for the gods who had descended. He felt that he was being transformed into a divine human being, that he himself was being transubstantiated by the gods in his physical body. This was the moment at which he spoke from the deepest depths of his heart: I am not now the one who walks about in the physical world; I am the one in whom the god who has descended is living; I am the One whose name comprises all the sounds of speech, the One who was in the beginning, who is in the middle and who shall be at the end. I am the Alpha and the Omega.

On the way his inner being took form, through his manner of feeling all these things, depended the degree to which he was actually able to participate in the secrets of the cosmos, in the divine working and creating in the cosmos, in the revelation of forces and substances and beings in the cosmos under the influence of divine, spiritual creativity. This was what it meant to do the work of the priest in the ancient Mysteries.

In the semi-ancient Mysteries the temples were no longer built underground—or if they were, this was done out of tradition no longer understood; the tradition lived on but the living content was lost. In the temples that had now risen to the surface of the earth great importance was attached to everything to do with consecrated water, with ablutions and other celebrations involving water.

These traditions still live on in the way baptism is performed by immersion in water. What the priest celebrated was now less to do with the actual element and more with the fact that through the inner strength brought to bear on the celebration the fluid human being, the one in whom the forces of the ether body were at work, now became one with the universe. When the Transubstantiation was achieved at that time and when everything that preceded it and came after it had to do with the fluid element in one way or another, the human being again felt how the organization of the etheric body was working in him, temporally this time. Through the accomplishment of the Transubstantiation the human being felt how his growth from childhood onwards took shape under the influence of the fluid element, how it shaped itself more and more and how the ether body is at work in this streaming from the past via the present and on into the future.

Just as through their physical body the priests of ancient times felt themselves to be at one with the earthly element, so did the one who celebrated the Transubstantiation in the semi-ancient Mysteries of the second Mystery age feel at one with all that is watery in the whole cosmos. Within himself he felt the forces of growth of all living things germinating, sprouting, growing and unfurling to become a developed organism, and then contracting again into a seed. In celebrating the Transubstantiation he felt this sprouting, budding, living, dying activity. At every moment he was able to say to himself: Now I know how beings arise in the world and how beings die in the world. The rising and falling forces of the etheric were active in him. You could say he sensed eternity in the holy Transubstantiation. 5ᵗʰ May 2016

Taking Transubstantiation and Communion once again as a single act of consecration, a single celebration, the communicating priest knew that the substances transformed in the way described yesterday were merging with his etheric, fluid human being. He felt himself to be at one with all that preserves immortality, that comes into being and dies away again, that is born and dies in the universe. Birth and death drifted above the altar and downwards from the altar towards and amongst the throng of the faithful. Feelings of eternity streamed through one, and it was this being-streamed-through by feelings of eternity that took the place of what had happened of old, when there had been a feeling of being-at-one with the whole cosmos through the earth.

When the third period came round, the human being was to experience consciously through the holy act of consecration how he became one with the airy element, and through the airy element with the cosmos.

Over in the Orient when an individual strove in solitude as a yogi he used a different method of becoming conscious of the stream of divine, spiritual supersensible cosmic forces in inhalation and exhalation. He took a direct hold of the breath. In Western Asia and, even more so, further west in Europe, there was no direct taking hold of the undiffer- entiated breath; here the magical Word was intoned into the breath. Thus the breath, the air streaming into and out of the human being, was taken hold of in the magical Word, the cultic Word. In this way it came about that the upward effort of human forces towards divine forces was experienced, was revealed, either in what was spoken into the sacrificial smoke or directly through the intonation of the magical, cultic Word. One felt as though one were oneself intoning the magical, cultic Word, the words of the prayer. On the whole every prayer means the following. It means that the human being is endeavouring to rise up with his forces into the divine, spiritual region; there he meets with the gods. And when he there intones the Word it is no longer he who is speaking; it is the god who is speaking in the cultic Word, revealing himself in the airy element. Through his astral body the human being felt himself to be within what rules the forces of the air.

Consider now how tremendous, how strong was the tran- sition from the semi-ancient Mysteries to the semi-new Mysteries, from the second to the third age. What the ancient 'Fathers' experienced was experienced in the physical body. It was an intensification of the activity of the physical body. What the sun priest in the second age experienced was an intensification of the ether body, the fluid human body. What the priest in the third age experienced, when he intoned the cultic Word and felt the streaming of the divine, spiritual forces, was experienced in the astral body. For ordinary consciousness the astral body even then was only in the least part a mediator of consciousness. Only in the earlier times of the third age were the priests still able to sense in the magi- cally spoken cultic Word: As I speak, the god is speaking in

me. But this waned. In the way it works the astral body
remained unknown by consciousness, which was on the
increase all the time. For today's consciousness it is entirely
unknown. Therefore, little by little, the verbal content of the
cultus became something that for the chosen meant the
presence of the god, and for those not chosen merely an
intonation of something that did not come into their
consciousness.

This became increasingly the case with a great number of
priests serving in the Catholic faith. The act of consecration
of man, the Mass, turned gradually into something celebrated
by the priest although he himself was no longer present in it.
One cannot, however, celebrate with these intoned Words
without the incorporation of air beings, or, in other words,
without the presence of spirit. Nowhere is there anything
materially shaped in which spirit does not immediately take
up its abode. So if the act of consecration is celebrated with
the true cultic Word, even by the most unworthy priest, there
is always something spiritual present, though perhaps not his
soul. Therefore whatever happens, the believers are present
at a spiritual event if the liturgy is right.

Once this had become increasingly decadent in the final
stage of the third age, the more rationally inclined denominations, the Protestant denominations, believed they could
do without celebrating the cultus at all. There was no longer
any awareness of the significance of the cultus, of the direct,
real collaboration of human beings with the gods. This led to
the times of inner experience in which we now live. The act of
consecration of man, which brings the divine, spiritual life
directly down to the earth, has gradually become something
incomprehensible. What ought to be experienced through it,
namely apocalypse or revelation, has become incomprehensible.

Such, basically, were the experiences which those of you
had had who came one day and said: There must be a

Christian renewal. You experienced what lives in today's civilization, what lives in today's religious life; you experienced the religious life of all the denominations as having been separated off from the genuine, real spiritual world. You were looking for the way back to the genuine, real spiritual world.

We have now reached the pointer that will lead us straight into the depths of the Mysteries that are connected with the Book of Revelation: that the Transubstantiation in the first age is linked to experiences made with the physical body, in the second age to experiences made with the ether body, and in the third age to experiences made with the astral body. It will depend on you and on your inner experience of the working and weaving of the spirit in the world whether the Act of Consecration and whether the Book of Revelation will be taken hold of by the human 'I'. *25th May 2016*

So a proper understanding of the task to be fulfilled through this movement for religious renewal will depend on what has to be done being directly seen as carrying out a task supersensibly allocated to us, a task that places what it does at the service of the supersensible powers. What you do must either peter out into nothingness, in which case it will have been merely a kind of inconvenience in the present evolution of the universe, if you fail to grasp the profound nature of your task. Or you do grasp the profound nature of your task, you do feel this task to have been linked from the outset not with the work of human beings but with the work of the gods throughout the earth's evolution. You would then have to say to yourselves: We have been summoned to share in shaping the fourth Mystery age of human evolution on the earth. Only if you have the courage, the strength, the seriousness and the perseverance to find your way like this into your task, only then will you have placed your task at the service of those powers who permitted the content of that cultus to flow down directly out of the spiritual world when we were gathered here two years ago. Only then will that which you have taken on through the content of this cultus, a revelation out of the spiritual world which as such rayed down upon you, *9 June* be real.

Then you will more and more feel and sense it to be true that the Christ first entered into earthly life through a cosmically real, telluric deed. The Mystery of Golgotha exists as a real deed. The time has now come for human beings to unite this with their 'I'. The earlier way in which the Holy Supper was remembered was still immersed in the third Mystery age, the age when the astral body took in and ruled the effects of the cultus that were accomplished in the airy element. Now, however, it is necessary for human beings to unite their deepest inner being with the Christ in full consciousness, and for them to begin to understand apocalypse, revelation in a new way.

How was revelation understood in the first Mystery age? It was experienced as the presence of the gods who exist at the beginning, in the middle and at the end, who are Alpha and Omega.

How was the presence of the divine powers understood in the second Mystery age? It was experienced in what resounded through the universe as the music of the spheres, in the cosmic Word streaming from heaven to earth, the Word that has created everything, that is creating in everything, that is alive in everything. In that age people experienced in an instant what is at the beginning, in the middle and at the end. They experienced Alpha and Omega in the cosmic, universal Word. Whenever in these various ages mention was made of Alpha and Omega—using different sounds of speech, perhaps, although ones fairly similar to those of the Greek language—there was always the endeavour to recognize what is really contained in this Alpha and Omega, in this First and this Last.

How was revelation, apocalypse, understood in the third

Mystery age? It was understood in that the human being unfolded the as yet only semi-conscious cultic Word. When the human being intoned this semi-conscious cultic Word and this then transubstantiated itself—which I shall illustrate in a moment—that is when apocalypse, revelation, was perceived during the third age. Perhaps one of you, or perhaps most of you, have had a day when you were receptive with your senses and your soul to impressions from the outside world. Perhaps you heard some music and then went to sleep still under the impression of this music, and then woke up again in the midst of your sleep. Maybe you then felt as though you were living in a billowing, but a transformed billowing, of the symphony you had heard during the day. This is how it was for the priests during the third Mystery age. What happened to them can be compared with the ordinary experience I have just described. They celebrated the act of consecration with the cultic Word, experiencing how the god became present in it. They had sent the cultic Word aloft, and the god had streamed into the cultic Word. They departed from the holy act of consecration in the mood in which it is fitting to depart from it. They experienced in what had undergone transubstantiation not only the human cultic Word in which the divine spirit had become present; they experienced also how what they had spoken had become transubstantiated, transformed. They experienced streaming towards them the supersensible echo of what they themselves had intoned in the liturgy of the Mass, transformed now, and bringing revelation, apocalypse, to them. As a return gift for the appropriately celebrated act of consecration the god revealed apocalypse. This is how apocalypse was sensed in the third Mystery age.

The individual who felt himself to have been made a priest through Christ Jesus himself, the writer of the Book of Revelation with which we shall be concerning ourselves, was the first to sense something that hardly any or only a very few others ever experienced again. He sensed how the apocalyptic content became absorbed into his own 'I'. For it was the astral body that absorbed the echo I spoke about, when the god gave the apocalyptic content as a return gift for the Word.

The one who wrote John's Book of Revelation felt his fully conscious 'I' to be at one with the content he wrote down in that Book. From the long-since extinguished consecration service of Ephesus came the inspiring stimulus for that priest, the author of the Book of Revelation, who felt himself to have been anointed by none other than Christ Jesus. He felt himself to be within a continuous celebration of the ancient, holy act of consecration. In feeling his 'I' to be entirely filled with the meaning of the act of consecration he now also felt entirely filled with the apocalyptic content.

The Book of Revelation is spoken out of John as, in ordinary consciousness, only the little word 'I' can be spoken out of the human being. When we say 'I' we express the whole of our inner being with this sequence of sounds. This cannot denote anything other than the single, individual human being, who is, however, richly filled with content. The content of the Book of Revelation is a rich content.

If we take everything that religious feeling and deepening can give the soul, if all illumination energetically striven for, all endeavour to comprehend the supersensible, is allowed to work in the human spirit, if we allow ourselves to be enthused by a contemplation of the three past Mystery ages, if what lived in the first, second and third Mystery age can become for us a living inspirer for the fourth, and if we let the power of God's spirit work in our soul in the way that is once again possible today, then shall we experience that quantitatively there is not only one Revelation but as many Revelations as there are human 'I's devoted to God, speaking from individual priests to Christ, who is to be found anew through this movement for Christian renewal.

In quality the Book of Revelation is unique, but quantitatively it can become the content of every individual priest's soul. Conversely, the soul of every individual who celebrates the Act of Consecration of Man can become a priestly soul by preparing to identify the 'I' with the content of the Book of Revelation. As human beings we are 'I's; we become priests in the modern sense of the word if the Book of Revelation is not merely written in the Gospel, and also if the Book of Revelation is not only within our hearts as a finished piece of writing, but if the 'I' becomes aware of the fact that in every moment of life it can through its own act of creation bring forth a reproduction of the Book of Revelation. 23ʳᵈ Jhe 2015

The following perhaps somewhat pedantic or philistine picture will help you to understand what I mean: Someone writes down the content of a book. The book is sent to the printers where it is printed. Then a given number of copies, each one separate although the content is identical, is sent out into the world. It is a unique thing to which your attention is drawn at the beginning of the Book of Revelation, a unique thing that was revealed to John by Christ himself. For this is 'the revelation of Jesus Christ' received by his servant John. (Rev.1,1) The content is unique, but it is reproduced when each one himself or herself brings it forth out of the wisdom of the supersensible worlds.

This is what it means to understand the Revelation of John. In the deeper sense of the words it also means understanding that the Christ has consecrated us and thus made us priests. You have felt what it means when the apocalyptist says that Christ himself has anointed him a priest. Becoming anointed as a priest takes place when one feels how the content of the Book of Revelation came into being in John. When it is felt that these people of today, who want to become priests, do so through creating within themselves the experience of the 'I' in the Revelation, then the 'I' becomes apocalyptic; then the 'I' is priestly.[1]

More of this tomorrow.

LECTURE THREE

Dornach, 7 September 1924

Yesterday we looked at the significant turning-point that came about in human evolution because from the third Mystery age onwards the human being's participation in the cosmic world through the act of consecration of man—namely in the Transubstantiation—took place in the astral body, that member of the human being which during sleep, for ordinary consciousness, departs from the physical body and which during the time of separation from the physical body is not receptive to perceptions of the surrounding world.

Let us be clear about how this astral body works in us today. It is the astral body that brings us the thoughts about our surroundings, the thoughts through which we comprehend the world. The moment the astral body departs from our physical and our etheric body, the thoughts about our surroundings are no longer there.

This realization can be supplemented by adding that the 'I'-organization, the 'I' in human beings as they are constituted today, is the recipient of the sense impressions. The sense impressions die away when the 'I'-organization withdraws from the physical and ether body. You could draw it like this: Here is the human being's physical body, and here is his ether body. (Plate 2) During sleep the astral body and the 'I'-organization are outside them. When we are awake this 'I'-organization provides us with sensations and sense impressions. The sense impressions are not there when we sleep because the 'I'-organization is not present in the physical and ether bodies and because the 'I'-organization is not receptive to impressions of our surroundings while we are asleep. The astral body only supplies the thoughts while it is in the physical and ether body. When it is outside these it is not sensitive for the things of the world and does not supply any impressions.

In the third Mystery age, when the human being [the priest] was to come into contact with the divine spiritual beings through the cultic Word by means of all the preparatory exercises, it was this astral body that became receptive to working out the Transubstantiation within itself in the Communion, and through this working out of the Transubstantiation it became receptive for apocalypse, for revelation. 30 / 6 / 2016

Beginning with our present age, the same kind of process must now take place in the 'I'-organization of human beings. This 'I'-organization must be constituted in a way that enables it to experience the Transubstantiation, even though in ordinary consciousness only sense impressions can be experienced through it. It must be constituted in a way that enables it to participate in revelation, in apocalypse, through the Transubstantiation.

The human being can indeed become receptive to this today; the human being can genuinely become a priest if he takes into himself inner pictures that are true spiritual images of the supersensible world. By saying this we have, basically, characterized the inner connection between an esotericism that rightly exists today and that which must live in the soul of the priest. We have characterized what can make The Christian Community become the bearer of an important part of the new Mysteries. We must take account, though, of how the Anthroposophy that is drawing near to human beings today is constituted.

I have often cited a certain image by saying: People today are inclined to accept as knowledge everything that can in any way be supported by external perception, by scientific experiments. They do not want to accept as knowledge what cannot be supported by external perception or by experiment. But people who have this attitude resemble someone who says: Every stone on the earth needs support if it is not to fall down; therefore the planets in the universe must also be supported so that they do not fall down. That the planets hold each other up in the universe without any supports is accepted as a matter of course today, because this is taught traditionally, on good authority. The fact, however, that anthroposophical truths are such that they do not need to be supported by external observation or by scientific experiments but mutually support and carry one another—this is widely doubted.

As soon as we can accept that anthroposophical truths are valid because one such truth supports another, so that the truths give each other mutual support—when the moment arrives in which we can accept this we can begin to desist from repeating that unfortunate turn of phrase which states: Since I cannot as yet see into the spiritual world, I cannot understand the content of Anthroposophy. When this moment arrives we begin to understand Anthroposophy through the way its truths support one another, and then we can delve more deeply into it.

This task of delving more deeply into the knowledge about the spiritual world given by Anthroposophy is the task that can, and indeed must, lead the priests to their inner path. We need only realize that the disposition, the attitude of soul we enter into, when we honestly take hold of Anthroposophy, is a fitting way of approaching something like the Book of Revelation. The Book of Revelation is unique, but as I allow it to work on me every one of its images, every Imagination becomes one with my own 'I'. The moment then comes when this revelation can be not only the experience of the human 'I' but also its creation. What we have to do is approach this Book of Revelation in an anthroposophical sense. Today there is no other way of gaining access to it.

7 July 246

Let us now endeavour to grasp a few main points of the Book of Revelation spiritually.

The sentence 'I am Alpha and Omega' (Rev. 1,8) is only comprehensible if you know that in olden times the sound A [Ah] was not the abstract, separate, meaningless part of a word we feel it to be today, but a sound of sufficient import to have its own name.

Humanity has treated the sounds of speech, which embrace such an immense mystery, in a peculiar manner. Humanity has treated the sounds of speech like the police treat criminals, giving each sound a number, just as criminals are numbered when they are shut up in their cells. By losing their names and gaining numbers instead, the sounds of speech have lost their inner nature. This is a pictorial way of putting it, but it is entirely true.

If we go back beyond those Roman-Latin times when the sounds of speech were given numbers, we come to ages when humanity was fully aware—and in Hebrew this was certainly the case—that it was perfectly appropriate for a sound of speech to have its own name, so that it could be called Alpha—or Aleph in Hebrew—because it was a being, something divine, a supersensible being. When we look more closely at this first sound of what we now call the alphabet we shall have to undergo a kind of spiritual development of concepts before we can arrive at what Alpha really is.

In Anthroposophy we describe how earthly evolution goes back to the pre-earthly, planetary conditions of consciousness known as Moon, Sun and right back to the Saturn condition. In considering the evolution of the world we try to bring forward whatever is linked with the evolution of the human being. In Old Saturn we find the first cosmic human seed which, after manifold transformations through the conditions of consciousness of Sun, Moon and Earth, has become the human physical body we know today. The human being existed in Old Saturn in a primal seed-beginning.

It is important for those of us who seriously and honestly want to penetrate to the truth in these matters to ask ourselves: What did this primal seed of the human being experience in Old Saturn? Life in Old Saturn took its course in variations of warmth. In differentiations of heat and cold human beings absorbed varying temperatures. They lived in conditions that told them much about the heat and cold of the cosmos and also much about the spirit, but only that realm of the spirit that worked in variations of heat and cold. *14 July 2016*

Moving on from Old Saturn to Old Sun we find that now human beings lived in a physical body that was differentiated into warmth and air, so that in Old Sun they had an organism consisting of warmth ether and the element of air. There was thus a differentiation within the human beings themselves. The human being became inwardly more rich. Not only are differences in temperature perceived, as in the Saturn condition, but now something appears that could be called an inwardness. Human beings in Old Sun perceived warmth, but they also perceived a kind of inner breathing rhythm within themselves, which in turn expressed secrets of the cosmos, was a mirror image of cosmic secrets.

We can see how the being of man grows richer as it develops from the Saturn condition to the Sun condition of the earth, and richer again as it develops from the Sun condition to the Moon condition and to the Earth condition. This being of man will grow richer still by developing further through the future planetary conditions up to Jupiter and on to Vulcan.

What was the human being's relationship to the world in Old Saturn? His relationship to the world in Old Saturn was such that quantitatively he experienced infinitely many variations in temperature, but not very much qualitatively. There was as yet little of the world in the human being. He existed, he was human; you could say he was just human, having nothing much of the world in him as yet. But as he moves forward through Sun, Moon, Earth, up to Jupiter his inner being will more and more become filled with world. His life will become ever more richly endowed with world. Now, here on the earth, we already have a good chunk of world in us. And when the Earth condition will have reached the stage at which it will dissolve once more, human beings will have a great chunk of macrocosm in them that will have been worked through in earthly images.

We already bear a part of the cosmos in us, only we do not know this with our ordinary knowledge. As we progress onwards towards spiritual knowledge through Imagination, Inspiration and Intuition, our inner experiences will become ever more wonderful and magnificent in our soul. Just consider the human eye as it is known to our ordinary consciousness today. Yet this human eye is a cosmos in every one of its details, wonderful and magnificent like the macrocosm. Even just in the physical body every organ is revealed as a whole wonderful world. When a human being looks around as an initiate, he sees a world down there with elements and up there with stars, with sun and moon. When he looks into himself he sees every organ, eye, ear, lungs, liver and so on, each as a world in its own right. This physical body of the human being is a tremendous weaving and interpenetrating of worlds, worlds that are complete, worlds that are as yet only present in seed form, worlds that are sense-perceptible, half supersensible and wholly super-sensible. As the human being progresses through many evolutions he gathers more and more worlds into himself.

We can discern the human being at the beginning of Old Saturn right at the outset of being human, with as yet no world in him. The first thing he felt during the evolution of Old Saturn was that he was a body of warmth; he perceived the dimensions of this body of warmth. Expressed in a diagram we could say that in Old Saturn the human being felt himself to be warmth, but gradually, having at first felt like a kind of warmth mollusc, he noticed something like a collection of different temperatures, and then something like an outer skin, a warmth skin, though somewhat cooler in temperature than the warmth inside. He felt the inside to be somewhat warmer, with manifold variations, while the outer warmth skin had warmth of the least intensity.

We can describe all this in today's language, but there is something abstract about our language. It lacks the power of enchantment with which to conjure before our souls the magnificence of such images when we look into past aeons right back to Old Saturn. Those who are touched even slightly by these visions will also be touched by the holy awe with which such things were seen in the ancient Mysteries. As late as the chthonic Mysteries of ancient Greece these things were spoken about in a way that recognized the human being of Old Saturn who did not yet possess the skin of warmth; and they knew about this human being of Old Saturn that the first thing he took to himself from the surrounding world was the skin of warmth which imitated the world in its configuration. That was the first thing the human being took on from the world.

When the human being was still a being of warmth, what did his inner experiences look like subjectively in the soul? His inner experience was pure wonderment about the world. The only way you can express what he experienced is to say that it was pure wonderment. Warmth cannot be comprehended as anything other than pure wonderment. Externally it is warmth, internally it is experienced as pure wonderment. It is only because people have become so clumsy in their concepts that they speak about the inexplicability of the 'thing in itself' as did old Kant. The 'thing in itself' of warmth is wonderment; and the human being of Saturn was just as much wonderment as he was warmth. He lived in wonderment, in astonishment about his own existence, for he was only just embarking on this existence. This is Alpha: the

Saturn human being, the warmth human being living in wonderment. And the first thing the human being experienced as world, as the outer housing provided by world, the skin, this is Beta, the human being in his house, in his temple. (Plate 2) The house was the first thing the human being received from the world: the skin—Beta.

If we proceed in this way through the whole alphabet, we proceed through the world. After gradually taking into himself everything that is world and filling his whole being with it, when he arrives at Vulcan having united with himself the whole content of the world, of this great All to which he belongs, the human being will have become the one he was at the beginning of the Saturn condition *plus* the whole world. He will be Alpha and Omega, man who unites in himself everything that is world. By saying 'I am Alpha and Omega' in the way John's Book of Revelation does, we have designated what the human being will be at the end of the Vulcan condition. At the end of the Vulcan condition the human being, too, will be permitted to say: I am Alpha and Omega.

Let us look at what we have imagined to ourselves as being the beginning, middle and end of humanity's evolution, let us look at this in conjunction with the Mystery of Golgotha. In the being who incarnated in Jesus through the Mystery of Golgotha we have—roughly half way through human evolution—a being in the world who is already at the stage in world evolution that the human being will have reached at the end of the Vulcan condition. We have a being as a god such as man will be as a human being at the end of the Vulcan condition.

What is it to be god as compared to being man? To be god as compared to being man means that in the stream of time the god is that which man will be later on. Do not say that this is tantamount to bringing the god down to the level of man or even making the god out to be man. The god does not become man. For supersensible vision time is simultaneous reality, although this may sound paradoxical. The interval between man and god is demonstrated by what occurred at the time of the Mystery of Golgotha. In trying to comprehend such things one must not directly relate different times with one another, nor beings who belong to different times.

In writings such as John's Book of Revelation many things are still expressed in the language of the Mysteries, so they can only be understood if the meaning can be extricated out of the Mystery language. It is not surprising that the writer of the Book of Revelation spoke in the Mystery language, for in his day people were still familiar with it. They knew that the sounds of speech are supersensible beings, that Alpha is the human being as a supersensible being at the beginning of his existence, that when you move from Alpha to Beta you move from human being to world, including the divine world, and that when you go through all the sounds of the alphabet to Omega you are taking into yourself the whole of the divine world. 22nd Sept 2016

It is a disturbing fact today that the sounds of speech are nothing but trifles as far as we are concerned. What are the sounds of speech but trifles nowadays? You do not know very much if you only know the ABC. Such things are trifles, but they are trifles that point back to a beginning where there were divine, spiritual beings. Our trifling letters of the alphabet are the descendants of what humanity once upon a time recognized as divine, spiritual beings. The whole alphabet was the sum of such divine, spiritual beings. The sounds were gods, resounding towards the human being from all sides, sounds such as A, B, Alpha, Beta: the human being, the human being in his house, and so on. Alpha and Omega: the human being with the entire world. When speaking them, human beings experienced the sounds of speech as that which filled them with spirit.

The last remnant of the divine spirit living in the sounds was still present when the cultus was intoned in the third

Mystery age. In the earliest part of that age this was still well understood. When human beings intoned, one after another, the sounds of what is today our abstract, traditional alphabet, they were intoning the cosmic Word. Through what they were intoning they united themselves with all the gods. In the beginning was the Word—this means the same as when Christ says 'I am the Word', or 'I am Alpha and Omega'.

The Book of Revelation is written in the language of the Mysteries, so it uses expressions that hark back to the great times when human beings felt the macrocosm to be a speaking universal All. The sounds of speech, which in olden times denoted the highest spirituality for human beings, have been reduced to trifling shadows today. We must learn to sense what has happened. The sounds are there, but the gods are no longer in the sounds as far as human beings are concerned. The gods have departed from the sounds. Ahrimanic beings are now hidden in a demonic way in the sounds of our speech. The popular myth that the sounds of our speech contain something of black magic if they can be held rigid is not without foundation. This is rightly maintained by a healthy popular imagination, for the divine sounds of the past have become ahrimanized. The gods of old have departed from the sounds and ahrimanic beings have entered into them. If we cannot find the way back in this connection, then even through speech human beings will more and more fill themselves with ahrimanic powers.

These are the kind of feelings with which we must approach the Book of Revelation. Only then will the content it places before our souls be revealed in all its might and greatness. For what is it that the apocalyptist wants? He wants what all those also want who rightly speak about Christ from genuine knowledge.

John wants to present the Christ to humanity. He draws attention to the fact that the Christ is here. He begins the Book of Revelation by saying that the Christ is here.

Translated into our language, the first words of the Book of Revelation signify simply: Behold the appearance of Jesus Christ! Look, I want to show you this appearance of Jesus Christ which God has given! 29ᵗʰ Sept. 2016.

The first thing the apocalyptist does in his own way, in the apocalyptic way, is to point out that the Christ wishes to appear before humanity. But then he immediately draws attention to the fact that he not only intends to announce the appearance, the Imagination of Jesus Christ, which to some extent presupposes the ability to see spiritually; he also intends to draw attention to the fact that the divine world power which has brought this appearance into the world has also brought a description in words of this thing that it has made visible to the spiritual eye.

These words, that are from God himself, are the interpretation of the appearance of Jesus Christ, and God has sent them through an angel to his servant John. This is how we must understand the beginning of the Book of Revelation.

Actually, two things are in question. Firstly there is the matter of an Imagination, an image of Christ, and secondly there is the matter of Christ's message. What is spoken of in the second sentence—that which John witnessed and of which he bore record—this is the appearance of Christ and the interpretation of his appearance: Christ in an image and Christ described in words. The apocalyptist's intention is to place before human beings Christ in an image and Christ in words.

This immediately points to something that was obvious to people of those times but which has meanwhile become entirely lost to humanity. In our poverty-stricken psychology we talk today of a sense perception and of a mental image. And to make the matter as impoverished as possible people say that sense perceptions are brought about by the senses, and that mental images are made by human beings in their mind. Everything is merely subjective; nothing cosmic is left.

People put Kantian interpretations on a rich world and forget entirely that the human being exists in the midst of the universe.

The intuitive element of the Word has shrivelled in us into impoverished mental images; the intuitive element of the Word is the second thing emphasized by John, testified to by John. The apocalyptist presents the appearance of the Christ to us as what we might call a perception of the supersensible. We must therefore say:

> See the appearance of Jesus Christ, given by God to show his servants what must come to pass in the course of a short time;

I shall explain these words later.

> God has put it into words and sent it through his angel to his servant John. John has testified to God's Word and to the appearance of Jesus Christ, which he has seen.

John wants to give to human beings what he has received from God in the letter and what he has seen. 5ᵗʰ Oct 2016

It is necessary that we reconsider the scripture of Christianity in this concrete way. And it is your task as priests—you who want to be priests from the deepest and most honest impulse of your hearts—to bring concreteness back into scripture. For it is a fact that people reading the Gospels in the language of today are dishonest if they say they understand them. What I have just explained to you is what it says at the beginning of the Book of Revelation. 30ct 2016

'The Revelation of Jesus Christ', we read in one translation, 'which God gave unto him, to show unto his servants things which must shortly come to pass; and he sent and signified it by his angel unto his servant John.'[1] This is what is written there, and this is proclaimed throughout the world as the wording of the Book of Revelation. Yet no one can actually imagine what it means. This is the case for the greater part of the Gospels. It is because of efforts to persuade people that there is meaning in a text that no longer represents what was originally written in it that people have gradually come to believe that one should not even try to go more deeply into the Gospels. Indeed, how should one set about doing so? If you read the Gospels in any modern language you no longer understand anything—if you are honest. What you read in the Gospels in these modern languages no longer expresses anything. One must go back to what was originally written, as we did just now for the first two sentences; and we shall do this for other sentences as well.

People also say that for certain passages in the Gospels one must go back to the Greek text. Well, with all due respect to our contemporaries who make such honest efforts to understand Greek, I have to say that in fact no one can understand ancient Greek today because we no longer have in us what the Greeks had in them when they spoke and when they listened. When we listen to someone, or when we speak ourselves, we are nothing but bags of flour. We remain as passive inwardly as the flour in a well-packed bag. This was not so for the Greeks. The consciousness of the Greek vibrated when he listened; he came alive inwardly, and out of this liveliness he spoke. The words he heard and those which he spoke were living bodies, they were alive for him. And look at the peoples of the Orient. There may be decadence in them today, but they are not like Europeans who can no longer inwardly hear anything at all that is alive when they speak or listen. Listen to an Oriental poet such as Rabindranath Tagore, listen to how such people, even in their few important examples, depict the inner weaving and life that can live in language.

Today people think they have language if they possess a dictionary with English words on one side and German ones on the other. They are perfectly happy to put down the German words to correspond with the English ones. They have not the slightest inkling of the fact that one is leaping across a chasm, that one is entering an entirely different world, and that what lives in language should be treated as something divine.

People must become conscious of this once more. Then, inwardly, they will demand to return to what vibrates within ancient communications such as the Book of Revelation that conjures up before our soul the appearance of Jesus Christ. As a mighty appearance, indeed, this will stand before our soul if we can see it as though the whole element of clouds were to draw together suddenly and present us with wonderful splendour, taking on human form and angel form. As if past, present and future were to well out from the cloud substance, revealing the spiritual substance content of the world which includes within it the human being—this is how the appearance of Jesus Christ is pictured.

The appearance is initially such that we fall silent before it, becoming one with the world and ceasing to exist for our own consciousness. We stand before the appearance in such a way that it alone is there, while we ourselves become nothing. Then, behind the appearance, we become aware of God who reveals, the Father God who has given us the appearance. Behind the appearance he gives the inspiring words. The words that are the interpretation of the appearance, this is his secret. But the time has come when the secret is given by God to an angel who brings it down to human beings as a message in a letter from God, along the same path taken by the Inspiration from God to human beings.

When the human being has fallen silent, has disappeared, has been absorbed into the appearance, beginning not only to be himself but also inwardly to take in the letter from God, of which he must first break the seals, the seven seals that close it, making it the letter from God that is sealed with seven seals—when this happens, the human being himself becomes what is written in the letter. Then the human being begins to regard what is written in the letter as his own 'I'-being. Then he stands before the appearance filled with divine ideas, with the divine concept, with the spiritual inner picture of the appearance.

When you imagine the Priest John before the appearance of Jesus Christ, losing his identity in selflessness, when you see him receiving from the angels the seven-times sealed letter from God, when you see arising in him the decision to break the seals and impart the content to humanity—then you have the picture, the Imagination, that stands at the beginning of the Book of Revelation. We must understand what he takes in to be the Word, and that it is as I have described it in the Imagination. This is what the apocalyptist wants to impart. Therefore he says: Blessed is he who reads and hears the Words of the macrocosm, who absorbs and preserves for himself what is written in the book—if he can understand it—for the time has come.

It has come indeed. There is nothing arbitrary about this. It belongs to the karma of the community for Christian renewal that we are now speaking in this connection about the Book of Revelation. 20 oct 2016

LECTURE FOUR

Dornach, 8 September 1924

Yesterday we brought before our souls the image shown to us by the apocalyptist, the image of Jesus Christ's appearance, given by the Father God; and I was allowed to remark that the explanation designed to lead to an understanding of the image can be conceived of as a letter sent by God himself to John.

It is integral to the Mysteries and to the manner in which one speaks out of the Mysteries and presents them, that henceforth the writer of the Book of Revelation is himself also regarded as the writer of the letter. It lay in the nature of the Mysteries for the writer of a document such as this not to feel himself to be its author in the sense in which we regard the author of a work nowadays. He felt himself to be the tool of the spiritual writer. He felt there was nothing personal left in the actual writing down. So John is perfectly justified in acting as though he were writing what he has to write at God's command, as a message from God. In all that follows this becomes obvious in a way that truly befits the Mysteries.

It is perfectly true to say that in our present time we need once more to understand such things as the transition from the appearance of Jesus Christ in the first few verses of the Book of Revelation to what then follows, namely the seven letters sent to the different congregations. Our present time has entirely forgotten any understanding of such things that once existed as a matter of course in the Mysteries and even still in the way the early Christians thought.

Once again, this is something it will be up to you to take

further as your priestly work continues to develop. Think now that what is said in the Book of Revelation, written down as it is through Inspiration, is directed to the Angels of the congregation at Ephesus, of the congregation at Thyatira, of the congregation at Sardis and so on. These letters are said to have been written to Angels. This is something that immediately trips up our modern understanding, so it is important for us to have a proper view of what follows. *(handwritten: // Jan 17.)*

A man who had spent the recent part of his life making tremendous efforts to reach an understanding of the anthroposophical view of the spirit once came to see me. In your priesthood you must know about such things for they are after all typical of our present age. This is only one example, but a striking one, to show what I mean. It is something you will often meet on your path as priests, and the important thing for you, is it not, is your path as priests. This man said: 'It seems to me that Anthroposophy strives to take the words of the Bible literally.' I replied: 'Yes.' He then proceeded to quote a whole string of examples which he considered could not be taken literally, but only symbolically. I said to him: 'Certainly there are very many so-called mystics, theosophists and so on who search the Bible for all kinds of symbols and suchlike, who dissect the Bible into symbols. Anthroposophy does not do this. Anthroposophy looks only for what can lead to understanding the proper meaning of the original text—although this might sometimes mean taking the symbolic language as the starting point. Working in this way,' I continued, 'I have never found, in all the passages I have been able to investigate, that the Bible cannot be taken literally if one juxtaposes the original text with all the misinterpretations that have arisen over the course of time.'

This, then, is the final aim: to take the Bible literally. You could even say that if you cannot take the Bible literally, you have not yet understood those passages that you are unable to take literally; and this is indeed the case with many people today.

We are touching here on something esoteric which has perhaps so far not come up so clearly in our meetings but which should certainly be brought before your meditative consciousness. It happens from time to time nowadays— perhaps not like lightning flashes, for they come from above, but like volcanic flashes, for they come from below—that things that are remnants of ancient Mysteries flicker up in one confession or another. I have often mentioned a pastoral letter in which an archbishop made the following claim:[1] The letter asked the question: Who is higher, the human being or God? In a rather roundabout way, perhaps, but on the other hand also quite bluntly, this letter drew attention to the following: When the priest stands before the altar—so went the letter—when a human being who is a priest stands before the altar (this is only the case with a priest, not with other people) he is higher than God, more powerful than God, for he can force God to take on earthly form in the bread and wine; when the priest celebrates, when he brings about the Transubstantiation, God is obliged to be present at the altar.

This is a discussion that reaches far back into the ancient Mysteries and it is also a discussion that is still quite current in eastern esoteric Brahmanism in so far as this derives from Mystery knowledge. The idea of man as a being who includes the divinity within himself, who is, actually, higher than the divinity, is familiar to and in agreement with all the Mysteries. When his soul was in this state, a Brahmin priest, especially in olden times, felt himself to be the suprapersonal bearer of the divinity, if I may put it this way.

This is an incisive statement flashing in to our time from the ancient Mysteries, and it should at least once be confided to a priest's meditative soul life. After all, it contradicts entirely what has gradually become established, particularly in Protestant consciousness. As far as Protestant consciousness is concerned, what is written in the pastoral letter quoted is of course nonsense. We shall be returning to this during our considerations on the Book of Revelation. Behind it is really only the idea, writ large, that comes towards us here at this point in the Book of Revelation.

At the behest of God, and inspired by God, John writes to the Angels of the seven congregations. In the state of soul in which he is writing, he certainly feels himself to be the one who is to pass on advice, admonition, their mission and so on to the Angels of the seven congregations. What does this mean in a concrete sense? When the Angel of the congregation at Ephesus, or at Sardis or Philadelphia was mentioned, who was actually meant? To whom was the message to be addressed? Though this is difficult for people to understand nowadays, there were in those days individuals like those of today whom we call well-educated individuals—individuals well educated in the Christian tradition we would say today of people in an analogous position—there was a core of individuals who understood the meaning of this: The one who is writing has a prophetic nature, a prophetic nature like that of John who, when he is writing in this state of soul is higher than those Angels. He is writing to the Angels of the congregations. But among those who understood there would have been no need to point to something supersensible when mentioning 'angels'. The picture people had was this: Christian congregations have been founded and continue to exist. The writer of the Book of Revelation considers that he is addressing his letters to future times in which what he has to say to the congregations will come to pass. He is not speaking at all of present conditions. He is speaking of future conditions. If those who at that time were taking into consideration the traditions that had arisen out of the ancient Mysteries, they would have pointed to the bishop of the congregation as the one to whom the letter was addressed.

On the one hand it was entirely clear to them that the

actual leader of the congregation was the supersensible Angelos, but on the other hand they would have pointed to the bishop, the canonical administrator of the congregation. People at that time had the concept that the one who was the administrator of a congregation such as that of Sardis, or Ephesus or Philadelphia, the one who exercised this office, was the actual earthly bearer of the supersensible Angelos-being. So when he writes, John does indeed feel himself inwardly taken hold of by a being higher than the Angelos. In writing to the bishops of the seven congregations he is writing to human beings who are not only filled with their own angel—which is the case with every individual—but also with the guiding, leading Angel of the congregation.

So he begins to speak about what he has to say to these congregations, and he is certainly pointing to the future. We must ask: Why are seven letters written to seven congregations? These seven congregations are of course the representatives of the various pagan and Jewish nuances out of which Christianity has been born. Concrete facts were much more thoroughly understood in those times than later on. At the time when the Book of Revelation was written people knew exactly: Here, for example, is the congregation of Ephesus that long ago brought forth the immensely great Mysteries of Ephesus which, as was quite common in olden times, had pointed to the future appearance of Christ. The cultus at Ephesus was intended to unite the celebrants in Ephesus, as well as those witnessing the celebration, with the divine, spiritual powers and also with the coming Christ. With its prophecy of the coming Christianity and with its pagan cultus, the ancient pagan congregation at Ephesus was perhaps the one that was particularly close to Christianity.

That is why the letter to the Angel of the congregation at Ephesus spoke of the seven candlesticks. The candlesticks are the congregations, as the Book of Revelation expressly states. The letter to the congregation at Ephesus, in particular, must be taken in its actual form just as it stands.   It is clearly indicated that this congregation at Ephesus was the one that took up Christianity most intensely, devoting its first love to Christianity. For it is said that it did not keep its first love. It is of a future time to come that the apocalyptist wishes to speak in his letter. So we see in the example of this admonitory letter to the congregation at Ephesus how the apocalyptist characterizes the development the congregation goes through as one in which it looks to what flames up again from olden times.

It was indeed the case that the different congregations spoken about here represent various pagan or Jewish nuances, that they had various ceremonials through which they approached the divine world in varying ways. Every letter begins in a way that shows how in each congregation Christianity has developed out of its particular brand of ancient pagan worship.

One must understand that in the early days of Christianity people's state of soul was entirely different from that existing today, especially in Europe—though not so much in the Orient. The way we now see religion with a content of concepts that can be described logically was very, very foreign, really entirely foreign to the ancient Mystery pictures of the early Christian centuries. In those days people saw the Christ as an appearance of the mighty Sun Being. But it was up to the congregation at Ephesus, the congregation at Sardis, the congregation at Thyatira and so on to strive towards him each in its own way, in accordance with its own cultus. Each has a different nuance in the way it approaches him. Everywhere there are intimations of this being acknowledged.

 Take the congregation at Ephesus, whose task it was to carry on the profound and ancient Mysteries of Ephesus. It could not help but be different from, for example, the congregation at Sardis. The congregation at Ephesus had a cultus that was profoundly permeated by the presence of divine, spiritual substances in earthly life. The priest walking in procession around Ephesus was able to call himself god or man in equal measure. He knew himself to be the bearer of the god. The whole religious consciousness at Ephesus was rooted in theophany, the appearance of the god in the human being. The different priests at Ephesus each respectively represented the corresponding god, and there was even a specific task of taking this theophany, this bringing-to-appearance of the divine, right into the souls of the congregation.

Assume that among the priestesses at Ephesus performing the rituals of the cultus there was one in the procession who was essentially the living, human form of Artemis, Diana, the Goddess of the Moon. The members of the congregation were expected to make no distinction between the earthly appearance and the goddess herself, so that the earthly, human appearance was regarded as the actual goddess. Events in the ancient Mysteries such as public processions took the form of people who were the gods walking one behind the other. Just as today we have to learn how to acquire appropriate concepts for things, so did the people then have to acquire images in their soul and feelings in their soul through which they could see the god in the human being who was the priest or priestess.

It is therefore no wonder, since the apocalyptist speaks in the Mystery language in the way I have described, that he should turn particularly to the congregation at Ephesus where this special way of thinking, of feeling, of sensing was most intensely developed. That is why it was natural for the congregation at Ephesus to regard the seven candlesticks as the most essential symbol of the cultus. These candlesticks represented the light that lives on earth while at the same time being divine.

The situation was entirely different in the congregation at Sardis. This congregation was the Christian continuation of an ancient, very highly developed astrological star religion in which the participants really knew how the passage of the stars relates to earthly affairs and where they read in the stars all the things the higher and less high leaders commanded to be done in all earthly matters. The congregation at Sardis had evolved out of a Mystery cult that counted to the highest degree on discovering from the starry sky at night the secrets of life and the requirements of life. Before it became possible to speak of the congregation at Sardis as a Christian one, it had to be spoken of as the one that adhered most firmly to the old dream clairvoyance, for it was out of this dream clairvoyance that the nightly secrets of the macrocosm were derived. At this place, where so much store was set by the continuing tradition of the old dream clairvoyance, little attention was paid to what the daytime brought.

In this sense the difference between the sun worship and sun teachings of Ephesus and Sardis is indeed significant, in so far as one can genuinely speak of the ancient wisdom of both these places. In all the ancient Mysteries the teachings— which were also passed on to the lay population—were also the science of the day, for there was no science that was separate from the Mysteries. The sun teachings of Ephesus differentiated between the five planets on the one hand— Saturn, Jupiter, Mars, Venus, Mercury—and the sun with the moon on the other. Nowadays we call the sun a fixed star in contrast to the planets, but then, especially in Ephesus, the sun was distinguished by being separated off from the planets and worshipped as the star of the daytime because from the moment it rose to the moment it set it was seen as the life-giving principle.

This was not the situation in the earlier days of Sardis. Here the daytime sun was nothing special, and its light was accepted as a matter of course. In the town of Sardis the daytime sun was nothing special, but the night-time sun, which the ancient Mysteries termed the 'midnight sun', was seen as being of the same degree of importance as the planets. The moon was not distinguished from the rest of the planets, and the sun was seen as being really of the same degree of importance as the planets.

The sequence in Sardis was: Saturn, Jupiter, Mars, Venus, Mercury, Sun, Moon. But not in Ephesus. Here they enumerated: Saturn, Jupiter, Venus, Mercury on the one side, and on the other the gods of day and night, Sun and Moon, who were close to the life on earth. This is the great difference, and it was to this that all the ceremonial at Sardis was related.

In these earliest Christian times the old pagan cultus lived on in Ephesus, but with a slant towards Christianity, while in Sardis the nuance of the old pagan cultus, tending towards astrology in the way I have described, also lived on. So it was quite natural for the apocalyptist to write of Sardis 'that hath the seven Spirits of God and the seven stars'. (Rev. 3,1)

Here we do not have the candlesticks standing on the altar, nor the light that is bound up with the earth, but the light that is up there in the macrocosm.

You can discover the degree to which the apocalyptist is still imbued with the ancient Mysteries when you answer the question: What is it that he chides the congregation at Sardis about; to what must they be especially attentive? They must, he tells the congregation at Sardis, be attentive to finding the transition to the daytime sun, the place from which Christ took his departure.

The meaning of each word must be taken exactly as it stands, if only one can press forward to the original meaning, knowing how the religious life was led in olden times, and that the apocalyptist was speaking in the grand style as the last of his kind—though there are always later effects that linger on. In the way he spread the culture of Hellas, Alexander the Great, for example, behaved impeccably when dealing with the religious life. This is obvious wherever we examine Alexander's campaigns. There are no endeavours to persuade the population, and no dogmas are given out. Each people is left with its own cultus and convictions, with only such additions being introduced as can easily be absorbed. Buddha's messengers to Babylon and Egypt also worked in this way. After they had fulfilled their mission there were few outer signs in the cultus or in the words used in the celebration by which one might have distinguished the later from the earlier time. Inwardly, however, there were immense differences, for there had been poured into the devotions these peoples brought to their gods everything that could possibly be absorbed in the way of nuances in the cultus, in the ceremonial and in their convictions. The same, basically, also happened in the European regions in older times. The people were not arbitrarily flooded with many dogmas, for the point of contact always remained the peoples' own ancient Mystery customs.

These things are the building bricks we need to know about if we are to read the Book of Revelation properly, without the intrusion of even a small remnant of those absurd conclusions modern theology has reached about it. This tolerant way of building on what is already there which a number of times has the apocalyptist saying, for example: 'You say you are Jews and are not' (Rev. 1,9; 3,9)—this is the way in which he wants to speak out of the hearts and souls of the people on the spot. Such passages and others have led to the Book of Revelation being considered not as a Christian but as a Jewish document. One has to understand how these things have arisen out of the old way of considering such matters.

We shall be having to go into more detail, but there is one conception we must still touch on today: The apocalyptist, writing through Inspiration, knew exactly how one can give a complete picture of some reality by describing a specific number of typical aspects. You can see how wonderfully individual are the characterizations of the seven congregations in the seven letters of the Book of Revelation. It is quite wonderful. Each one is described in a way that distinguishes it clearly from the others, so that each presents itself to us with its own individual features. The writer of the Book of Revelation knew perfectly well that if he had described an eighth congregation he would have had to describe something that resembled one of those already existing. And the same would have happened with a ninth. The seven nuances he has given provide the fullest possible description. He knew this.

Here is another wonderful conception coming to us from those olden times. It came to me recently in such a living way when we drove over from Torquay—where we had been holding our summer courses in England[2]—to the place where King Arthur's castle once stood, King Arthur with his twelve knights. You can still see what vibrant life there must have been in this place. You see the headlands jutting out into the sea. They still have on them the last few remaining ruins of Arthur's ancient castles, which were wonderfully formed. You look out to sea—there is sea here and here, with a hill in

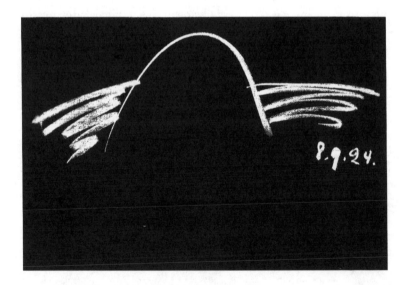

the middle—and you realize how strikingly the sea brings soul into that locality. The picture gives an impression of incessant change. While we were there sunshine and rain alternated quite rapidly, which of course also happened in olden times. In fact, things are quieter now, for the climate has altered in this respect. You watch this wonderful interplay, the way the elemental spirits of light enter into relationships with the water spirits who spray up from down below; and again you see quite special spirit phenomena when the waves break on to the land and, tearing themselves away, are thrown back again, or when the surface of the sea is ruffled. Nowhere else on the earth does the cosmic elemental realm ebb and flow in such a remarkable way.

What I was permitted to observe there was the instrument of Inspiration for the participants at Arthur's Round Table. They received the incentives for what they had to do through what was told to them with the help of those beings of sea and air. These knights of King Arthur could number only twelve. This came to me because one can still perceive today what it was that formed the basis for that number twelve. There are just twelve nuances of perception when you are concerned with this kind of cosmic perception that comes into being with the help of elemental beings; twelve modes of perception. If you want to embrace all twelve as a single human being, you find that one of them always makes another indistinct. So the knights of Arthur's Round Table shared the tasks among themselves in such a way that each could be regarded as one of these twelve nuances. They were convinced that in this way each of them possessed a clearly differentiated feeling of the universe, the tasks of which they took upon themselves. There could not have been a thirteenth knight, for he would have had to resemble one of the twelve. *16 March 2017.*

The conception on which this is based is clear: When human beings want to share out the tasks to be done in the world, there must be twelve of them. Together they form a whole, representing the twelve nuances. If human beings confront the world in communities, in congregations, this calls for the number seven. These are things that were known in those days.

The apocalyptist is writing out of this supersensible understanding of numbers, and he continues to do so in the further course of the Book of Revelation. Today I simply want to speak about reading the Book of Revelation. John shows us how among the appearances there is one in which he sees the throne of Christ, the throne of the transfigured Son of Man, around whom are seated the four and twenty elders. (Rev. 4,4) Here we see something in which twenty-four have a part to play. What does it mean when there are twenty-four nuances?

Congregations have seven nuances; human beings incarnated on the physical earth have twelve nuances. But when we are talking of human beings as representatives of human evolution in supra-earthly life, then we come to yet another number. There have been leaders of humanity whose task, from age to age, has been to reveal what humanity needed to receive as revelations. These revelations are simply written into the cosmic ether, which can also be termed the Akashic Record. If we take the sequence of great revealers in evolving humanity, we find inscribed into the supersensible realm what each one of them has had to give.

One should seek an individuality such as Moses not only in what he was as the earthly Moses, and also not only in what he was as documented in the Bible, for these are depicted in accordance with the Akashic Record. One should seek Moses where he is seated on the throne of Christ. The eternal element of his earthly existence, the abiding part *sub specie aeternitatis*, is firmly engraved in the cosmic ether. Only twenty-four such human powers chosen for eternity can exist, however, for a twenty-fifth would merely constitute a repetition of one of the others. This was known in prehistoric times.

If human beings want to work together on the earth, there must be twelve. If human communities want to work together, there must be seven; the eighth would be a repetition of one of the seven. But if, *sub specie aeternitatis*, those work together who have made themselves spiritual, who represent a stage of human evolution, there must be twenty-four, and these are the four and twenty elders.

If we take all twenty-four elders together—some of whose revelations already exist, while others are still to come—we have surrounding the throne of Christ a synthesis, like a summary of all revelations to humanity. Before this throne of Christ there stands the human being as such, the human being in juxtaposition with what is merely one link in the chain, a single stage of humanity. What I would like to describe as 'the human being in himself', in the way he must be comprehended—this is depicted beneath the image of the four beasts.

A grand picture is there before us. The transfigured Son of Man in the centre, on the throne the separate stages of humanity, through the sequence of ages, as the twenty-four guides of the twenty-four hours of the great cosmic day, and, spread out over all this, beneath the picture of the four beasts, the human being himself, who has to embrace all the separate stages. Something important, something essential draws near to us in this.

What is taking place there before the seeing eye of the apocalyptist who brings the messages of God to the Angels of their congregations and thus to the whole of humanity? What is taking place? When the four beasts begin to act, which means when the human being discovers his relationship with the Godhead, the twenty-four guides of the twenty-four hours of the great cosmic day fall upon their faces. They worship that which is higher, that which is the *whole* human being, as opposed to what each of them represents, which is merely one stage of humanity. The elders were really seen as this picture which the apocalyptist has to place before humanity. In olden times it was said that the one seated on the throne will come, whereas the apocalyptist has to say: The one seated on the throne has already been.

I wanted to speak about what it means to read the Book of Revelation. But we can only learn to read it correctly when we put ourselves in the position of starting to learn how to read by beginning with the ancient Mysteries.

We shall now endeavour to read on in the Book of Revelation, for it contains profound secrets, and not only those that you ought to get to know, but also some that it will be for you to carry out, some which you must do.

LECTURE FIVE

Dornach, 9 September 1924

Our prime concern should be to read the Book of Revelation in the way that is appropriate for today. Today the spiritual development of the human being is to unfold in the sign of the consciousness soul; for this reason alone, therefore, it is appropriate that the guidance of spiritual life must become fully conscious, so it is therefore up to us to adopt with full consciousness the appropriate orientation about what the apocalyptist tells us.

In earlier ages the revelations of the apocalyptist no doubt meant something only to the highest initiates, of whom there were fewer and fewer as time went on, and nothing to the ordinary priests. Today what the Book of Revelation contains must enter fully into the consciousness of priests.

Yesterday we spoke of seven congregations, and from one point of view we pointed to the congregation at Ephesus. The world is most certainly full of viewpoints and many of these can play a part in one and the same matter. We can describe the congregation of Ephesus as we did yesterday, and find how in this particular congregation Christianity developed out of previous pagan conditions. Another way of looking at it would be to show how these impulses contained a great deal of the basic structure of the first post-Atlantean cultural age, even more than was there in the India of later times. So one can in a sense regard the Christianity that developed at Ephesus as a Christian continuation of the world view and view of life of the first post-Atlantean cultural age. The second congregation mentioned in the Book of Revelation is the one at Smyrna where the ancient Persian culture thrived before the transition to Christianity.

Then comes Pergamos, which is introduced as the congregation that lived during the third post-Atlantean culture. Specifically in the letter to the congregation at Pergamos we can discover references, more or less unveiled, to the Hermes Mystery that was alive in this culture.

In the letter to the congregation at Thyatira we are referred to the fourth post-Atlantean culture, the age in which the Mystery of Golgotha itself took place. When we allow the effect of this important letter to work on us we are everywhere reminded of the direct message the Mystery of Golgotha had to impart.

Then comes the congregation at Sardis about which we spoke yesterday when I showed you how this congregation had a specifically astrological orientation, how it was oriented towards a star religion. Of necessity this congregation of Sardis would have to have a good deal of past history, but above all this congregation in particular carries future things within it. So let us now try to bring this into our spiritual view of today. We are living in the fifth post-Atlantean cultural age. When you look at Sardis you see that there are elements that were already past at that time; but you also see something germinating like a seed, something that was not yet complete at the time when John was writing the Book of Revelation. The whole tone of this fifth letter is different from that of the four preceding ones. In his letter to the congregation at Sardis John points to the future. The future to which he was pointing, which was there like a seed in Sardis, is our time now; it is the time in which we are now living.

The sequence of post-Atlantean cultural ages, and at the same time the inner development of Christianity, is hinted at in another way in the seven seals, and this letter bears hidden within it the development of the post-Atlantean ages mingled with the development of Christianity. In the seven seals, too, the seven congregations are hinted at. We are shown—and we shall look at the other meaning of the seven seals later— how when the fourth seal is opened, the one corresponding to the fourth post-Atlantean age, a pale horse appears, and now the talk is of death entering into the world. (Rev. 6,8) With this we are touching on one of the most important secrets of the Book of Revelation in so far as our own age is concerned. In the fourth post-Atlantean age death really does in a sense enter into humanity. You must be very clear about this. You get to know human nature very well when you consider death.

Let us initially go back to the first, second and third post-Atlantean ages. The make-up of the human soul, in fact the make-up of the whole human being, what he felt himself to be, was very different in the earlier ages from what it became later on. Long ago there was a distinct inner feeling of growing into one's sojourn on the earth. In their ordinary consciousness human beings had a clear memory of having lived in the spirit world prior to life on earth. This awareness had become considerably dimmed by the time the Mystery of Golgotha was approaching, but in the first, second and third post-Atlantean ages it was so significantly present that every human being knew: I was a spirit being before I became a child. There is not much of this state of soul to be found in external documents, but it was so. One reckoned not only with a time spent on earth, for there was also a continuation of one's earthly time backwards into the spiritual world to consider. What came into play in the age that coincided with the Mystery of Golgotha was that earthly life began to be seen as clearly bounded by two gates, the gate of birth or conception and in addition the gate of death.

This awareness, this kind of soul make-up, did indeed only set in during the fourth post-Atlantean age. From about the eighth pre-Christian century to the fifteenth century after the

Mystery of Golgotha a consciousness unfolded that sees the human being strictly enclosed within the boundaries of earthly life. Since then another new consciousness has been in preparation, of which we are only at the beginning. You must take into account that only four or five centuries have passed since this began to develop, so we are about at the stage the fourth post-Atlantean age had reached by the third century BC, when consciousness was still quite different compared with the consciousness of the fully evolved fourth age that developed later. People today on the whole are not yet clothed in the garments of the new consciousness; for the most part their consciousness is still that of the fourth post-Atlantean age. Our civilization as a whole is the cause of this.

Think how much that belongs to the fourth post-Atlantean age is still with us, how much people are either still living as a matter of course in the fourth post-Atlantean age or at least are still flirting with it. The whole of our grammar school education still has the fourth post-Atlantean age working in it. So long as Latin was the language of scholars—this was the fourth post-Atlantean age. In public life, too, we still think in the way people thought in the fourth post-Atlantean age. You could say that for the fifth post-Atlantean age we have not even reached the stage humanity needs to be at for the consciousness soul to begin developing. That is why people today still see their life on earth as being bounded at either end by the gate of birth and the gate of death.

There is of course some development going on in the new consciousness, only in most people it is not having much of an effect yet; it is only showing in some individuals who are particularly gifted in that direction. I have met quite a number of these during my lifetime, but on the whole little notice is taken of them. The consciousness to be developed by human beings in the fifth post-Atlantean age is such that the time between birth and death is not quite sufficient for it, so that death constantly plays into one's life on earth. People will become aware that they die a little bit every day, so that dying is constantly present in the human being, so that death is constantly present. There are some individuals who live in great fear of death, sensing that it is constantly eating away at their earthly humanity. But I have also met people who love death because it is their steadfast companion for whom they continuously long.

An awareness of being accompanied by death is something that will become more and more prevalent in the fifth post-Atlantean age. Let me describe this more concretely. Human beings will perceive in themselves the intimate fire process which is bound up with the development of the consciousness soul. Especially at the moment of departing from sleep consciousness and entering waking consciousness they will experience the waking consciousness like a kind of fire process within them which is consuming them. For the consciousness soul is something highly spiritual, and the spirit always consumes what is material. The manner in which the consciousness soul consumes what is material and what is etheric in the human being is a kind of intimate fiery process, a process of transformation. It is this that human beings will more and more perceive within themselves as the fifth post-Atlantean age proceeds. However, one must not imagine this fire to be burning like a candle flame; this would be too physical a picture. It is in a moral way that people will feel this being-accompanied-by-death taking shape in their soul.

When people notice a good intention, or a strong purpose they may have, evaporating again immediately, or in an hour or after a day or a month, most of them within our current materialistic view of the world find this acceptable as a part of the way things are. But it is something about which we shall more and more learn to feel differently. We shall learn to feel how a good intention that we have been too weak to carry out begins to consume our life, begins to diminish our moral weight. We shall learn to feel how such a thing makes us more of a moral lightweight, more insignificant for the universe. Nowadays we see such a thing as no more than a weakness of soul, not as something that works on in the cosmos, which in the future, however, we shall indeed feel it to be. In a similar way people will begin to feel how certain intellectual activities consume them, like a fire in the soul consuming them. Such things are indeed already happening even on a grand scale, but hitherto they have not yet been sensed for what they are.

One can find one's way step by step into the spiritual world, for example by taking account of the suggestions in the book *Knowledge of the Higher Worlds*.[1] By this means it is possible to achieve harmony between spirit, soul and body. But the way most people today carry on their inner life, without these exercises, and indeed even the way the religious life is carried on in the different denominations, causes the religious life to work in the human being in such a way that his moral weight is diminished, made lighter.

These things are being perceived consciously more and more, and human beings will undergo great changes during this fifth post-Atlantean age. It is a very great change when one feels either strengthened or diminished in one's whole humanity through what one is in one's soul life, when one senses destiny to be not merely a matter of outer circumstances exercising their influence on one, but when one feels destiny to be something that makes one morally heavier or lighter.

This is the consciousness that is in the process of coming about in human beings, and it can be seen happening quite externally and empirically. We are entering a time in which priests will have to take account of such things when they have their congregation before them. It will be necessary to treat what is rising up in people's consciousness—something of which they are not yet fully aware, but which shows in all kinds of restlessness, nervousness and inharmonious feelings—in such a way that individuals receive comfort and strength.

It will become less and less appropriate for priests to treat individual human beings according to some general pre-conceived ideas about how this should be done. Please do not be offended when I say that in some ways stereotyping has been and still is the norm. When you speak to a person who is perhaps suffering from some kind of delusion and has sought refuge with a minister, you can hear exactly what that minister has said to him or her. You can hear how the minister has sought to awaken in that person a sense of being sinful. In another case again you can hear how a minister has sought to awaken a person's sense of being sinful. This kind of stereotyping is to be found everywhere.

When I once had to attend three funerals on the same day I noticed how the minister began each service with the same sentence: 'However high above the earth the heavens are, so high are my thoughts above your thoughts.' Three times the same stereotype which would, however, have been more or less justifiable during the fourth post-Atlantean age. This is the kind of thing, as I have mentioned, that is reaching over into the fifth age so that it is still happening now, whereas in this age there ought to be a much more subtle way of observing, there ought to be a transformation in the way things are done.

Priests must begin to do this now. They must begin to learn how to direct the glance of their soul right into the heart of the other person. Hardly anyone is capable of this nowadays. Human beings remain terribly unknown to one another these days. If you read the Book of Revelation with a degree of reverence—in fact you cannot read it without reverence—if you read with reverence the passage about the white raiment (Rev. 3,4–5) in which those will have to be clothed who have fulfilled the task of the fifth cultural age, you gain the impression: It is a matter of looking deeply with the eye of the priest into this special type of human consciousness; it is a matter of getting to know the human being as he appears before you now in the fifth post-Atlantean age. This is the admonition: Get to recognize the human being not by the clothes he wears, not by what he presents to the outside world, but by the raiment of his soul. In the letter to the congregation at Sardis the apocalyptist speaks this admonition to the present time in which we are now living.

A priest in our time must penetrate to a person's soul through all the external circumstances in which human beings find themselves. In a sense a priest must look at a person in the way I described the day before yesterday with regard to wanting to find that person's karma.[2] I said that to reach a person's karma one must disregard his profession, his social standing, his ability and his incompetence and must instead go deeply into his soul, into those characteristics and capabilities that can find expression in any profession a person might have. This is because you have to look to what the individual was in his former life on earth. Well, there is no need for the priest to go quite this far, but he must begin to see through everything external and find the individual's inner being, that which is purely human in him, that which makes the person human inwardly, an individual human being.

It is definitely the case that when we have read in the Book of Revelation as far as the letter to the congregation at Sardis we can sense that what is written there is a direct summons to our present time. As we read on we can then gain an even profounder impression.

Let us now think about the time when the fifth post-Atlantean age will have passed. During the course of this age human beings will have changed their consciousness in a way that will enable them to see how death works on them. They will learn to understand this, but not to the extent that makes them aware all the time of the exact age they are going to reach. They will see how death works on them. They will have death as their constant companion. Death will be with them naturally. The new element that must enter into all the different fields of life will be that the human being's content of soul must enable him to regard this having-death-beside-one as something natural. To have awakened in oneself the powers of eternal soul alertness means: to have death as a good friend and constant companion always by one's side.

When you look about you, you are still seeing things entirely in the light of the fourth post-Atlantean age. On the whole you are seeing life which has death within it, in every plant and every stone, but you are not seeing death because you do not yet see death in yourself. But human beings will begin to see death all the time. One will increasingly have to speak to people in this vein, for as a person increasingly perceives death his whole way of looking changes.

To perceive death means to perceive many things that are today still entirely hidden behind outer appearances. In a sense we regard nature as being very stable because we cannot see into its finer, more intimate realms. You might take a walk in the countryside and come across a notice stating: Foot and Mouth Disease Area. In reality something more intimate has been taking place over the whole of the area, something that might be compared with a stormy sea or a volcanic eruption. This is the kind of thing that human beings will face in the sixth post-Atlantean age.

Because human beings do not yet see death, they only notice an eruption of Vesuvius, say, or a strong earthquake measured by a seismograph. But they do not notice the tension in the etheric sphere that arises for example when an important genius lives or is born in a particular place. They equally do not see that mighty working and weaving of spirits of which the stars and their constellations are merely an outer sign.

To see all these things in some way is what human beings can expect in the sixth post-Atlantean age. The sun as it is today will have fallen down from the heavens and the stars will have fallen down as well. Where the stars now shine in, like material abstractions, one will see a mighty working and weaving of spirit. In the course of the fifth post-Atlantean age, therefore, there will be a great change in the way human beings see themselves, and in the course of the sixth post-Atlantean age the whole world surrounding them will change. Do not imagine that the initiate, for example, sees the world in the same way as one who is not initiated. And the same applies to the sequence of stages in consciousness. Human beings in different stages of consciousness do not see the world in the same way.

That we as human beings are living in a process of transformation, a process of transformation of the human being and of our image of the world, is indicated in the Book of Revelation, among other things, by the way there is a relative similarity in the first four letters. The first seal is opened and a white horse appears, one horse. The second seal is opened and a red horse appears, another horse. The third seal is opened and a black horse appears, yet another horse. The fourth seal is opened and a pale horse appears, again it is a horse. (Rev. 6)

When the fifth seal is opened there is no longer any talk of a horse. The import of this letter is indicated in quite a different way. So as we proceed in our reading of the letters we find an indication of a fundamentally significant transformation that will take place in our own age.

There is only one thing to be said, which is that we must prepare ourselves to become the new, transformed congregation of Sardis. This new, transformed congregation of Sardis will have to understand that there is little value in knowing plants, animals and minerals unless one can find the stars working in every one of them. In the spiritual sense the stars must fall down from the heavens, and this can already be perceived.

Let me give you one specific example of this. People usually notice the external configuration of such things without taking much account of the way they fit into the whole spiritual evolution of humanity. Each one of us can only do something at the place where we find ourselves, and for me the following took place here just before my last trip to England. You know perhaps that when I am in Dornach I set aside one or two hours each week for the men working on the building here when I talk to them about science and spiritual science during their working hours. The men like it very much if I get them to suggest the subject. They like choosing the subject themselves and among other things they want to know about today's spiritual life and culture. This is also something that you as priests will surely have to understand.

Before I set off for England I had one of these sessions with the workmen, and one of them had prepared the question: What is the reason for some plants having fragrance and others not? Where does the fragrance of flowers come from?[3] Well, these lectures have been going on for years and the workmen are by now sufficiently well primed not to put up with the usual chemical explanation about some substance or other being what spreads this or that perfume—you know what scientific explanations usually amount to: poverty comes from *la pauvreté*. No, these workmen are after real explanations.

So here in brief is what I told them over the next hour or so. Something that has fragrance first of all draws our attention to our sense organs; we perceive the fragrance through our organ of smell. We should then ask ourselves whether our sense of smell is subtle enough to allow us to work as a sniffer dog for the police. Of course you will agree that it is not. On the contrary, you will have to admit that we human beings have rather a blunt sense of smell, not a subtle one, and that as you go down the scale in nature you come to more sensitive organs of smell.

Take the dog with an organ of smell so delicate that it can be trained as a sniffer dog. Look at the way its forehead slopes backwards following along the continuation of the olfactory nerves which carry the scent into the very being of the dog. We human beings have a forehead that is puffed up. Our intelligence apparatus is a transformed organ of smell, especially in its capacity for apperception. This alone makes it obvious that as we go down the scale to lower animals we come to more sensitive organs of smell.

Spiritual science teaches us that in their flowers and in the way they develop fragrance very many plants are nothing other than organs of smell, real vegetable organs of smell of immense sensitivity. What do they smell? They smell the cosmic fragrance that is always present. And the cosmic fragrance that emanates from Venus is different from that emanating from Mars or from Saturn. For example the fragrance of the violet is an echo-in-fragrance of what the violet perceives of the cosmic fragrance. Plants that smell nice perceive the cosmic fragrances that come from Venus, Mercury or Mars. *Ferula fetida* perceives the smell of Saturn and passes it on in the asafetida derived from it.

This is something these people want to know, for in a sense they want to know how the stars fall down to earth. What, after all, are the beings in the world but what the stars send down. If you want to speak realistically about these things, you have to say: The stars really are falling down, for they are in the plants. It is not only the fragrance that is in them, but the plants themselves are actual organs of smell.

My first talk today[4] was once again to the workmen, and I asked them to state the questions they wanted answered. One question was as follows: If what you said last time about fragrances is right, so that plants are sensitive organs of smell, where then do the plants' colours come from?

So I had to explain that the fragrances of the plants come from the planets, while the colours come from the power of the sun. I expanded on this, giving examples that show this to be the case. One member of the audience was not satisfied, asking why I had not mentioned the minerals, and why were they also coloured. I can understand why the plants have colours, he said, and that a plant growing in the cellar without sunlight might have the right shape and fragrance but no colour—why it would remain pale or even colourless from lack of sunlight. But what about minerals?

So I had to explain further. The sun has a daily course arising from one revolution of the earth in 24 hours. It also has an annual course that brings about the seasons during which it reaches the zenith and then falls back again. But there is another cycle as well, and I went on to explain the Platonic cosmic year. I explained how the sun now rises in Pisces at the vernal equinox, but that in former times it rose in Aries, and before that in Taurus, and then Gemini, and so on, taking 25,920 years to complete one cycle round the Zodiac. In this way the sun has a course that takes one day, another course that takes one year, and a further one lasting a whole cosmic year. Whereas it gives the plants their colours during the course that takes one year, the minerals need a cosmic year of the sun to gain their colours. In the colours of the minerals, in the green of the emerald, the wine-yellow of the topaz, the red of corundum, there lives a force that develops during the sun's cycle through the Platonic cosmic year.

So you see: If you take from the spirit what you have to say about the world, people begin to ask questions about earthly things in a way that shows they are no longer satisfied with attempts to explain the earth by means of the trivia emanating from our laboratories and dissecting rooms. They want to understand in the proper way, and are well satisfied to be shown things in the 'Sardian' way that involves including the stars and their effects as well. In doing this one is doing what the apocalyptist does; one is bringing Sardis into our present time.

What I have been telling you is merely one example. We must begin to bring this sense for the stars, this sense for the beings of the stars into our present time. We must begin to help people understand anew that the Christ is a Sun Being. This is the fact that meets with the greatest opposition of all.

When I tell you these things, and especially when I tell you how our modern fifth post-Atlantean age must become, in a way, a re-awakened Sardis such as we find described briefly, concisely and marvellously in the fifth congregation and the fifth seal that must now be opened—when I tell you these things you will sense that it is our task today to develop this special way of understanding the Book of Revelation, namely that the Book of Revelation be a *task* that is knocking daily at the door of our heart. There is no point in merely interpreting the Book of Revelation. It is necessary that we *do* the Book of Revelation in all things, otherwise we might as well leave it alone. Merely to interpret it is almost valueless.

Herewith I have now told you the second aspect that must be involved when we read the Book of Revelation. Yesterday I sought to explain the form, today I am seeking to show you that to read the Book of Revelation one must be present with one's will. This is only natural, for revelations have always arisen through Inspirations of the will. With this we are touching on a truly apocalyptic point, a living apocalyptic point.

There are people today who are in some ways educated in an apocalyptic manner. They are educated apocalyptically in a way that gives them an education of the will that is oriented specifically towards the Roman Catholic church. These are the Jesuits. Jesuit education, the exercises of the Jesuits, have a strongly apocalyptic aspect. The exercises of the Jesuits involve a schooling of the will such as is always at the foundation of any apocalyptic, any revelatory vision.

Educating the will is the most important aspect for anyone who takes seriously a genuine priesthood in the sense of a Christian renewal. Such a person must understand the Book of Revelation if he is to see in it the right impulse for the will, whereas a very one-sided impulse for the will was given by Ignatius of Loyola, a grand impulse no doubt, but an extremely onesided one. Today this has become ahrimanically rigid, but especially in looking at Ignatius of Loyola we are shown how wrong it is to look at the world in any other way but through spiritual science. People still attribute the development of the Jesuits today to Ignatius of Loyola, but this is wrong. Ignatius of Loyola has long since been reincarnated and has of course extricated himself entirely from that earlier stream. He lived anew as Emanuel Swedenborg, and the development of the Jesuits since then has slid right into the realm of Ahriman; it no longer harks back to Ignatius of Loyola but works now in accordance with Ahriman's purposes.[5] You could say that this is the shadow, the counter-image of what you yourselves must train yourselves to be by, as I have said, taking the Book of Revelation into your 'I' in such a way that your 'I' becomes the sum of powers that work in an apocalyptic way.

LECTURE SIX

Dornach, 10 September 1924

When someone was initiated in the ancient Mysteries, he first experienced having his understanding, his whole human soul make-up, guided towards the meaning of the cycle of world cultural evolutions, a cycle that runs in sevens. In the Book of Revelation we have a clear after-echo of what results from the initiation principle of the ancient Mysteries. The number seven is contained in the Book of Revelation in many different ways, including its structure, its composition, and its content. At the time, of course, things linked with the number seven were not linked with it in any external sense in the manner we might imagine today. Instead, the person in question was initiated into the whole way in which numbers work and interweave.

I want to draw your attention here, dear friends, to something I explained in quite a different context in the other course of lectures I am giving on the science of speech.[1] I had to explain how it is possible to have experiences in the sounds of speech, but that today humanity has lost the capacity of having experiences through the sounds of speech. Consider how a sound of speech contains elements of the formative, living Word and how through experiencing such sounds the most wonderful cosmic content can be formed through combining those sound elements, of which there are approximately 32. Put yourselves into a time—and there have been times when this was a reality for human beings—that lived and moved in these elements of the sounds of speech, vividly experiencing the wonder of being able to fashion a world through experiencing these 32 sound elements. In the formation of speech, in the formative shaping of the Word, one felt the weaving of spirit that accompanied the experience of speaking. One experienced how gods live in the sounds of speech.

Of these 32 sounds it is easy to work out that about 24 are consonants and about seven are vowels—of course such things are always approximate. In the sense of the opening of John's Gospel—'In the beginning was the Word'—you can then throw light on the image, which can also be thought of as an apocalyptic image, of the Alpha and the Omega surrounded by the seven angels—the vowels—and the 24 elders—the consonants. In this sense it was also felt that the secret of the universe lived entirely—in the way I have already explained—in what was intoned in the holy speech of the cultus. So while celebrating the cultus one felt the mighty presence of the cosmic content existing in this symbolic picture.

Humanity must anyway begin to feel again *where* the gods were sought by the wisdom of the Mysteries. They were not sought in such a distant, transcendental realm as is imagined today. Their incorporation was looked for in such things as the sounds of speech. 'Cosmic Word' denoted that which weaves throughout the universe, that in which human beings share through their own speech.

It is the same with numbers. Our present idea of numbers is thoroughly abstract as compared with the way they are still seen in the Book of Revelation. In the early Christian centuries there were some individuals who understood things like the Book of Revelation to some extent because there was still a feeling for the secret of numbers, because the specific relationships in the structure of a sequence of numbers were still experienced. A number sequence was not taken in the way we take it today as being a stringing together of one number with the next. People experienced what was contained in the three, in the four; they experienced the closed nature of the three, the open nature of the four, the nature of the five, so closely related to the being of man. Something divine was felt to be in numbers, just as something divine was also found in the written letters and in the sounds of speech.

Once an individual had reached the stage in the ancient Mysteries when it was time for him to be initiated into the secret of numbers it was his duty to think and to feel in the sequence of these number secrets. Consider what this involves. In music we have the seven notes with the octave, the eighth, being like the first. In the rainbow we have seven colours. There are also other phenomena in nature involving the number seven. Imagine it occurring to nature to make the colours of the rainbow appear in a different order; the whole universe would be upset by this. Or think of ordering the notes differently in the musical scale; music would become intolerable.

The one to be initiated was shown that, as in nature, there is also a law applying to the soul being of man. After his initiation he was expected not to cast his thoughts hither and thither arbitrarily, for he was now obliged to think in accordance with numbers, to experience the secret of numbers inwardly in the way it lives and weaves in all beings and all processes, in the way it lives in nature.

The Book of Revelation was written in an age when it was still entirely valid for the human being to be in the midst of the cosmic secret of the number seven or twelve or twenty-four, or the number three. Since the beginning of our era of the consciousness soul, which means since the first third of the fifteenth century, the importance is returning of what existed prior to the strict validity of the number seven, and furthermore shifts are also beginning to occur in the number seven itself. We are no longer in the happy position of experiencing an evolution that runs strictly in accordance with the number seven. We have reached a stage in earth evolution when irregularities are beginning to come into the secrets of numbers, so that for us the secrets of numbers have attained a new significance.

While we enjoy finding out how the secrets of numbers live in a document such as the Book of Revelation, it is also the case that when we enter in a living way into material such as this Book we become capable of comprehending through our senses also those things that take place outside the secrets of numbers. You could say that in some ways we are extricating our life from the secrets of numbers. We must, however, learn how to use them in forms that are appropriate for human happenings on the earth nowadays, and how they should be taken into consideration by priests in the field of religion.

This being said, I shall, however, now speak about certain phenomena as though they were still proceeding in accordance with the secrets of numbers, for it is in a sense a slow process for world events to extricate themselves from the secrets of numbers and enter into a way of proceeding that is not bound by them. The way of thinking in the ancient Mysteries was to see great cycles of time following their courses in the number seven, and also other, smaller and very small cycles.

In the seven congregations that existed contemporaneously as actual concrete groupings on the earth we also see the continuation of the old cultures as well as the beginning of new cultural ages. But there is on the other hand also a smaller cycle that we can learn to understand through the Book of Revelation. It is this smaller cycle, dear friends, that I would like to consider with you now.

Looking back to the time when the Mystery of Golgotha took place on the earth we find, with regard to the spiritual evolution of human beings, the archangelic regency of Oriphiel,[2] that archangel who receives his impulses predominantly from the forces of Saturn. After this we come to an age when Anael was the reigning archangel, then to the age of Zachariel, then to the age of Raphael, then to that of Samael, then Gabriel, and then to the present age of Michael. We have a first, second, third, fourth, fifth, sixth and seventh age, so that with regard to this smaller cycle within our larger fifth cycle we are in the seventh age. We are living in an age we would have to describe as follows if we were to use today's way of formulating things: We are living in the age of five/ seven, the fifth post-Atlantean cultural age, the fifth larger cycle of human evolution, and—with regard to a smaller cycle of the ages of archangelic regency—we are living in the seventh age, which interweaves with the larger one.

A seventh age, dear friends, signifies an end stage. The age we are now in was preceded by the sixth, that of Gabriel. In a sixth age a great many things are decided, and preparations are made for the end. But the age prior to it also still works into that sixth age. The Michael age began around 1879, the Gabriel age around 1471. Before that was the age of Samael, the archangel who receives his impulses from Mars; that was the fifth age.

The point in time when the fifth post-Atlantean cultural age began occurred during the age when the archangel of the fifth shorter age was regent. During the fifth archangelic regency, that archangel had already been preparing the onset of the fifth post-Atlantean cultural age for three to four centuries. So being already in progress, the smaller age coincided with the beginning of the larger age. This signifies nothing less than that the larger ages are prepared by spirits of the middle hierarchy. The third hierarchy, to which the archangels belong, are the serving members of the higher hierarchies. The law of numbers thus brings it about that at the beginning of the fifth age the fifth archangel coincides at the height of his smaller age with a higher being from a higher hierarchy who is also in the number five.

It is a good while, relatively speaking, since people spoke about such things, but they were spoken of for longer than one ordinarily imagines. In places like the School of Chartres these secrets were even being mentioned in the twelfth century. At that time there was still an apocalyptic language. It is always the case that the universe is seen, so to speak, in the perspective, in the aspect, of number.

When Plato says: 'God mathematizes, God geometrizes,'[3] he is referring not to our little bit of abstract geometry or mathematics but to that profound experience people in ancient times had regarding forms and numbers. Materialism derides this today, but in fact we can everywhere see that the law of the number seven is also at work in organic life.

Consider the time it takes for something to develop and then follow this up by looking at butterflies or larvae emerging or the incubation period of certain illnesses. You will find the law of the number seven at work everywhere. The initiates were shown that numbers are derived from the very nature of things, and this in turn drew their attention to the way things stand in the overall cosmic context.

It makes us sit up and take notice, dear friends, when we hear: The archangel who is in the number five begins his period of regency in connection with the fifth post-Atlantean age with forces emanating from Mars. If an age begins with Mars forces—even quite superficially this is hinted at—then there is something warlike in it.

We see that the cultural ages are separated from one another by important events. But we also see that there was an important event that separated the Atlantean period from the present, post-Atlantean period—which as a fifth period has now reached its fifth cultural age—and this event is the ice age known as the Great Flood, the fall of old Atlantis and the rise of new continents. We are now living in the fifth post-Atlantean age, and a sixth and seventh age will follow. The catastrophe that will separate the next great period—after the fifth, sixth and seventh ages—will not be merely an external event in nature such as the ice age and everything we are told about the Great Flood. The separation between the fifth and sixth period will show itself more in the moral realm. A war of all against all, about which I have often spoken, will be a moral catastrophe that will separate the fifth from the sixth great period of earth evolution. It will certainly also be connected with events in nature, but these events in nature will be more in the background.

The fifth cultural age was introduced by what comes through Samael from Mars, the quarrelsome spirit, in that elements of conflict were fetched down out of the spiritual world. At the beginning of the consciousness soul era we see also in the smaller sequence how our fifth post-Atlantean age contains something of a premonition, a prophetic premonition of what will happen at the close of the greater post-Atlantean period as a whole, once the fifth cultural age will have been followed by the sixth and seventh.

Listening to the voices of those speaking at the turn of the fourteenth to the fifteenth century who still knew something of the secret processes behind the visible ones, you will even then, in that time of Samael's Mars regency, hear indications about the end of our greater post-Atlantean period, though only in tiny hints. Once you make a correlation between number and what is happening, you begin to think apocalyptically. You learn to read the universe apocalyptically and you will find that countless secrets reveal themselves if you learn to look at the world in this apocalyptic way.

Think now of how our time lies in the small Michael age and also in the fifth post-Atlantean cultural age as well as in the greater cycle of the post-Atlantean period. Let us investigate the meaning of this. We are living in the fifth greater period of the earth, the post-Atlantean period. This fifth period is the one that has to a considerable extent disengaged the human being from the divine world. The people of Atlantis still definitely felt themselves to be filled with God; rather than feeling like individual human beings they felt themselves to be enveloped in the mantle of God. A human being during Atlantis felt that it was God who existed rather than the individual.

The purpose of our post-Atlantean period is, essentially, to make the human being independent, to disengage the human being from the divinity, and this is what has been happening slowly and gradually through four cultural ages. It began slowly in the ancient Indian cultural age which could definitely still be sensed in the Mysteries of Ephesus. In the ancient Indian cultural age the human being still felt himself to be within the divinity, whereas he disengaged himself quite strongly during the second cultural age, that of ancient Persia. In the third cultural age he felt even more separated, so that he began to feel death approaching in the distance. In the Greco-Latin cultural age death was felt to such an extent that the saying came to be coined: 'Rather a beggar in the land of the living than a king in the underworld.'[4]

Now that we are destined in the fifth post-Atlantean cultural age to find death more and more by our side as a companion, as I mentioned yesterday, we shall need moral powers if we are to endure this constant presence of death. So it is important for us that our time in the immediate present should see the consciousness soul—accompanied by the constant presence of death beside the human being—coinciding with the Michael age, that archangelic regency which signifies a kind of end, a kind of culmination of perfection, but involving at once both decadence and perfection.

Michael, the Spirit who lived in the sun, the most important servant of the Christ-Spirit in the sun, experienced the Mystery of Golgotha from the other side. Humanity on earth experienced the Mystery of Golgotha in such a way that they saw Christ approaching. Michael and his hosts, who were still in the sun at the time, experienced it through having to take leave of Christ.

Dear friends, we must permit the two poles of this supreme cosmic event to work on our souls: the hosanna on earth, the arrival of Christ on earth, and the leave-taking from Michael's hosts in the sun above. The two belong together.

In this very age of ours Michael has experienced a great metamorphosis. The beginning of his regency entailed his following after Christ in coming down to the earth, whereas in future his regency will entail his striding ahead of Christ's deeds on earth. One will learn to understand once again what is meant by the words: Michael goes on before the Lord. Before Oriphiel there was of course also a Michael age, and in the Old Testament the initiates in Asia spoke of Michael as going on before Yahweh; just as the countenance as a person's foremost part goes on before him, so did they speak of Michael being the Countenance of Yahweh, and so must we learn to speak of Michael as the Countenance of Christ. But we are now in a different age. Certain things now have to attain their highest perfection. We must in a sense learn to make something fruitful that was hitherto not able to be fruitful.

Take the seven congregations of the Book of Revelation. We can allocate each to one of the archangelic regencies, and if we take the first age, which paralleled the Christ-Event and the beginning of Christianity and which was still going on when the Book of Revelation was written, we shall find that it is represented for us by the congregation at Ephesus. In accordance with the Book of Revelation we can also see this congregation at Ephesus as the one which was bound to Christianity with its first love. All this can be comprehended through the secret of numbers.

The next age we come to is that of Anael who derives his powers from Venus. In that age we find the great deeds of love that were accomplished for the spread of Christianity, countless deeds of love, especially those that still live in the traces of the Irish monks who spread Christianity across Europe. In the other aspects of Christian life, too, we find love to be supreme under the regency of Anael.

Then follows the regency of Zachariel who draws his powers from Jupiter, chiefly powers of wisdom, powers that were, however, little understood in that age. Also, instead of an actual reign of Jupiter, the archangel regency began to withdraw into the background. Humanity in a way no longer reached up to the region of Jupiter; it denied the Jupiter spirit. The significant Council of Constantinople, that Eighth Council which deprived the evolution of humanity of so much by abolishing the trichotomy, falls in this age.[5]

Now comes the age when something little noticed in

external history was at work. After the conclusion of the Zachariel age humanity was fundamentally sick in soul. Humanity was really quite ill, and substances of disease spread from East to West, terrible substances of disease that endangered Christianity because they stemmed from materialism, for it was materialism that pushed its way into Christianity. Because the age of Jupiter wisdom was finished it became possible for materialism to make itself felt within Christian culture.

Something remarkable that was present on the earth only as a projection was behind all this. Behind all these remnants that were like sickness there was something remarkable in the age that followed that of Zachariel from the tenth, eleventh century onwards, the age of Raphael, the physician among the archangels. This was the age in which healing took place behind the scenes of world history, not visibly in public but very much within. Much was healed with regard to rescuing certain moral qualities that were about to perish. In opposition to the substances of disease that had been brought to Europe through Mohammedanism, something else was called for that also had to come from the Orient but in another form, something steeped in the Christian principle. Behind the Crusades—and in fact in principle this was the cause of the Crusades—one must look for the will to heal humanity, to cure it of the materialism threatened both by Mohammedanism and by Roman Catholicism. Basically it was Raphael, the physician among the archangels, who inspired those who first taught humanity to look to that Orient towards which the Crusades were directed.

In this, dear friends, we find ourselves in the fourth smaller age that fell within the fourth larger post-Atlantean cultural age, the Greco-Latin age. This fourth larger age was destined to have within it the Mystery of Golgotha. The fourth smaller age, the Raphael age, is intimately related to the whole basic structure of the fourth larger age. We see how the Archangel

Raphael—by inspiring human beings to undertake the Crusades, turning their attention powerfully towards the Orient in order to find the Mystery of Christ there in the Orient—we see how Raphael took up the impulses of Christ, how a spiritual atmosphere floated above the ground, floated above all that was happening. Those who were able to look behind the scenes of external happenings even only a little bit were separated from the immediate spiritual world by the merest gossamer web, just as we were when Michael began to work visibly on the earth in the last third of the nineteenth century.

Outstanding spirits were alive in that Raphael age, among them Joachim of Floris and Alanus de Insulis.[6] They were able to observe Raphael's work, this work of healing humanity carried on behind the scenes of external happenings. This was the background to that age when the spirit was substantially sick. Witness to this is also the fact that precisely at this time people began to gain an understanding specifically for the Gospel of Luke, the Gospel of Healing. Thus when we look at the times in accordance with the secret of numbers we gain important knowledge to help us understand the significance of events.

Then followed the age of Samael that received its fundamental impulses from Mars. Powers of conflict began to work; they were inoculated into humanity. The number five became opposed to the number four. Whenever there is a transition from a four to a five there is the peculiar situation of the five always getting into opposition to the four. Back in the ancient Mysteries there were long ages when the pupils, the adepts, were initiated into the secret of numbers, and there came a time when these pupils emerged from their lessons filled with a deep conviction that they expressed in the words: Now I know the number of evil, it is the number five.[7] Wherever the number five is at work in the universe we are always up against the world of evil. The five rebels against the four, and in consequence great decisions have to be taken which culminate in the transition up into the six, coming about in either a good way or a bad way.

We shall reflect tomorrow on the extent to which this can lead into more concrete considerations, into the wisdom of the heart and of the human soul. I wanted to show you how one can use numbers as a guideline in trying to fathom events.

LECTURE SEVEN

Dornach, 11 September 1924

Before going any further in our consideration of the Book of Revelation we must now add a number of points regarding the proper way to read it, points that are, however, more external. We shall certainly then reach our own present time with what we read in this Book. First we must look at the spiritual background out of which the Book of Revelation has emerged. Of course I do not mean this in the sense of today's way of explaining a work against the background of its time in a superficial historical manner. Such a method is not applicable in the case of works that have been conceived out of the spiritual world in the way described in the Book of Revelation. We must be clear about the fact that the Book of Revelation came into being in the way it did according to the spiritual conditions of its time and not according to external, historical conditions.

Let us now look at that time of the early Christian centuries, and let us connect it with general cosmic evolution in the spiritual sense.

Looking at evolution taking place behind the scenes of external happenings we see that the year AD 333 is an important one. That year represents the point in time when the 'I' entered into the intellectual or mind soul of the human being that had gradually evolved between 747 BC and the beginning of the era of the consciousness soul in the fifteenth century. The year 333 falls in the middle of this period. The development of Greek culture was an important aspect of the era of the intellectual or mind soul, and it continued to have its effect until the era of the consciousness soul. The Mystery

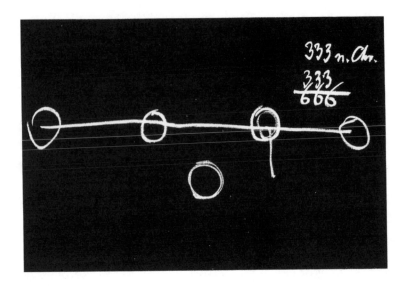

of Golgotha took place in the era when the intellectual or mind soul was evolving.

We must understand that the entry of the 'I' into the intellectual or mind soul is an immensely significant event. The coming of the 'I', which took place around the year 333, had a very profound and serious effect in the souls of those in particular who were suitable for receiving the influence of the spirit. Those who want to participate in the life of the spirit and want to work in the same direction as the life of the spirit must relate the external facts of historical evolution to their spiritual background.

What important external events took place during the period when the 'I' was entering into the human soul behind the scenes of external happenings? What light does the entry of the 'I' throw on these events? Dear friends, it is at such a point that the human being finds the whole relationship between God and man becoming incomprehensible, insecure and open to dispute.

One event that happened at that point in time was the

important controversy between Arius and Athanasius.[1] With the entry of the 'I' into the intellectual or mind soul, ambiguities arise in the inmost soul of the human being, although these remain unconscious for the time being. But they lead to the question: In what way does the divine 'I' live in the nature of man? People at that time became uncertain as to what they should think about how the divine relates to the world and to the human being. In this matter Arius and Athanasius differed drastically, and we find that the view represented by Athanasius gained the upper hand in Western Europe, while that of Arius underwent a gradual decline.

Let us now look at this from the spiritual point of view, for this is the most important one if we want to understand the inner meaning and the inner spirit of something like the Book of Revelation. Arius saw the human being on the one hand rising higher and higher and, as it were, having to come closer and closer to the divine; and on the other hand he saw the divine being. In conjunction with these two great cosmic principles he then had to reach an understanding of the Mystery of Golgotha, of the nature of Christ. He wanted to find an answer to the question: How is the human and how is the divine nature contained in Christ himself? Should we really regard Christ as a divine being or not? The answer he came up with was, actually: No. Basically he occupied the same ground as that which later became the general opinion amongst the population of Europe, which was that a barrier must be erected between man and God, that the indwelling of God in the human being is not admissible, and that one must place an abyss between God and man.

Without prejudging things let us now return to the time of early Christianity which in the main has nothing in common with later Roman Catholicism, for as time went on Christianity became decadent in Roman Catholicism. For this reason we must also be clear about the fact that for the sake of humanity's further development it was essential for the whole controversy to be decided in favour of Athanasius, who saw Christ as a directly divine being, who saw in Christ the truly divine Sun Spirit. Later, though, this view was relegated more to the background because of the aversion to imagining Christ as a cosmic being. Athanasius in his whole turn of mind was predisposed to seeing in Christ a God who was equal to the Father God.

This view continued to have its effect, except that it was deprived of its ultimate point in AD 869 by the Eighth Council of Constantinople,[2] which basically destroyed the dogma of the Council of Nicaea by declaring the trichotomy a heresy. Herein lay the beginning of decadence in ecclesiastical Christianity; it meant that for subsequent centuries of Catholic ecclesiastical development it was no longer possible to grow into the spirit.

The revolution that occurred in the human being when the 'I' entered into the intellectual or mind soul is certainly coloured by this event, but at the same time it also gives that external event an inner significance of its own.

Looking more closely at the historical situation, we have to say that after the year 333 there came times—significant above all for European development—when contact with the culture of ancient Rome was discontinued. We see how the culture of ancient Rome, such as it had by then become, was basically unable to accept Christianity. A grand vista unfolds before us when we study this year 333. It is also the year in which the period begins when the culture of ancient Rome shifted further eastwards from Rome. Christianity fled eastwards from Rome under the Roman Emperor, the Roman Caesar who wanted to adopt Christianity.[3] It is less important to study the abuse and damage caused by the Council of Constantinople than to try and find the meaning of why there had to be a flight eastwards from the West when Christianity entered Rome. This is immensely significant. Seen from the spiritual world it is so significant and shining an event that by comparison all the damage done by Byzantianism hardly comes into consideration.

One cannot help saying how tremendously significant it is that Christianity had to flee at the moment when, in its external manifestation, it came into contact with the culture of ancient Rome. Nevertheless, after it had fled eastwards under Constantine, Christianity did flourish on the soil of ancient Rome, on the soil of what ancient Rome had been preparing for a long time. But as it flowered it was squeezed into external, secular forms.

We should try to imagine what it means when the apocalyptist turns his prophetic vision towards Christianity preparing itself in Rome, and sees how at the very moment when the culture of ancient Rome declares itself in favour of Christianity, Christianity takes on the ancient Roman forms. This is the aspect we see: On the one side there is the controversy between Arius and Athanasius, and on the other ancient Rome converting to Christianity. But in travelling eastwards, Christianity takes on the form that has been left behind in Rome, the Roman state structure, and becomes, also in the way it works externally, a continuation of ancient Rome.

We will now leave on one side for the moment certain things that we shall have to explain at a deeper spiritual level, and turn instead to history. The apocalyptist foresaw in a grand and powerful manner what history would bring. Although he did not express it clearly, he had it in his feeling life, and it underlay the composition of his Book: He showed how the growth of what was to take place both within humanity and externally in history would need 333 years after the Mystery of Golgotha, and how a strange semblance of development would then take place in Christianity. The soil on which everything was to be prepared that would then take another 333 years up to the year 666—this soil was that Christian Romanness, uprooted and moved eastwards, and that Roman Christianity which had comfortably adjusted itself to those Roman forms.

Dear friends, call up before your souls once more what we said yesterday about someone still inspired by the ancient Mysteries, such as the apocalyptist, becoming immersed in numbers. You see the apocalyptist contemplating the next 333 years, in which Christianity will seem to be flourishing externally, but in which it will in fact have to develop while shrouded in mist on two sides, driven eastwards in Constantine's day and preserving something old and ahrimanic from the West. Something is being prepared in the womb of evolution, something that had been left over from non-Christian ancient Romanness.

What was this non-Christian Romanness? If we look into the Mysteries, we find that in the greatest, most developed Mysteries the trichotomy, the sacred number three, was deeply significant. So let us have a closer look at what this meant. People thought of being born into the onward flowing stream of heredity; this was how the human being was thought of in, for example, the world order of the secret Hebrew doctrine. People thought of the human being with the capabilities and characteristics he had brought with him through heredity, through his ancestry. People imagined human life as a development going in a straight line with which nothing important interferes except what comes about through the impulse of heredity: You stem from the physical powers of your parents; in you the spiritual impulses of your physical parents are at work. That, essentially, was the doctrine of the 'Fathers' in the ancient Mysteries. This is as far as this dogma went, for example in the secret Hebrew doctrines, but also in other secret doctrines.

In the higher Mysteries, however, something else was added. These Mysteries spoke of the human being carrying the impulses of heredity and developing through them. But they also spoke of how during physical existence between birth and death the human being can take in another impulse as well, the impulse that enables him to extricate himself from heredity, to find his way out of this in his soul life. This is the Son-Impulse, the Christ-Impulse. These Mysteries said: The impulses of heredity are within the human being and bring about an evolution between birth and death that runs in a straight line. They come from the Father, from the Father who is the ground of everything. The impulses of the Son, however, do not enter into the forces of heredity. They have to be absorbed by the soul and worked on by the soul, they must expand the soul to such an extent that it becomes free of bodily forces, free of the forces of heredity. The impulses of the Son enter into human freedom—in the way freedom was understood in those times—they enter into freedom of soul, where the soul is free of the forces of heredity. These are the forces that allow the human being to be reborn in soul. They enable the human being to take himself in hand during the life given to him by the Father. All those ancient Mysteries saw the Father Human Being; they saw the Human Being who is the Son of the Father, the Brother of Christ, who takes himself in hand, who takes into himself what is in a sense free of the body, who has to bear within himself a new kingdom that knows nothing of physical nature, that represents an order different from that of nature: the kingdom of the spirit.

In speaking of the Father God in *this* sense, we would be entitled—although not in the external, materialistic way we do today, but more after the manner of the Hebrew teachings—to speak of natural phenomena that are also spirit phenomena, for the spirit is everywhere at work in natural phenomena. Science as we know it today, in the way it came into being not so very long ago and in the way it works, is only a one-sided science of the Father. We must add to this the knowledge of the Son, of Christ, *that* knowledge which relates to how the human being takes himself in hand, how the human being receives an impulse that can only be taken in through the soul and that does not come from the forces of heredity. That the human being enters into this is at first without any law, without the force or effectiveness of any law. The effectiveness comes in for him through the spirit, so that in the sense of the ancient Mysteries we have two realms: the realm of nature which is the realm of the Father, and the realm of the Spirit. The human being is carried from the realm of nature into the realm of Spirit by the Son, by Christ.

When we become properly aware of how such contemplations still ruled the apocalyptist and indeed the souls of his contemporaries, then we shall be able to see into his prophetic soul which was able to survey the future in broad outlines. This will enable us to understand how he now saw what came down upon Christianity—degenerating as it was in two directions into a semblance of its true self—round about the year 666.

His prophetic glance now fell on those teachings which were coming into being around the year 666 and which harked back to those Mysteries that knew nothing of the Son: the Mohammedan teachings. The Mohammedan teachings do not know the structure of the world I have just been speaking about, they do not know the two realms, that of the Father and that of the Spirit; they know only the Father. They know only the rigid doctrine: There is one God, Allah, and none beside him; and Mohammed is his Prophet. From this angle, the teachings of Mohammed are the strongest polarity to Christianity, for in them is the will to do away with all freedom for ever, the will to bring about determinism, for nothing else is possible if you can imagine the world solely in the sense of the Father God.

This gave the apocalyptist the feeling: The human being cannot find himself in this; the human being cannot become filled through and through with Christ; if he can comprehend only the old doctrine of the Father, the human being cannot take hold of his own humanness. For such an inwardly rigid and closed-off view of the world the external form of the human being becomes an illusion. The human being only becomes human by taking hold of himself through making Christ alive within himself; he only becomes human when he is adapted to the spiritual order in realms of spirit that are entirely free of nature. He does not become human if he regresses into a view that reckons solely with the Father God.

Now that the 'I' has been entering into man since the year 333, there is a danger—so says the apocalyptist—of humanity growing confused about this 'I' becoming filled with the Son God, with the Christ. After a period of time that is as long as the period up to then from the Mystery of Golgotha, something begins to rise up, something that threatens to keep humanity down at the level of the beast; 666 is the number of the Beast.

The apocalyptist foresaw quite decidedly what was threatening humanity. Christianity was going to collapse in two directions into a semblance of Christianity or, more clearly expressed, it was going to degenerate into a Christianity shrouded in mist. That which was threatening to flood over it in this way is indicated in the designation of the year 666, for the spiritual world the significant year in which what lives in Arabism, in Mohammedanism, sprang up everywhere. The apocalyptist names this year 666 as clearly as can be. Those who can read in an apocalyptic manner understand what I mean. By designating in his mighty words the number 666 as the number of the Beast the apocalyptist was foreseeing what would flood into evolution.

Thus, basically, he foresaw in a revelation everything that then followed. One thing was the streaming of Arabism towards Europe. Another was the way Christianity became filled with a doctrine that could only bring about a failure to understand the human being in his humanness. This arose because the doctrine of the Father was translated into materialism, leading to the assumption more recently that human evolution can only be explained by following the evolution of a sequence of animals up to the human being.

Darwinism surely was a case in point: As the number of the Beast, 666, appeared, the human being could no longer comprehend himself as a human being but only as some kind of higher animal. Surely we are seeing ahrimanic forces of opposition to the Son God at work in the way Christianity has become impregnated with the materialistic form of the Father doctrine. Are not such things still at work now, in our own time? I have often pointed to Harnack's *What is Christianity?* as an example of recent theological literature.[4] Wherever the name of Christ appears in this book you might just as well replace it with the name of the Father, for Harnack's *What is Christianity?* is nothing but a doctrine of the Father God and not a concrete teaching about Christ at all. In fact, it is a denial of the Christ doctrine, for in place of Christ it puts a generalized Father God, and it does not make any kind of approach to all that would come under the heading of Christology.

The apocalyptist saw this time approaching, and in its approach he saw in essence something that oppressed his soul: the difficulty about the Transubstantiation—if I may use a human expression that does not quite coincide with the spiritual, but there is no other way of putting it. Dear friends, you are well aware of how you yourselves had to struggle with the difficulty about the Transubstantiation when this movement for Christian renewal was inaugurated; and you know how much you are still having to struggle with the difficulties inherent in understanding the Transubstantiation. Think of the hours we spent discussing this matter of the Transubstantiation over there in the room where the fire in the Goetheanum started. The Transubstantiation encompasses the whole question of Son and Father. You could say that the controversy about the Transubstantiation as it arose in the Middle Ages also contained something of the oppression experienced by humanity in the controversy between Arianism and Athanasianism.

Transubstantiation can in fact only be meaningful if it is founded on a genuine comprehension of Christology that is in keeping with the spirit, a comprehension of the way in which Christ is united with humanity and with the earth. But because Arianism flooded in, Transubstantiation has always been exposed to being likened to the Father doctrine, which sees the metamorphosis taking place in the substances that are suitable for the Transubstantiation as having to be a part of the processes in nature, of the spirit in natural processes.

All questions connected with the Communion arise from saying: How can that which comes about in the Transubstantiation be grasped in a way that allows it to be compatible with what comes from the Father and is working in evolution and with what comes from the Spirit and is working in the laws of nature? It is not a question of a miracle but a question of the sacrament, which goes in a direction quite different to the trifling matter of a miracle that presented people in the nineteenth and even in the eighteenth century with such peculiar difficulties. One must think of the ordering brought about by the Father and the ordering brought about by the Spirit; and between them stands the Son who in the world of human beings lifts up the realm of nature into the realm of the Spirit. If we place this before our soul we shall find that the Transubstantiation does indeed appear as something that there is no need to see as belonging to the ordering of nature but that is no less possessed of reality, of a spiritual reality, a truly spiritual reality about which one can speak in the same way as one speaks about the reality of the ordering of nature.

The apocalyptist foresaw how difficult it would become for humanity, because of the violence with which the number 666 plays into human evolution, to say: Beside the ordering of nature there is also another ordering, the spiritual order.

But now—one would like to call it the most modern deliverance—there is something approaching out of Anthroposophy that can throw light on such a thing as the Transubstantiation. It is through Anthroposophy that we bring to life once more how human beings live repeatedly on the earth. We show how, by having their field of activity in the external, physical world, they have in them impulses coming from the line of heredity, and how through heredity they are linked with the power of the Father. Seen only externally, there is a great deal in human destiny which is linked with these forces of heredity and which is brought about by the powers of the Father hidden in nature. By acting, however, in a way that brings Spirit into their physical bodily nature which they have brought into being for this present life, human beings also have working in them all the results of their former lives on earth. These also work in them; these forces, too, are a foundation for their actions.

You can look at something a person does from two viewpoints. It can be an action born of father, mother, grandfather, grandmother and so on, but it can also be one in which forces harking back to earlier lives on earth are at work. The latter is an entirely different ordering and it can therefore not be understood on the basis of any science of nature, which is the science of the Father.

It is possible to consider two things which in their underlying reality are the same, though in outer appearance they are different. Look on the one hand at the human being and see how his karma, his destiny develops as the consequence of earlier lives on earth; it does this according to certain laws that exist, but they are not the laws of nature. And now look towards the altar where we see that the Transubstantiation is also not externally visible, for it takes place in the physical substances as a spiritual reality. The same laws are at work in both these processes, and we can bring them together: The one is the way in which karma works, and the other is the way the Transubstantiation takes place. If you understand one, you can also understand the other.

This is one of the mysteries, dear friends, that you in this new priesthood must grasp. This is one of the mysteries under whose light this community of priests must develop out of Anthroposophy. It is one of the inner reasons why this must be.

In saying this, one is also pointing out the immense difficulty that arose, with regard to comprehending the Transubstantiation, from the fact that people could not understand the kind of law which is at work in human karma and which provides the foundation for the Transubstantiation. That year in which the 'I' entered the human being, allowing him to achieve freedom in physical life, that year of 333 in which Christianity on the one hand had to flee eastwards, which meant on the other hand that it was fleeing into the arms of ancient Romanness that could never become entirely Christian—that year of 333 not only brought with it the entry of the 'I', but it also had to cast a shadow, a darkness, over the connections between different lives on earth. This is something that was a part of human evolution.

What would have happened if the 'I' had not entered into the human being at that time? Julian the Apostate—who would be better named Julian the Confessor where the ancient Mysteries are concerned—would have won the day.[5] With the teachings of the ancient Mysteries that he had wanted to introduce it could have happened that the 'I' entering in from spiritual worlds might have been absorbed by humanity in such a way that it would have been possible to grasp the teaching about karma. (Of course this is purely hypothetical; we are only considering what might have happened.) Humanity, however, had to scale higher barriers and was not able to enter into a comprehension of Christianity so easily as would have been the case if Julian the Apostate had won the day.

Humanity was thus exposed to the rise of the Beast, to the consequences and results of the number 666. As I said, we shall be speaking more about the inner aspects of this over the next few days. So humanity was deprived of teachings about karma but placed into the midst of teachings about the Transubstantiation. This meant that there was nothing in the external world that was analogous to the teachings about the Transubstantiation, for it is teachings about karma that are analogous to the teachings about the Transubstantiation. The power through which the destiny of a human being is 'made' in successive lives on earth is not a power of nature, not a power of the Father—it is the power of the Spirit mediated by the Son. This is the power that is also at work on the altar during the transformation of the Host.

We must certainly inscribe such a thing very deep down in our soul if we are to understand it correctly. If we can raise our soul, our inmost being to the spiritual impulses that work from earthly life to earthly life, then we can also comprehend what happens at the altar in the Transubstantiation, for it is no different there.

If we look at the consecrated Host with our ordinary understanding we see nothing of what is really happening, just as in the destiny of an individual we see nothing of what is really happening if we look only at what the strength of his muscles and blood achieves in the material sense, by which I mean out of the stream of heredity—I am not speaking of the spiritual forces that are at work in muscles and blood.

These things, dear friends, provide the context, and if we cannot understand them we shall understand neither the Book of Revelation nor the apocalyptist. The impulses we can read quite clearly in the Book of Revelation bring us right up to the present day.

LECTURE EIGHT

Dornach, 12 September 1924

By bringing before our souls the central points in which the apocalyptist's revelations culminate—as we have already done with certain aspects—we can soon arrive at the overall composition as well as the consecutive content of the Book of Revelation. Today we shall therefore continue in our consideration of the central points, so that tomorrow we can really get down to the content consecutively.

Yesterday I spoke about how the apocalyptist in a sense saw something that was threatening to engulf Christianity—that which he felt to be the true Christianity—something that would turn it away from the Christ-Principle and lead it back to the Father-Principle which, if it were to win the day, could take on only materialistic, naturalistic forms in this time.

The apocalyptist saw things and processes in accordance with the secret of numbers or, better, he both looked and felt in accordance with the secret of numbers. Just as the musician senses the way notes sound together in accordance with the secret of numbers, although he becomes conscious of this at most in the occasional passage, so did the apocalyptist sense more or less consciously the secrets that are linked to a number such as 666.

Let us now ourselves look into the cosmos in order to glean from it more of those secrets of the number 666. Let us consider that the Christian revelation as a whole is actually a Sun revelation, that Christ is the Being who comes from the Sun and who sends Michael with his hosts on ahead, just as in a different way Jehovah of old sent Michael on ahead. If we consider that we ourselves are now living in a Michael age we shall find that the Christ-Impulse as a Sun Mystery appears very profoundly indeed before our soul.

We must become profoundly aware in our soul that in the fight against Christianity what is being fought against is the fact that the real spiritual element of Christianity is connected with the Sun. Nothing would please the opponents of Christianity more than if human beings entirely lost their vision of the Sun as a spiritual being and retained only the view of the Sun as it is in physical existence—as I have already mentioned elsewhere during these lectures. When Arabism broke in upon humanity it brought with it the immense danger of humanity forgetting the Mystery of the Sun as the Mystery of Christ. The whole of human evolution would then be sent off in a direction different from the Michael direction which has the task of preparing the Christ-Evolution in a way that would make it comprehensible for human beings.

The apocalyptist who can see behind the scenes of external history realizes that what is happening externally in the order of the world is taking place on the foundation of super-sensible processes. So let us have a look at these super-sensible processes perceived by the apocalyptist as standing behind external happenings.

Every star in our planetary system, including the sun, has a collection of beings within it. On the earth we have the collection of human beings in their evolution. If we want to gain a very profound view of human beings on the earth we could take a look at a later point in evolution when humanity will have attained a much higher stage than the one we occupy today. We could look, for example, to the Vulcan condition, which will follow later after the Earth condition.

Dear friends, imagine what kind of a picture someone would have of the earth if he were to see before him a cosmic body containing a collection of Vulcan human beings. Yet this would still be the earth with its human beings, only it would be in a different stage. It is most important for the human soul to imagine the earth as a totality in this way, to imagine not only humanity in its present stage on earth but what is already present today in seed form, to look at what the human being carries within him and therefore what he *also* is: the human being at the Vulcan stage. The other planets everywhere also have a collection of beings living in them. To the earth has been assigned the task of being the place where the human being evolves, which is why it stands in the middle. We also have other planets, for example today's Jupiter which shows us quite clearly that its beings are entirely different. After all, we meet these beings when we are working out our karma between death and a new birth. If we take the totality of all the beings who are at work in connection with the individual planets including the Sun, we have what was seen right up to the fourteenth century as the spiritual Intelligence of each of the planets; even by the teachers of the Catholic church it was seen as the Intelligence of the planets. We can speak about the Intelligence of the planets as a reality, just as we can speak of humanity on earth being the earth's Intelligence. Every such planet possesses not only its Intelligence but also its Demon. The teachers of the church knew this right up to the fourteenth, fifteenth century. The totality of all the opponents of the Intelligences on a planet are Demons. And thus it is also on the Sun.

If we regard Christianity primarily as an evolution that accords with the Sun Genius, the Sun Intelligence, then we have to see that which is opposing this evolution of Christianity as the Sun Demon. The apocalyptist saw this. He saw what was happening behind the scenes when Christianity fled eastwards from Rome, and he saw Christianity taking on different ways of knowing. He saw the mighty counter-principle of Arabism bursting in on a Christianity that was threatened from two sides by illusion. And what he saw behind the scenes of external Arab and Mohammedan deeds made him realize that the Sun Demon was working there against the Sun Genius, against the Sun Intelligence. So he had to depict the Sun Demon as working and living counter to the Christian principle in the human being in such a way that if a human being succumbed to this Sun Demon he then no longer wanted to make contact with the divinity of Christ but wanted instead to remain in the sub-human realm. If asked, the apocalyptist would have called the representatives of Arabism in Europe 'human beings who have surrendered to the Sun Demon' in their soul nature. It was clear to him that from this Arabism everything arises that brings the human being close to animal nature, first of all in his views but gradually also in his will impulses. Who could deny that this also lives in the will impulses? With things that happen as realities in the world one does not always have both cause and effect side by side; one does not see the purpose nor that towards which the purpose is directed.

We may therefore ask ourselves: What would happen if Arabism, the teaching of the Sun Demon, were to be entirely victorious? Humanity would be withdrawn from being able to experience conditions that human beings must experience if they are to comprehend the working of karma from earlier incarnations or if they are to comprehend the Transubstantiation. In the final analysis, that which flowed from Arabism was directed against an understanding of the Transubstantiation. Certainly external facts do not look as if this were the case, but by allotting validity only to the old Father Principle, to the natural world-order, the Sun Demon does indeed intend to sweep away from human view that kind of union which is active in the very highest degree in a sacrament such as the Transubstantiation.

For the apocalyptist, then, the Sun Demon was particularly active around the year 666. He describes him in a way that allows any initiate to recognize him. All such spiritual beings, the Intelligences of the planets, the Intelligences of the Sun, and the Demons of the planets and the Demons of the Sun, have their key sign within the Mysteries where they are present during important ceremonies, and the Sun Demon has this sign:

The apocalyptist describes the Sun Demon as the two-horned beast. In the Latin era, during which Greek and Latin were joined together in the language of the Mysteries, the kind of reading that involved reading in numbers had already become external to some extent, but nevertheless, people did still read in numbers. The apocalyptist used the special mode of reading that was current in his day. He wrote the number 666 using Hebrew characters.

400	200	6	60
ת	ר	ו	ס
tau	resh	vau	samech

He wrote the characters by giving their number values, and he wrote them to be read from right to left. The consonants, to which the appropriate vowels must be added when speaking, give the name of the Demon that has this sign of the Sun Demon: Sorat. Sorat is the name of the Sun Demon at that time, and the apocalyptist describes this sign which we can easily recognize.[1] The apocalyptist sees everything that works against Christianity in this way—such as Arabism—as an outflowing of that spirituality which is represented by Sorat, the Sun Demon.

Dear friends, the number 666 was there in one instance at the time when Arabism was flowing into Christianity in order to impress the seal of materialism on to western culture. But it was there for a second time after a further 666 years had passed, in 1332, in the fourteenth century. At that time once again the Beast rose up out of the waves of world events. To one whose vision is like that of the apocalyptist, world events appear as continuous waves of timespans measuring 666 years. The Beast rises up to threaten Christianity in its search for true humanity; beasthood asserts itself against human-hood: Sorat stirs. In the fourteenth century we see Sorat, the adversary, rising up once again.

It was the time when—out of the deepest depths of soul much more than out of orientalism—the Order of the Knights Templar[2] wanted to found a sun view of Christianity, a view of Christianity that looked up again to Christ as a Sun Being, as a cosmic being, a view that knew again about the spirits of the planets and stars, a view that knew how in cosmic events Intelligences from worlds that lie far apart from one another work together, not only the beings of one particular planet, a view that knew about the mighty oppo-sitions that are brought about by such obstinate beings as Sorat, the Sun Demon, who is one of the most mighty demons in our system. What is at work in the materialism of human beings is, fundamentally, the demonic work of the Sun Demon.

It is of course difficult now to consider what might have become of European civilization if that powerful, that externally powerful Order of the Knights Templar—their riches were confiscated, as we know—had been able to achieve its goals. But in the hearts and souls of those who could not rest until the Order had been destroyed in 1312 and until Jacques de Molay[3] had met his death in 1314, in the hearts of those who were the adversaries of the Christ who looked to the cosmos, in these hearts Sorat lived again, not least by making use of the Roman Church's attitude of mind at that time to bring about the death of the Templars. The appearance of Sorat was more visible than it had been the previous time, and the demise of the Templars is shrouded in a stupendous secret. When you can see into what went on in the souls of the Templars while they were being tortured you can gain some idea of how what lived in their visions was instigated by Sorat. As a result they slandered themselves, providing their enemies with a cheap indictment through what they themselves uttered. People were confronted with the terrible spectacle of seeing individuals being unable to speak about what they genuinely represented, while different spirits from among the cohorts of Sorat spoke through them instead, accusing the Order of the most disgusting things out of the mouths of its own adherents.

The number 666 has twice been fulfilled. And now the time has come in the spiritual world when Sorat and the other opposing demons are preparing to prevent the Sun Principle from entering into the earth. Michael, on the other hand, preparing for his new regency, is fighting with his hosts for this entry of the Sun Principle. Michael was regent of the earth before the time of the Mystery of Golgotha, around the time of Alexander. The other archangels then in turn took over from him: Oriphiel, Anael, Zachariel, Raphael, Gabriel. Since the last third of the nineteenth century he has again been regent of the earth in order to continue working in his way for Christ, for whom he worked until his previous regency ended, approximately until the end of Alexander's rule. Michael is on the earth once again, this time in order to serve here on earth the preparation for Christ and for the deeper comprehension of the Christ-Impulse.

As time has gone on I have spoken here and in various other places about how Christianity has been introduced spiritually through Michael. I mentioned one aspect of this two days ago when I spoke in a lecture[4] about Michael's regency in the time of Aristotle and Alexander, during which a genuinely Christian impulse was already introduced, and when I also pointed to the year 869 in which a kind of supersensible Council took place. This continued further. And at the beginning of the new era, when the consciousness soul is beginning to take effect, we now have—if we look up to spiritual events belonging to earthly humanity and running parallel with earthly events—the wonderful sight of a supersensible school with Michael as its teacher. Those who were to work towards a real development of Christianity—souls not at the moment incarnated on the earth, and also other spiritual beings—were gathered in great numbers around Michael, from the fourteenth to the sixteenth century, as though in a great, supersensible school in which those souls were being prepared who were to appear on earth at the beginning of the twentieth century during Michael's regency. When we look at what was being prepared there we find that it was the anthroposophical world view, which wants to work for this evolution.

From what the ancient Mystery wisdom saw, and through the prophetic sight of future Mystery wisdom, we gather that human beings who take in what we call the inner Christianity, the spiritualized Christianity, those who look to the Genius of the Sun with regard to Christ: these individuals will experience an acceleration of their evolution and reappear on the earth again at the end of the twentieth century. Dear friends, everything we are able to do now in our time by way of taking in the spirituality of these teachings is of great significance, for we are doing it for the human beings who are, *sub specie aeternitatis*, alive at this time. It is a preparation for what is to take place at the end of the century, initially in the form of great, all-embracing, intense deeds of the spirit, after a great deal will have happened that is inimical to a spiritualization of modern civilization. The great revolutions that came about in Europe as a result of the Crusades belonged under the sign of the second occurrence of the number 666. This fact found its expression in the demise of the Templars. Sorat continues to work on and on

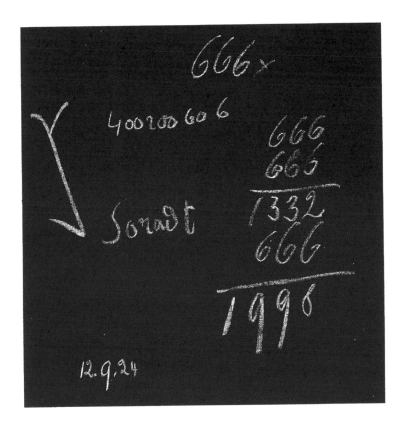

against the forces coming from the Genius of the Sun that are battling for a genuine Christianity.

Before us lies the time of the third number 666: 1998. At the end of this century the time will come when Sorat will once again raise his head most strongly out of the waves of evolution to become the adversary of that appearance of Christ which those who have been prepared for it will already experience during the first half of the twentieth century when the Etheric Christ becomes visible. Only two thirds of the century have still to run before Sorat once again raises his head most mightily.

During the first 666, dear friends, Sorat was still hidden

away inside the evolutionary process of events; he was not seen in any external form, for he lived within the deeds of Arabism, and initiates were able to see him. When the second 666 years had passed he showed himself in the thinking and feeling of the tortured Templars. And before this century is out he will show himself by making his appearance in many humans as the being by whom they are possessed. Human beings will appear of whom it will be impossible to believe that they are real human beings. They will even develop externally in a peculiar manner, for outwardly they will have intense, strong dispositions with savage features and furious destructiveness in their emotions. Their faces will be like the faces of beasts. The Sorat human beings will be recognizable by their external appearance; in a terrible way they will not only scoff at everything but also oppose and want to push into the pool of filth anything that is spiritual. This will be experienced, for example, in the way something that is at present concentrated into a small space in seed form as today's Bolshevism will become incorporated into the whole of human evolution on earth.

That is why it is so important that all who are capable of doing so should strive for spirituality. What is inimical to spirituality will be there anyway, for it works not through freedom but under determinism. This determinism has already decreed that at the end of this century Sorat will be on the loose again, so that the intention to sweep away anything spiritual will be deepseated in large numbers of earthly souls, just as the apocalyptist has foreseen in the beast-like countenance and the beast-like strength that will underlie the deeds of the adversary against the spiritual. Even today the rage against spiritual things is already immense. Yet it is still only in its very early infancy.

All this was foreseen by the apocalyptist. He saw the true unfolding of Christianity as a matter connected with the Sun, but he also foresaw how terrible would be the unfolding of the Sun Demon. All this appeared before him. The entry of Michael into the spiritual evolution of humanity at the end of the nineteenth century, and the appearance of the Etheric Christ during the first half of the twentieth century are events that will be followed by the arrival of the Sun Demon before this century comes to an end. In this Michael age of ours, especially if we want to work in the realm of theology and religion, we have every reason to learn above all from the Book of Revelation how to think and feel in an apocalyptic way, how not to remain stuck in what are merely external facts but how to rise up to the spiritual impulses that lie behind them.

The trail is being blazed for the entry of the demons, the adherents of the great Demon Sorat. To gain an idea of this you only need to speak to people who understand something of what led to the World War. It is fair to say that of the approximately 40 people who are guilty of causing that war, almost all were in a state of lowered consciousness at the moment when it broke out. Such a state of consciousness is always a way in for ahrimanic demonic powers, and one of the greatest of these demons is Sorat. Such are the attempts Sorat is making to gain at least temporary access to the consciousness of human beings in order to bring about calamity and confusion. Not the World War itself, but what followed it and what is even more terrible and what will become more terrible still—for example the present state in which Russia finds herself—this is what the Sorat spirits who invade human souls are aiming at.

We must be aware of the fact that this is so. For in times when there was true spirituality on the earth, what did it mean to work as a priest? It has always meant, dear friends, that one worked not only within the sphere of earthly events but also in full consciousness of how one stands in the spiritual world, in intercourse with the divine world. This and no other was the spirit in which the apocalyptist wrote his

Book of Revelation. Someone who wants to lead human beings into the spirit must himself be able to see into the spirit. Every age has to do this in its own way. Look at the inner laws according to which—although perhaps somewhat alienated from the spirit—the sequence of Egyptian pharaohs appears to be so logical. We can glean from this that the succession of pharaohs was indeed not arbitrary. Ancient scriptures told which task each pharaoh following on the previous one must regard as his specific obligation and that the impulse for the formulation of that obligation emerged from what later came to be called the Hermetic revelation, the revelation of Hermes. I do not mean the Hermetic revelation we know today in a somewhat bowdlerized version, but the ancient Hermes wisdom that also belongs to the great Mysteries in which one spoke of the revelation as being three times holy: a revelation of the Father, a revelation of the Son, a revelation of the Holy Spirit. All this points to the fact that priestly work everywhere meant working out of the spirit into the material world; this is what priesthood was always understood to signify.

This is what the impulse of priesthood must once again become, now that the period of time is over when it was not felt to be true that one can work out of the spiritual world. With the culture and education we have today, which in the era of the consciousness soul has gradually come to take on materialistic forms in every field, people are very far from being able to comprehend such a thing as the mystery of the Transubstantiation and with this the spiritual mysteries of Christianity. For individual priests today, contemporary education makes it seem like a kind of untruth to speak of the profound contents of the Mysteries that are connected with the Transubstantiation. Hence the rationalistic discussions about Transubstantiation that began at the time of the second attack by Sorat and continue today up to the time of the third attack. There is absolutely no point in taking the

Book of Revelation as something about which commentaries can be written. The only meaningful thing to do is to learn through the Book of Revelation how to become an apocalyptist oneself, and in becoming an apocalyptist to get to understand one's own time so well that the impulses of that time become the impulses of one's own work.

As a human being of the present time and as a priest one can enter into this by looking directly at the beginning of the Michael age in the 1870s, at the appearance of Christ in the first half of the twentieth century and at the threatening rise of Sorat and his adherents at the end of the twentieth century. As human beings who understand these things and know how to interpret the signs of the times, let us arrange our lives in accordance with these three mysteries of our time: the mystery of Michael, the mystery of Christ, and the mystery of Sorat. If we do this, we shall work in the right way in the field to which our karma has led us, and so will the priest in his priestly field. We shall continue from here tomorrow.

LECTURE NINE

Dornach, 13 September 1924

Now that we have brought a number of elements together in order to delve further into the essence of the Book of Revelation, let us turn our attention to the Book itself. We shall begin by addressing some questions relating to the end, the goal of what the apocalyptist sees in his vision and wants to impart to humanity. You will see later why I have chosen to structure our considerations in this particular way.

What the apocalyptist gives us is what you might call a communication to humanity, a revelation to human beings, but a revelation that is very different in its essence from other communications not arising out of clairvoyance. So the apocalyptist points out that the event which enabled him to make his communication to humanity was a special one, a mighty enlightenment. The Book of Revelation is thus shown to be an event, a fact belonging to the further development of Christianity.

The great starting point of Christian development on the earth, which before it happened could only be foreseen and hoped for, is of course the Mystery of Golgotha itself. After this come the various facts that must come about if Christianity is to go on developing from the Mystery of Golgotha onwards through all time and eternity. One such fact is the content of the Book of Revelation. The apocalyptist is fully aware that he is not only telling others something that he himself has experienced and that will contribute to the development of his time; he knows that the very receiving and passing on of the content of the Book of Revelation is a fact in itself.

The important aspect that distinguishes Christianity from other religious creeds is that the old religions were teachings, whereas the essential aspect of Christianity is the deed of Golgotha, and this essential aspect must be followed by further deeds. It is therefore not a primary and fundamental priority that people should have the Gospels explained to them. What is essential is that Christianity should seek a real and genuine connection with the Mystery of Golgotha. Under the influence of intellectualism in recent times, Christianity has adopted intellectualistic forms of its own. This has even led to the famous statement that Jesus has no place in the Gospels.[1] This would mean more or less that the content of the Gospels may be accepted as teachings while no account need be taken of the teacher from whom they stem. God the Father alone has a place in the Gospels, so it is said. This is tantamount to implying that the important thing about the Mystery of Golgotha was that Christ Jesus appeared and gave teachings about the Father. But this is not the essential aspect at all. The essential aspect is that the Deed was done on Golgotha, that Christ Jesus lived on the earth and accomplished the Deed on Golgotha. The teachings are the accessories, they are secondary and inessential. Christianity must fight its way back to a recognition of this, and also to actually carrying it out.

So while he is receiving the revelation, the apocalyptist is aware that this fact has happened and that it is working further through him. This is what is important to him. What is it that continuously takes place through this? Looking at the make-up of the human being as it is today, we know that during the daytime he wears his four 'garments', physical body, etheric body, astral body and 'I', in quite a normal way. When he sleeps, on the other hand, astral body and 'I' are outside the physical and etheric body, they are in the spiritual surroundings of the earth that are there behind the phenomena we perceive with our physical senses. They are not as yet perceptible to the human being, for this is only possible through initiation. During sleep the human being leads a dim existence of which only a generalized sensation remains on awakening, or he sees dreams that rise up out of sleep in the way I have often described. Astral body and 'I' are in the spiritual world in such a way that they can have no impressions, no direct impressions of Christ and his whole being. If there were nothing more to this than what I have just described, the 'I' and astral body would enter into the spiritual world each night but would have no direct contact with Christ. But because the Mystery of Golgotha has taken place during the course of earth evolution, when the 'I' and astral body returned to the physical realm of earth each morning they would immediately have an impression of Christ, for Christ is present in the earth's aura. But this impression would remain dim. Just as the night-time impressions remain dim for the day, so would this impression of Christ existing within the physical and etheric body as they sleep only be perceptible in the way the state of sleep is perceptible to someone on waking up, and there would be no clear experience of Christ.

We have to imagine that immediately after the completion of the Mystery of Golgotha on the earth there were individuals who had experienced it and who were able to pass on to others the immediate experiences they had had of it. Christ himself also gave his disciples an esoteric schooling after his resurrection; he gave them many profound teachings. All this continued to spread during the first few decades after the Mystery of Golgotha. It would have had to come to an end at some point, and indeed we see how it gradually did draw to a close in certain circles. In the notorious writings of the Gnostics and in other older explanations by the first church fathers who were still the pupils of the apostles, or pupils of the apostles' pupils, there were immense esoteric teachings about Christianity. These were rooted out because the church wanted to be rid of something that was always a part of these teachings, namely: anything cosmic. Immensely significant things were destroyed by the church. They were destroyed, but by reading in the Akashic Record they will be restored down to the last dot on the i when the time is ripe.

So for outer history these great impressions would have drawn to a close, but just as this was threatening to happen the Book of Revelation came into being. And when this Revelation is rightly taken in—and indeed examples of this were provided by a number of individuals during the second stage after the Mystery of Golgotha—when this grand, prophetic vision of evolution is rightly taken in, which means when it has been taken into the astral body and especially into the 'I'-organization, then 'I' and astral body will carry this Revelation—which, as I told you in the first lecture, comes directly from the spiritual world and is actually a kind of letter, a direct verbal Revelation including visions—then 'I' and astral body will carry it out into the world of the earth's aura when they are in the sleeping state. This means, dear friends, that all those who have taken the Book of Revelation into their inner understanding have gradually been enshrining it in the ether of the earth's aura, so that now the presence of Christ working on in the earth's aura provides this aura of the earth with its fundamental keynote.

Each night when the astral body and 'I' are outside the physical and ether body, this Christ-Impulse influences initially the ether body of the human being in a profound manner. But on returning with his 'I' and astral body into his physical body in the morning, the human being is usually not capable of finding what there is of the Christ-Impulse in his etheric body.

As the pupils of John gradually take in the content of the Book of Revelation, the meaning of the words becomes enshrined in the ether of the earth's aura. So what is thus enshrined in the earth's aura, indeed what was already enshrined there through the great and significant impressions received from the divine, spiritual beings by the author of the Book of Revelation himself, or perhaps one should say by the one who received the Book of Revelation—all this works on the human being's ether body between going to sleep and waking up. This means that those who have an inclination towards the Mystery of Golgotha can expose their ether body to the content of the Book of Revelation while they are in a state of sleep. This is a fact. Through a right disposition towards Christ one can generate a kind of sleeping state that enables what the content of the Book of Revelation has brought about in the earth's ether and what lies in earthly evolution through the coming of Christ into the earth's ether to become enshrined in one's ether body. This is the actual process, this is the ongoing deed of the Book of Revelation.

In one's work as a priest it can be quite possible to explain to someone requiring one's help in that capacity: Christ entered into earthly evolution through the Mystery of Golgotha; in order to prepare human beings he first brought about what is given in the Gospels, so that in their astral body and in their 'I'—you will have to use the kind of terminology comprehensible to your congregation—they can absorb the content of the Gospels; this prepares them to receive the Christ-Impulse into their ether body on waking up. The apocalyptist himself, however, by being placed within Christianity as it develops, becomes able to incorporate into the human ether body what he describes so concretely, that which is in the evolution of Christianity throughout the various ages right on into the future.

This brings an essentially new element into earth evolution, in contrast to the teachings of the ancient Mysteries. What was it that the ancient Mysteries imparted to the initiate? They imparted that which can be seen when one surveys the spiritual essence of what has been present in the world for all eternity, that which can be seen when one finds the eternally working divine being in external physical forces. The initiate of the ancient Mysteries made no demands as to receiving anything else into his ether body except what came anyway as the result of initiation.

The Christian initiate goes further than this. He wants to take into his ether body what has only gradually come into being during the course of earthly evolution, everything connected with the Mystery of Golgotha and with Christ. The revelation of the apocalyptic Book thus contains the beginning of an initiation for Christendom. This revelation is a kind of early stage of an initiation, not for individuals but for the whole of Christendom; and individuals can prepare themselves for participation in this.

This opens the path along which the principle of Nature, of the Father, can be transcended. Basically all the old initiations took the form of Father initiations. One looked for nature and for the spirit in nature and was satisfied with that, for human beings were themselves part of that world of nature. But now Christ has been here on the earth, and here he will remain. He has fulfilled his Deed on Golgotha and will remain here. One cannot take into oneself what happened through the Mystery of Golgotha merely by taking part in the old initiation. One must first raise oneself into a world of spirit that is different from the one that streamed through the ancient Mysteries. What streamed through the old Mysteries was merely the hope that the Mystery of Golgotha would one day stream through the new Mysteries. Now, however, the human being makes contact with the spirit not through nature but directly through Christ.

The old initiate always chose a roundabout route via nature. What the new initiate did—this was the view of many half or partially initiated individuals not in the first century but especially in later centuries after the Mystery of Golgotha—was to seek contact with the Spirit Being of the world via what had flowed into the world through Christ and through what is built on Christ.

This was how a new initiate viewed the Book of Revelation. What he saw in it made him say: Nature is one way of going into the spiritual world; the immense wisdom revealed in the Book of Revelation is the other way. It is a wonderful surprise and delight in spiritual research when one comes upon individuals—not in the first Christian century, but in later ones, from the second to the sixth—who say: Nature is great—they mean what the ancient world saw as nature—but that which is revealed out of the supersensible realm by the apocalyptist, or by the apocalyptists, is equally great or even greater; for nature leads to the Father, but what is revealed through the apocalyptists leads through the Son to the Spirit. Those were times when a path to the pure, immediate spirit was sought via the Book of Revelation.

This was at the same time a pointer towards the real change that must and will come about during the course of human evolution once human beings have made themselves worthy of it. In olden times there was a strong feeling of the human being having stemmed from the spiritual world but having to go through a development that would strongly bind him to what came towards him from the physical, sense-perceptible world. This link with the physical, sense-perceptible world was strongly felt, and the view was that humans had become sinning and sinful beings through their links with the material nature of the earth.

A different age was to be prepared in contrast to this, and the apocalyptist foresaw and proclaimed it. He was searching for the picture, the right Imagination in which to place this secret before human souls in imaginative pictures. So he enhanced and summarized a picture that was quite customary in the secret teachings of the Hebrews. This is what was shown by these secret teachings:

Souls come from the spiritual world; these souls coming

from the spiritual world clothe themselves with what comes from the earth; when they build houses for the most external tasks of the spirit, the result is cities; but when they build homes for the inner tasks of the human soul the result is the human body, built from bricks provided by the earth.

The concept of building dwellings merged with the concept of building one's body. This was a beautiful, a wonderfully beautiful picture, for it is also quite practical. The body in which deeds were done and where soul processes and functions took place was a house, and the external house provided protection for all of this. There was this wonderful picture: If I build a house from earthly materials for my external activities, then the walls of the house, the house as a whole, provides a protection for what I do. This is merely an expanded, or you could say a hardened, more sclerotic continuation of the first house the human being built—the first house, the one that contained the inner processes of soul, is his body. Having built his body, which is a house, he then builds a second house, which uses ingredients from the earth as building materials. It was considered a perfectly everyday matter to regard the body as a house, and this house as the protective garment donned by the human being here in the physical, earthly world. What is formed out of the soul like this was regarded as the housebuilding done by the human being.

In olden times the human being did indeed grow very attached even externally to what he felt was his house. Here is a drawing of it (Plate 3, bottom right): This is the human being's body with its skin. If he were to grow another skin for the external activities of his soul, it would be like a tent, only this tent does not grow of its own accord, for the human being makes it for himself.

In Hebrew secret teachings this confluence of having command over the earthly realm and of taking in earthly ingredients for human development was viewed in a particular way. As far as the physical earth is concerned, you have to admit that there is a North Pole and that a degree of coldness is concentrated there. This North Pole can be described quite physically as part of the geography of the earth, something that belongs to the earth and is an essential part of it. The Hebrew secret teachings also did this with regard to the soul activity in the forces of the earth. Like the geographical North Pole, they saw another pole on the earth where all culture was concentrated, in other words where the most perfect houses were gathered, and they regarded Jerusalem, the entirely physical city of Jerusalem as this place. This was the pole where external culture was concentrated around the human soul, and the crowning glory of this city was Solomon's Temple.

It then came to be felt that this aspect of the earth's evolution had come to an end. Those who understood something of the Hebrew secret teachings did not regard what happened after the Mystery of Golgotha, in the destruction of Jerusalem, as an external event brought about by the Romans. The Romans were merely the accomplices of the spiritual powers, carrying out on their behalf what was entirely the plan of those spiritual powers. The idea they had was that the old way of gathering ingredients from the earth in order to build the human body as a house had come to an end. With Jerusalem's attainment of its full greatness the substance, the material from the earth that could be used in building the human body as a house, was exhausted.

Translated into the Christian way of thinking, this Hebrew secret teaching meant: The destruction of Jerusalem would have happened even if the Mystery of Golgotha had not taken place, but that which can become a new creation would not have been planted in this destruction of the being of man who creates with the help of the earth. The seed for an entirely new creation is laid in the Jerusalem that was doomed to perish. Mother Earth dies in Jerusalem. Daughter

Earth lives in expectation of another seed. It is no longer the ingredients of the earth that are taken to build bodies and the houses of the Old Jerusalem, which had stood as the crowning glory of all that takes place on earth, for now the earth rises up as a spiritual pole of the Old Jerusalem. One will no longer be capable of building something like the Old Jerusalem out of earthly ingredients. Instead the new era begins, for which the seed was sown by the Mystery of Golgotha. Now human beings receive from above what will envelop their inner being (Plate 3) more from the outside. The New City descends from above and pours itself out across the earth, the New Jerusalem. The Old Jerusalem was made from the earth and its substances, the New Jerusalem comes from heaven and its spiritual ingredients.

You will probably find such a picture rather strange in comparison with all the things that are normally thought these days and what you have learnt from these. What do people imagine the anatomical and physiological human being to be like? He eats, takes the substances of his food into his stomach, digests these, discards some of them, and replaces what needs replacing with the substances he takes in.

But this is not how things are at all. The human being is threefold and has in him a human being of nerves and senses, a rhythmical human being, and a human being of metabolism and limbs. None of the substances taken in through food enter the system of metabolism and limbs, for all of it goes into the system of nerves and senses. The system of nerves and senses absorbs the salts and other necessary substances that are always finely distributed in the air and light, and steers these towards the system of metabolism and limbs. The system of metabolism and limbs is nourished entirely from above downwards. It is quite untrue that this part of the human being receives the substances it needs directly from food. If earthly substances enter the system of metabolism and limbs, then the human being is ill. All the substances taken in and digested in food provide solely the organs belonging to the system of nerves and senses. The head in particular is built from earthly substances. The organs of metabolism and limbs, on the other hand, are built from heaven. And the rhythmical human being brings about balance in both directions. The human being does not eat the oxygen in the air, he inhales it. The way he takes in substances through his system of nerves and senses is coarser than the way he does this through his system of metabolism and limbs. What the human being needs for his system of metabolism and limbs is absorbed through an immensely delicate breathing process. Ordinary breathing is quite coarse by comparison. And what the human being does with oxygen—namely producing carbon dioxide—is once again something more delicate than what happens so that the foods passing through the stomach can supply the head. The transition takes place in the rhythmical human being.

This is the truth about the structure of the human organism and its processes. What anatomy and physiology teach today is nonsense in the face of the truth and comes about as a result of the materialistic outlook. As soon as you know something about this, you realize that what builds the human body comes not only from below, from the plant, mineral and animal kingdoms of the earth, but that what nourishes the organs which are often regarded as the coarser ones comes from above.

Knowing this, one will be able to see quite clearly that up to the time when Jerusalem perished there was a kind of surfeit of nourishment from below. Then, with the Mystery of Golgotha, what comes from above begins gradually to assume importance.

Although people have reversed these facts in the manner described, what happens today is that development comes about in many ways as a result of the old nutrition from below being replaced by nutrition from above, which is now more important. This causes the human form to change. Our head is no longer like the heads of old. The human head in ancient times had a forehead that sloped back more. (Plate 3) The forehead today is more domed; the outer part of the brain has become more important. This is the actual change, for the part of the brain that is becoming more important is more akin to the organs of digestion than the part that lies beneath it. The peripheral part of the brain is becoming more similar to the organs of digestion than are the more delicate tissues in the middle part of the brain, i.e. the continuation of the sensory nerves towards the centre of the head. The organs of metabolism, in particular, are nourished from above.

One can really look into these things down to the tiniest detail if one is willing to say about certain things what the apocalyptist says: Here is wisdom. In the ordinary knowledge that lives amongst people there is not wisdom but darkness. What people today call the results of science is, in fact, the result of Kali Yuga, the utmost darkening of human mentality. This should be regarded as a secret and not talked about on every street corner, for esoteric things are things that remain within a specific circle.

The growth of the New Jerusalem has been ongoing since the Mystery of Golgotha. When the human being has entirely fulfilled his time on earth he will have reached the stage in which he not only weaves the heavenly substance into his own body through his senses, but in which he extends the heavenly substance through what we call spiritual knowledge and art into what will be the external city, the further extension of his body in the sense I have been talking about. The Old Jerusalem was built from below upwards; the New Jerusalem will be built in all reality from above downwards. This is the immense perspective arising out of a more than gigantic vision experienced by the apocalyptist. The mighty vision he saw told him: Everything human beings have succeeded in building has risen upwards out of the earth, and this was concentrated in the Old Jerusalem; but it has now come to an end. He saw the rising up and the melting down of the Old Jerusalem, and he saw the city of man, the New Jerusalem, descending from above, from spiritual worlds.

This is the aim, the final goal of the revelation in the Book of Revelation. It contains truly Christian paths for humanity and Christian aims for humanity as well. In endeavouring to understand them we arrive at certain peculiarities in the Book of Revelation about which a good many individuals have inklings but which they cannot quite understand. Someone making serious efforts to understand the Book of Revelation cannot help saying: What can I do to enter into such a picture of the Old and the New Jerusalem? How can I get inside it? I cannot simply go on talking about these pictures which initially have no content comprehensible to me; I must somehow get inside the content. In order to enter into the content we need a cosmology and a view of the human being that is given only by a new world view such as Anthroposophy, by true insight into the spiritual world. We come to Anthroposophy through the Book of Revelation because we need the means provided by Anthroposophy in order to understand the Book of Revelation, because we notice: John received the Book of Revelation from regions where Anthroposophy dwelt before descending to human beings.

If one wants to understand the Book of Revelation honestly and earnestly one has to understand it anthroposophically. This is most obvious in connection with the final goal, the New Jerusalem. You must understand the secrets of how the human being is structured from above and from below, but not only as if this were an external science. Then you can expand your comprehension to include the entire activity that human beings carry out on the earth, an activity that is directed from below upwards and then changes into one that goes from above downwards. The building of the Old Jerusalem will be transformed into the spiritual building of the New Jerusalem, which will be built from above downwards. People must work their way into something that is constructed spiritually. They must not merely see the Book of Revelation as something symbolic or theoretical that speaks in pictures, which is the habit of the Biblical exegetists. They must see it in a way that allows the spirit to be every bit as real as the physical earth has been for thousands of years.[2]

We must hold firmly to the following: The Book of Revelation does not contain pictures, it contains indications of wholly concrete facts, indications of what will actually happen and not merely pictorial hints of what will happen. This is most important. It is thus that we must feel and find our way into the Book of Revelation. More of this tomorrow.

LECTURE TEN

Dornach, 14 September 1924

We have brought before our soul the apocalyptist's ultimate goal, and when we have rightly understood it we see that this ultimate goal is described in a way that entirely accords with everything the most exact spiritual science can say about evolution. We have seen how the Book of Revelation shows the change of direction that took place in the building of the human being and of cultural manifestations from below upwards, into a way of building them that goes from above downwards. At the end of the last lecture I also stated that anyone honestly seeking to understand the Book of Revelation cannot avoid finding out what spiritual research has to say about world evolution.

There are some passages in the Book of Revelation that only make sense and are only comprehensible if they are approached according to what Anthroposophy has to say about the human being. It is understandable that this is the case when the revelation in question is founded on experiences of the spiritual world. But one must first grasp the fact that the pictures presented in the Book of Revelation are revelations of the spiritual world. This will enable us to get beyond the question of whether the apocalyptist was in fact capable of understanding intellectually all the details we find in his book, for this question misses the point. The real question is: Was he a true seer? He looks into the spiritual world, but the things he sees there are not true on account of his seeing them; they are true because their content is true. The things he sees revealed have their own content; they do not acquire this content through him. So let us not be put off if some rationalistic scholar comes along and proves that the writer of the Book of Revelation had such and such a degree of learning and could therefore not be expected to carry such a broad perspective in his soul. I do not even want to discuss whether the writer of the Book of Revelation possessed this broad perspective or not. I merely want to show that it is immaterial whether the apocalyptist is the one who brings us pictures that are revelations from the spiritual world. The important thing is that we ourselves must place these pictures before our soul as they are and let their content work on us.

So let us turn to that grand final picture of the New Jerusalem which has behind it the background of experiences I spoke about. It will now be a good idea to work backwards a little way from that picture. We come to the important passage where another grand picture rises up before our soul. The apocalyptist sees the grand picture of the heavens opening (Rev. 19,11). On a white horse there rides towards him a power about whom the apocalyptist speaks, and by the way he speaks he shows that he bears the trichotomy of the Godhead not only in his understanding, in his intellect, but also in his whole human being. The way he speaks shows how he knows with his whole soul that the three Persons are three forms of the One God and that if you go beyond the physical world you cannot speak of the one or the other, for they merge into each other. Placed into the physical world, however, the picture shows three Persons, so that we have to distinguish between the Father God, who is at the foundation of all natural facts including those that work into human nature, the Son God, who has to do with all that leads into freedom of soul experience, and the Spirit God, who lives in a spiritual, cosmic order that is far away from nature, entirely foreign to nature. Here on the physical plane these three Persons appear thus sharply differentiated.

On stepping across the threshold to the spiritual world, the human being enters a condition I have described in my book

Knowledge of the Higher Worlds, a condition in which he becomes structured into three beings, so that thinking, feeling and will each attain a degree of autonomy. In contrast to this, when we leave the physical plane and arrive in the higher worlds we see the Threefold God coming towards us more and more as One God. It is with this especially in mind that we must read the Book of Revelation. We must not follow the pattern of the physical world and distinguish between Father God, Son God and Spirit God.

The one who rides towards us on a white horse in that grand picture is the One God. The image of the Son God is more the one we see in the form of the human being's free development of soul on the earth. But now something highly extraordinary happens, something that makes this picture appear so grand. It is perfectly natural and self-evident that John, the writer of the Book of Revelation, sees heaven opened, and what is new that now comes forth, comes forth downwards from the spiritual world. This means that all culture must now be ordered in such a way that it comes from the spiritual world downwards to the physical. When we see this clearly, it is of course obvious that the condition which precedes the final picture of the New Jerusalem is that of John looking into the spiritual world. This means that heaven is open to him. By telling us this he wants to point to a future condition that will come about for human beings. He is, in fact, saying nothing less than this:

Before the situation comes about on earth in which spiritual ingredients for the building of the New Jerusalem descend from the spiritual world in order to be taken in by human beings, before it comes about that human beings become aware that they must now build from above downwards and no longer as in earlier times when material ingredients from the earth were lifted upwards, before the situation comes about—which John regards as a real one, as I said the other day—in which the human being will be involved mainly with his will, before this happens there will be another situation in which the human being participates solely with his knowing, in which he must look into the spiritual world: Heaven is opened and the One who lies at the foundation of all beings, sending them, creating them, making them holy, reveals himself.

Then follows the significant passage that makes the picture so grand: And he had a name written that no one knew but himself. (Rev. 19,12) This is very significant. When we reach the passage in the Book of Revelation where this is written we see another significant sign of it being one of the greatest spiritual revelations.

People designate their 'I' in all kinds of ways in different languages. I have often pointed to the spiritually rather ordinary fact that you can never say the name 'I' and mean someone other than yourself. I cannot call someone else 'I'. The name by which we designate ourself is thus different from all other names, for these are given to objects outside ourselves. But when I say 'I', in whatever language, I can only mean myself. I can only say it to another person if, in a real spiritual process, I have moved over and entered into him. But we need not speak about this just now.

In older languages the self was not specifically designated, for it was contained within the verb. The 'I' was not directly mentioned. The verb was used to show what one was doing, and this was what indicated that one was speaking about oneself. There was no name for the self. It only came about in later times that the human being gave his self a name, and in our German language that name contains the initials of Jesus Christ, which is an important symbolic fact.[1] If we take this fact of a language having a name that each of us can only apply to himself, and if we further intensify this fact, we come to what is now said in the Book of Revelation: The one who descends from the supersensible world has a name written on him which he not only speaks solely for himself but which only he and he alone can understand; no one else can comprehend it.

Think of the bringer of the revelation going to John and showing him the prophetic picture depicting what will one day come about for humanity, the picture of the One who comes down in the future, the One who has the name only he alone can understand. What can all this possibly mean? It appears to be meaningless when you first make an honest attempt at understanding it. Why does it say: '... he who is to bring healing to the world, he who is to bring justice to the world' as the Book of Revelation puts it (Rev.19,11), 'he who makes faith and knowledge true', as the Book puts it, not what some translations say: 'he that was called faithful and true', but 'he who makes faith and knowledge true'.[2] This is like a game of hide and seek. And what does it mean that he has a name written that only he understands? We are encouraged by this to ask more probing questions.

Let us think of this quite graphically: He bears a name that he alone understands. How can we participate in this name? This name must gain some meaning for us, it must be able to live in us. How can this come about? When the being who understands this name becomes one with our own self, enters into our own self, then within us this being will understand the name and with him we shall understand it too, for then with him in us we shall always be conscious of 'Christ in us'.

He alone understands the things that are connected with his being, but it is in us that he understands them; and the light that streams out in us through his understanding—because in us, in our own being he becomes this light—this gives the insight of the Christ-Being in our own self. It becomes an indwelling insight, an insight that dwells within the human being.

Something has now taken place. First of all, what has taken place is a necessary and intended consequence of the Mystery of Golgotha. This Being who has gone through the Mystery of Golgotha, this Being who must enter into us, so that we shall comprehend the world with *his* understanding, not with our understanding, this Being wears a garment that is sprinkled with the blood of Golgotha. So now we take this second picture. John the apocalyptist tells us that this garment sprinkled with the blood of Golgotha also has a name. It is not the name we were speaking of just now. The name of this garment sprinkled with blood is the Logos of God, the Logos, the God, the Word of God. (Rev. 19,13) The One, therefore, who is to dwell in us and who through his own understanding within us is to give us the light that comprehends the world, this One fills us with the Word of God.

The pagan peoples used to read the Word of God in the phenomena of nature. They had to receive it through external revelations. Christians must receive the creative Word of God by taking Christ into themselves. A time will come when events will have proceeded to a stage when all human beings who honestly take Christianity into their souls will know that the Word of God is with Christ and that this Word of God has its origin in our understanding of the Mystery of Golgotha and of the garment sprinkled with blood. In the language of the apocalyptist, Christ is embedded within the Mystery of Golgotha.

But there is a third aspect as well. Christ in three guises: once through himself, then through his garment, and thirdly through the deeds he accomplishes for human beings on earth. This is a description of a situation that must come about, although one can of course not name a specific year when this will happen; but it is something towards which Christian development must strive. The third thing towards which attention is drawn is a sword with which he works; it is the sword of his will, the sword of the deeds he accomplishes on the earth amongst human beings through the fact that he dwells within them. What he now does bears the third name: King of all Kings, Lord of all Lords. This is the third guise. What is the nature of a king, the nature of a lord?

If we get to know the essential inner meaning of the Latin word *dominus* we shall discover what language itself means in this instance, quite apart from what spiritual science has to say: A lord is someone on the earth or in the world who has been chosen to point the direction for another. How long will outer lords be needed on the earth? How long will the commandments of outer lords be needed, even the commandments of those who are outer spiritual lords of the earth? They will be needed only until the moment when Christ, with the name none but he understands, shall dwell within the human being. Then every human being will be able to follow Christ in his own being, in his own soul. Then everyone will strive to realize *that* in himself which desires to realize the will of the human being out of inner love. Then will the Lord of Lords, the King of Kings live in each individual.

Seen spiritually, this is the time in which we ourselves are now living. The fact that we are living in this time is merely disguised by the way human beings continue to live in their old ways, denying as much as they can in every field the fact that Christ now dwells in them. It has to be said that there is much in many human beings that is preparing them in the right way for the etheric appearance of Christ, who is of course a being descending from the divine world. But people must prepare for this by finding the wellspring of their actions and deeds within themselves.

This brings us through the spirit of the Book of Revelation to the difficulty of working as a priest today. In a certain sense the priest is expected to be the *dominus*, he is expected to lead and guide. The priest has the congregation before him, and his priestly dignity presupposes that he is the leader, that he is in a sense the king for those he has to lead. He is the one who administers the sacraments, he is the one who cares for souls. On the other hand we are living at a time when human beings bear the essence within themselves that enables them to take Christ into themselves to an extent that allows them to become more and more their own leader.

This is the position you put yourself in today when you want to assume the dignity of priesthood. Nevertheless, this dignity of priesthood is entirely justifiable, especially today, because although the essence human beings have in them is there, it needs to be called forth from them, the very best needs to be made of it. Everything that stands behind the dignity of priesthood is needed today to call forth from human beings what is in them. We are living at a time that poses quite specific requirements, but the outer world cannot yet entirely face up to these requirements. This is because the outer world is concerned with what human beings are through the fact that they wear a physical body. But it would be a terrible prospect if human beings were to live over into their next life on earth only in the form they now have in our present civilization.

We know that in anthroposophical circles efforts are made to avoid this. Human souls are offered something that will enable them to absorb what they are supposed to carry with them into the life of their next incarnation. But this must become possible for all humanity. Human beings today must build an 'I', they must build an individuality with which they can live on into their next incarnation. This is only possible if there can be added to their experiences as human beings something that is given through the grace of the offering, through the grace of the sacrament. Their karma will not become detached from human beings through this, but something will be loosened that is at the moment most strongly of all attached to them. Human beings wear a mask today. They go around in disguise. And if the desire arises to see the real individuality of a human being, this can lead to tragic conflicts.

One such tragic conflict was encountered by Hölderlin who once said all he could see when looking at his fellow Germans was 'craftsmen but no human beings, thinkers but no human beings, priests but no human beings, masters and servants, young and old but no human beings',[3] and thus he went on. Human beings, in a way, bear a seal of something that is outside them.

Today we need priests who work in a way that speaks to the human being as such, and that cultivates what belongs to humanity as a whole. Basically none of the confessions is capable of this today. Think how dependent they all are. The community for Christian renewal must grow beyond this dependence of the confessions. It must do this through its own destiny. No other profession growing from Anthroposophy is in a position comparable to that of the priests. They are in a unique position, and it is perhaps a good thing if out of the spirit of the Book of Revelation we for once express what this means. You only have to consider that in every other kind of work growing from Anthroposophy people are in some way or another dependent on the world around them because of the external pressures that exist. If you become a schoolteacher out of Anthroposophy, well, you know about the enormous difficulties facing us there. It is an illusion to imagine that we shall ever found a second Waldorf school so long as the requirement is for teachers to have some kind of seal of approval from the state. We were only able to found the Waldorf school because we did so before the state of Württemberg passed its education laws.

Or take the medical profession. We cannot simply create physicians out of the foundations of existence through the anthroposophical movement. Well, we could do so, but they would not be authorized, they would remain unqualified. In some ways we even have this difficulty where art is concerned. Although it has not quite happened yet, it will not be long before things tend towards what they are already trying to do in Russia where they expect even artists to acquire some sort of seal of approval from the state. Priests emerging from the anthroposophical movement are the only ones who can disregard all that. It is fine if they have been trained in some way, but for their work as priests they can disregard all of it. In the theology they represent they can truly lay the first foundation stone of the New Jerusalem, for they represent a theology that calls for recognition from no one but themselves. This is what is so important.

You are the only ones who are in this position. You should feel that this is the position you are in, for it is a position in which you will sense the specific nature of your priestly dignity. In countries like Russia they can drive priests out, but in countries like that they will never do anything to make priests acquire a seal of approval from the state. Either priests will be left to their own devices or they will not be wanted at all, which is what is tending to happen in Russia today.

So priests can for the first time feel the approach of the New Jerusalem, the approach of the indwelling Christ, of Christ who will become the King of Kings, the Lord of Lords. It is therefore rather fitting if the priest pauses at this forward-looking passage in the Book of Revelation, if he pauses with a fervent heart and unfolds all the enthusiasm of his priestly soul that he must unfold by contemplating this particular passage in the Book of Revelation. For the Book of Revelation is not a teaching, it is active, working life in all our souls. We should feel at one with the Book of Revelation. We should be able to bring the work we do and the life we live into the prophetic stream of the Book of Revelation. Then we find ourselves gathered around John the apocalyptist who sees before him the vision: Heaven is opened; he comes who alone understands his name, whose garment bears the name of the Word of God, who is the King of Kings, the Lord of Lords. Those priests who unite themselves with the cultus that has once more been drawn directly from the spiritual world, those priests who are themselves once again re-establishing the Transubstantiation in keeping with the Holy Spirit, those priests who have the new Act of Consecration of Man which is the transformed old one, having within it that which is valid of the old, but having the form that flows today from the spiritual world—these priests are now permitted to gather around John the apocalyptist who looks into heaven opened. We may regard the initiation which took place here, in the hall over there which was then devoured by fire, as being lit by the light that shines out when heaven is opened and the white horse appears with the One who is seated upon it, whose name only he himself knows and who must be embodied in us if this name is to mean anything to us. This is what is meant by understanding the Book of Revelation; the Book of Revelation requires understanding that is alive, it does not require mere knowledge.

Bound up with all that appears in a picture as grand as this, bound up with all this is deep, deep wisdom. Consider what makes its appearance in the immediate vicinity of this important vision. We are shown how the Beast begins to work, the Beast I have described, the Beast who shows the human being the way down from the spiritual to the physical, the Beast the apocalyptist has seen approaching in three stages, the Beast one of whose forms is not only the materialistic view of life but the materialistic attitude in life. The apocalyptist indicates two points in time. He points to the Beast being overcome, and he points to the stronger adversary of humanity being bound for one thousand years before becoming unbound for a short space of time. So we are actually faced with two adversaries of the good principle, with the Beast and with the one whom tradition calls Satan.

In a certain sense the Beast has been overcome as far as the outer physical world is concerned. It has been overcome by the way it is possible to confront materialism with a spiritual view of the world. In a certain sense Satan is bound at the present time. But he will become unbound again. Satan is bound, and those who see what matters in evolution know that he is bound. For if Satan were not bound at present, then all those things would come about that could mean the full outpouring of the phials of wrath. If Satan were not bound, there would be seen in the external world in the most horrible way how this is connected with the materialistic attitude and way of life on earth. Profoundest inner cynicism would proclaim materialism to be the truth, and this would arouse such greedy desire in the unbound Satan that one would see this materialistic attitude and way of life and the way ahrimanic powers seize on it, as the most horrible, the most frightful diseases.

If Satan were not bound, one would have to speak of materialism not merely as an attitude and way of life but as being the most evil of diseases. Instead of this, people make their way in life with the cynicism and frivolity of materialism, even religious materialism, and nothing befalls them. That nothing befalls them is due solely to the fact that Satan is bound while God is still giving human beings a chance to find their way to the spirit without falling prey to Satan. If Satan were here now, there would be many a teacher in one creed or another that had fallen for materialism who would present a frightful, a terrible sight to humanity. The inner picture pointing to the possible disease of materialism, the leprosy of materialism that would be here if Satan were not bound is indeed a most terrible one.

There is no other context except that of the Book of Revelation in which someone with spiritual responsibility towards this knowledge would bring up this picture. I myself would not use the expression 'the leprosy of materialism' in any other context except here where I have linked it to the Book of Revelation. As one finds one's way into the Book of Revelation one does have these frightful pictures before one's eyes which do indeed represent a spiritual reality.

The Book of Revelation must not only fill our life, it must also fill our words. If we take it into ourselves, the Book of Revelation not only brings life into our work as priests but also allows us to point to things we would never dream of mentioning in exoteric life. The Book of Revelation must live not only in our 'I' if we want to comprehend it; the Book of Revelation also wants to speak in our words. There is much that you will say to one another when you are gathered together alone in true priesthood amongst yourselves, so that it may live in you and be kept among you. From this you will draw the strength to speak the right words to those who are your congregation.

To be priests today means to be the first human beings who are permitted to speak freely amongst each other about the Book of Revelation. The Book of Revelation is the book for priests that follows on from the Gospels. You will all the more become priests, the more you live your way into this inner spirit of the Book of Revelation. More of this tomorrow.

LECTURE ELEVEN

Dornach, 15 September 1924

Let us put ourselves in the world into which the apocalyptist wants to place humanity through his description of the next age of the earth. He describes his visions of spiritual worlds coming in and taking hold of the earthly human being. He describes three stages prior to this, and we must get to know these. Each of these three stages represents something that must fall down before human beings will be worthy enough and capable enough to take the spiritual world, in all purity, into their working, their thinking and their feeling.

The first stage is the fall of Babylon—we shall for the moment use the apocalyptist's terminology. The second stage is the fall of the Beast and his associate, the False Prophet, who spreads the teachings of the Beast. The third stage is the fall of the divine adversaries, as they are usually called, namely the downfall of Satan. When we look at the future evolution of humanity with spiritual eyes we see these three stages very realistically, very concretely. In our century in particular, during which much will be decided regarding human evolution, there is every reason to direct the eyes of our soul towards these three downfalls. They will come upon us in a particular form after the time when Christ appears on the earth for the first time in the ether body, in other words actually after Christ's second appearance on the earth. Humanity must prepare for this, so that human beings will be strong enough to go through this threefold downfall of the adversaries of the Christ-Impulse without endangering their development of soul.

We must not forget how accurate the apocalyptist is. Every

time such a fall occurs he describes an angel coming down from the spiritual world, and we notice—and this is rather disconcerting for those who do not go more deeply into a spiritual understanding of the world—we notice that he depicts the angel as rejoicing at the great tortures, at the frightful things that then come about through the fall. It is important that we should understand this rejoicing.

First let us look at the three stages in the downfall of Christ's adversaries, beginning with the one termed the fall of Babylon. We can call up before our soul the sum total of all the errors into which human beings can fall as a result of their human nature. What the apocalyptist calls the Babylonian temptation includes everything that takes human beings down below what is actually their spiritual standard.

The human being is only truly human—although of course this is not possible in every moment of his evolution, for he must first achieve it—when he has within him a complete harmony between the principle of the material and the principle of the spiritual, when the material does not rise up in emotions that are not under the control of the spirit. This is what is so important and we must understand it very thoroughly. For even the apocalyptist would be unable to speak as he does if he had to presuppose that all feelings and passions and everything that comes from the will sphere and the centre of the heart were entirely unjustifiable. In particular to call feelings and passions unjustified—this false kind of asceticism in itself arises from the emotions and passions. If someone does not feel strong enough to imbue his passions with spirit in such a way that he can place them at the service of good world evolution—then this is the very way in which he pays homage to his emotion of weakness. Even if such a person really wants the good evolution—if he allows his feeling and heart sphere to become impoverished he will pay homage to his weakness.

The apocalyptist is not concerned with banishing emotions

or with banishing feelings and passions but with ensuring that they to not remain uncontrolled by the spirit. Everything emotional in human life, all the emotions, whether hefty or slight, that remain uncontrolled by the spirit, these are what the apocalyptist summarizes under the name of that city of Babylon in which people's passions turned them away from the spirit—if I may stereotype the matter in this way. You need only translate the coarse expressions—which were not coarse in their time—into the language of our own time. In the old way of picturing things one did not use abstractions; one characterized things quite concretely, so this is the way the apocalyptist speaks about Babylon. But why Babylon?

In Babylon, or rather at the Mystery centre of Babylon, there were very exalted Mysteries in which one could be initiated into the secrets of the supra-earthly cosmos, and in which one could learn about the secrets of the starry worlds and their spiritual content. The oldest priests in Babylon used the powers of dream-clairvoyance in a way that we would call mediumistic clairvoyance today. The wonderful teachings of old Babylon came into being through the use of this mediumistic path.

Today we can see that even mediums who seem suitable to mediate spiritual teachings—which is often done, only it ought to be under the guidance of initiates with the necessary insight—even such seemingly suitable mediums are susceptible to influences that are highly questionable morally. Because there is often a disproportion in mediums between what they reveal and what they are, they can often in the end not distinguish between truth and untruth; and this can intensify to an incapacity to separate what is moral from what is immoral.

You must understand what happens with a medium. A person becomes a medium—and this was the same with the Babylonian priests—when an external power draws the 'I' and astral body out of the physical and ether body. The

moment the medium's 'I' and astral body have been withdrawn from the physical and etheric body, another power
enters into this 'I' and astral body. Depending on whether the
initiator doing this has good or evil intent, whether he
belongs to the left-hand or the right-hand path, this power
will be either good or evil. In the time of ancient Babylon,
excellent knowledge and revelations came about by this
means. Later on, and today, there began to be a dis-
advantage: What happens when the medium re-enters the
physical body?

You see, the logic we have in the physical world by which
we distinguish between untruth and truth is no use in the
spiritual world. It is a complete mistake to believe that one
can use in the spiritual world the concepts of untruth and
truth that are current here in the physical world. There is
nothing in the spiritual world that can be distinguished in this
manner. There are beings who are good and others who are
evil. You have to recognize them for what they are, for they
do not tell you. But even the evil ones are true in their own
way. This is difficult to understand, of course, just as everything we encounter on entering the spiritual world is difficult
to understand. Here in the physical world we can state that a
straight line is the shortest distance between two points. In
the spiritual world this could be the longest distance, with any
other one being shorter. None of the logic we most certainly
need here in the physical world is any use in the spiritual
world.

So a true initiate needs to have a special disposition of soul
in order to see into the spiritual world. He must be fully
responsible in the way he immediately works with physical
concepts as soon as he returns to the physical world. A
medium, however, is not capable of doing this because he or
she does not enter the spiritual world consciously. When the
medium returns, 'I' and astral body fill the physical and
etheric body with a way of thinking that is appropriate for the

spiritual world but which corrupts all moral feelings and sensations that are valid in the physical world. That is why a medium is corrupted with regard to truth and untruth, and this then works on in everything else.

We can say that in fact Babylon went through this process and that thus even the highest, most significant revelation from the spiritual world became terribly corrupted. What initially applies to the principle of spiritual revelation can also extend to include ordinary human life, so that strong corruption sets in. Having entered spiritual life in this way, a human being then becomes more immoral than he was previously as an ordinary person. That is why Babylon was taken to be the representative of moral corruption, and the expressions used in the Book of Revelation are simply the usual expressions by which corruption was described at that time.

Since that time the whole of humanity, in so far as it has carried on what lived in Babylon, has become a city of Babylon spread out across the whole world. This is what the apocalyptist is saying: The city of Babylon is to be found amongst all of mankind on earth. It exists wherever human beings have fallen victim to the Babylonian temptation, and it is this attitude that must undergo its downfall before that final stage can come about of which the apocalyptist is speaking. When we investigate what it is that is at work in 'Babylonian corruption' we find that it is the ahrimanic principle that is at work in this corruption. Ahriman is inside human beings, and he is a power who is close to the human being within the cosmos as a whole. He is in the emotions that are corrupted in this way. The opposite pole to Ahriman is Lucifer. Ahriman lives in the things that must fall in Babylon, and these are the things to which Lucifer is opposed. What is the picture that arises for the apocalyptist when he sees this? It is the picture of the luciferic angels rejoicing. We must not gloss over this, my dear friends.

A good many world views have adopted the great error of thinking that the bad is necessarily the opposite of the best, for example that the evil principle down below is always met by the good coming from above. This is not the situation at all. In this chapter of the Book of Revelation (Rev. 19) the ahrimanic beings—Babylon—are down below, and the angels above who rejoice at the fall of Babylon are luciferic. It is the voice of Lucifer that gives tongue up above as a rejoicing of angels. The Christ-Principle always holds the balance between these two.

What the apocalyptist is saying here will only be understood when the threefold constitution of the world is properly comprehended. It is incomprehensible for ordinary human sentiment that pure, good spirits should shout for joy up there when down below such horrors come upon humanity as are portrayed here. But it is immediately understandable once you can see the shouts of delight as emanating from beings who had originally opposed the creation of a world in which human beings were to undergo their spiritual development. The luciferic beings want to maintain the whole of evolution at quite a different spiritual level. They do not want that union, that marriage of spirit with matter that has come about in earth existence. So they feel in their souls: Since that which Ahriman has taken hold of is now being thrown out of earth existence we can be pleased that at least a part of earth existence will not continue and will drop out of earth evolution. So you see that in this connection the picture painted by the apocalyptist is an immensely honest portrayal of the cosmos.

The first downfall, the fall of Babylon, is the fall of errors which human beings have themselves brought about. Although these errors are influenced by the initiation principle they are nonetheless human errors. When Babylon falls as the result of human error, a part of humanity is separated off from world evolution at a point in time which we shall

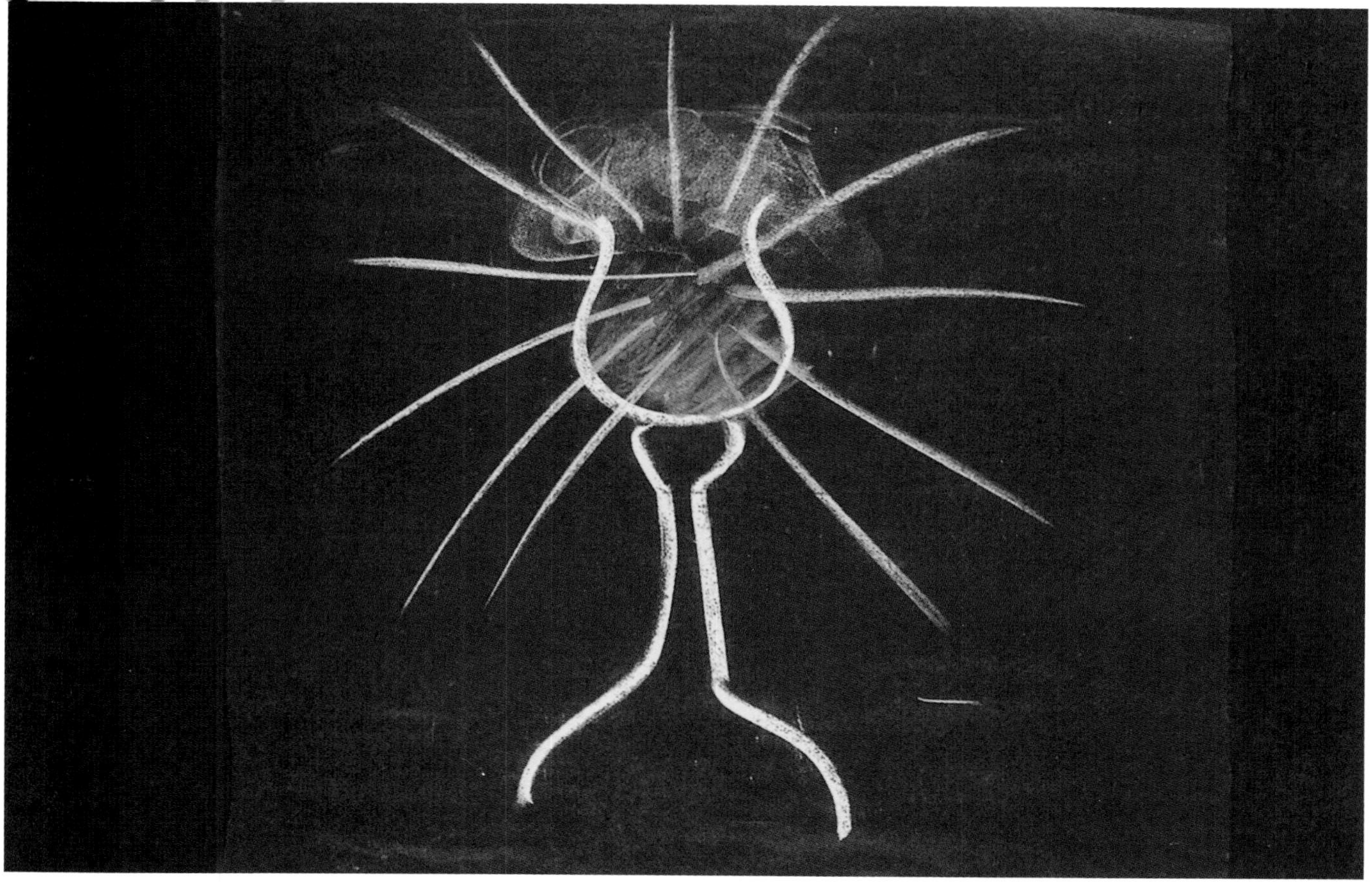

PLATE 1 Lecture 1, 5 September 1924

PLATE 2

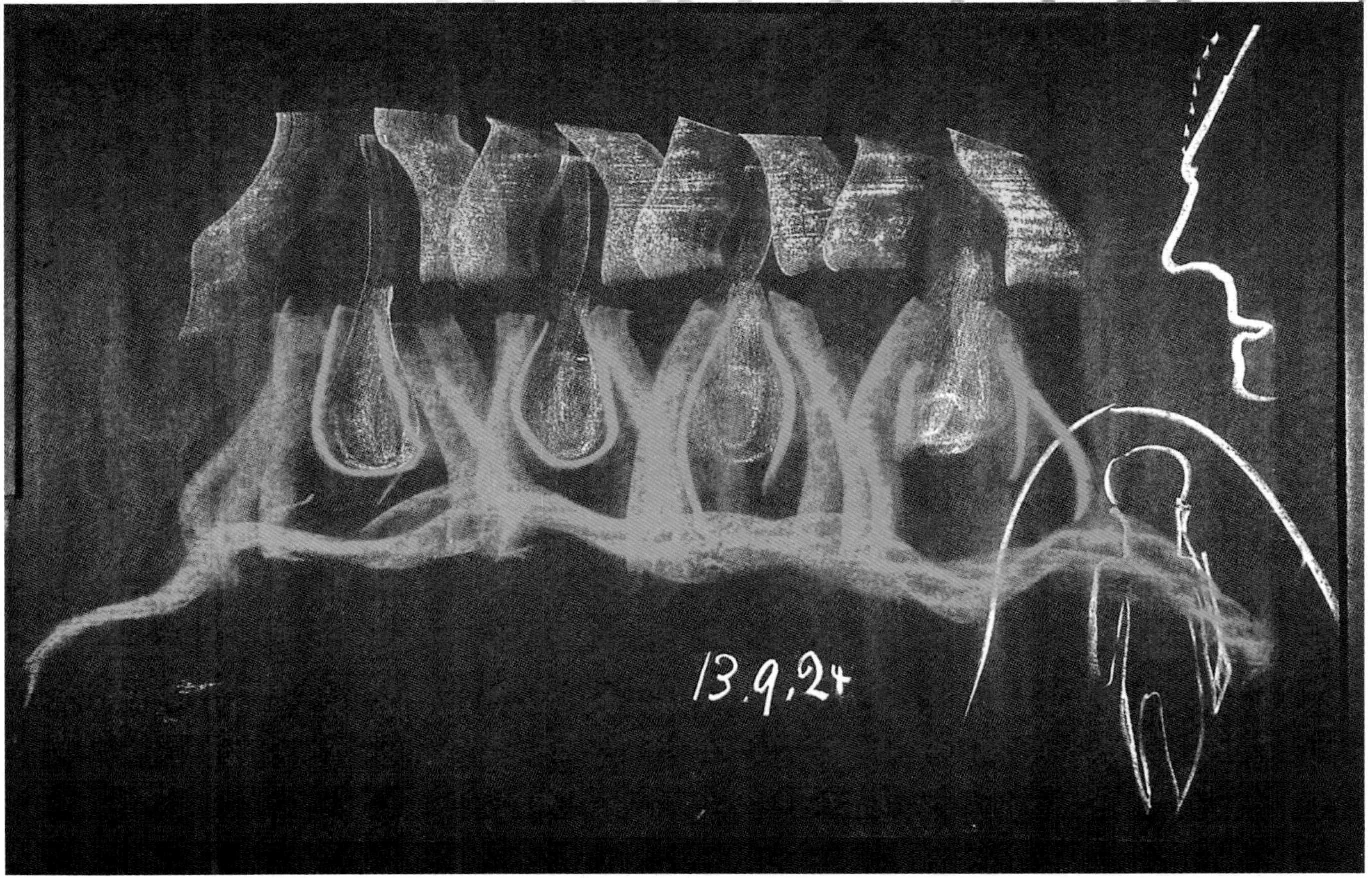

PLATE 3

13.9.24

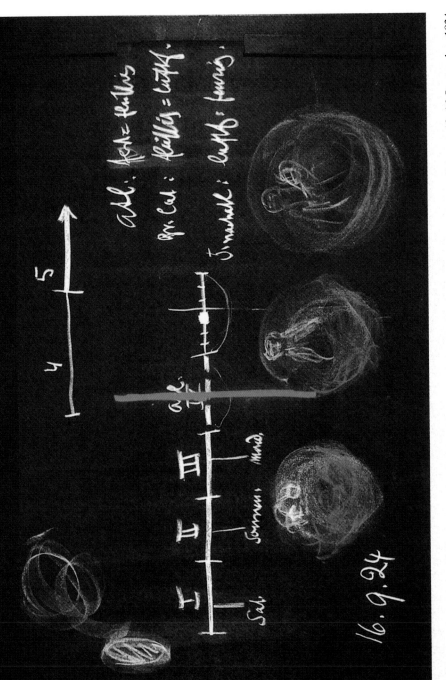

PLATE 4   Lecture 12, 16 September 1924

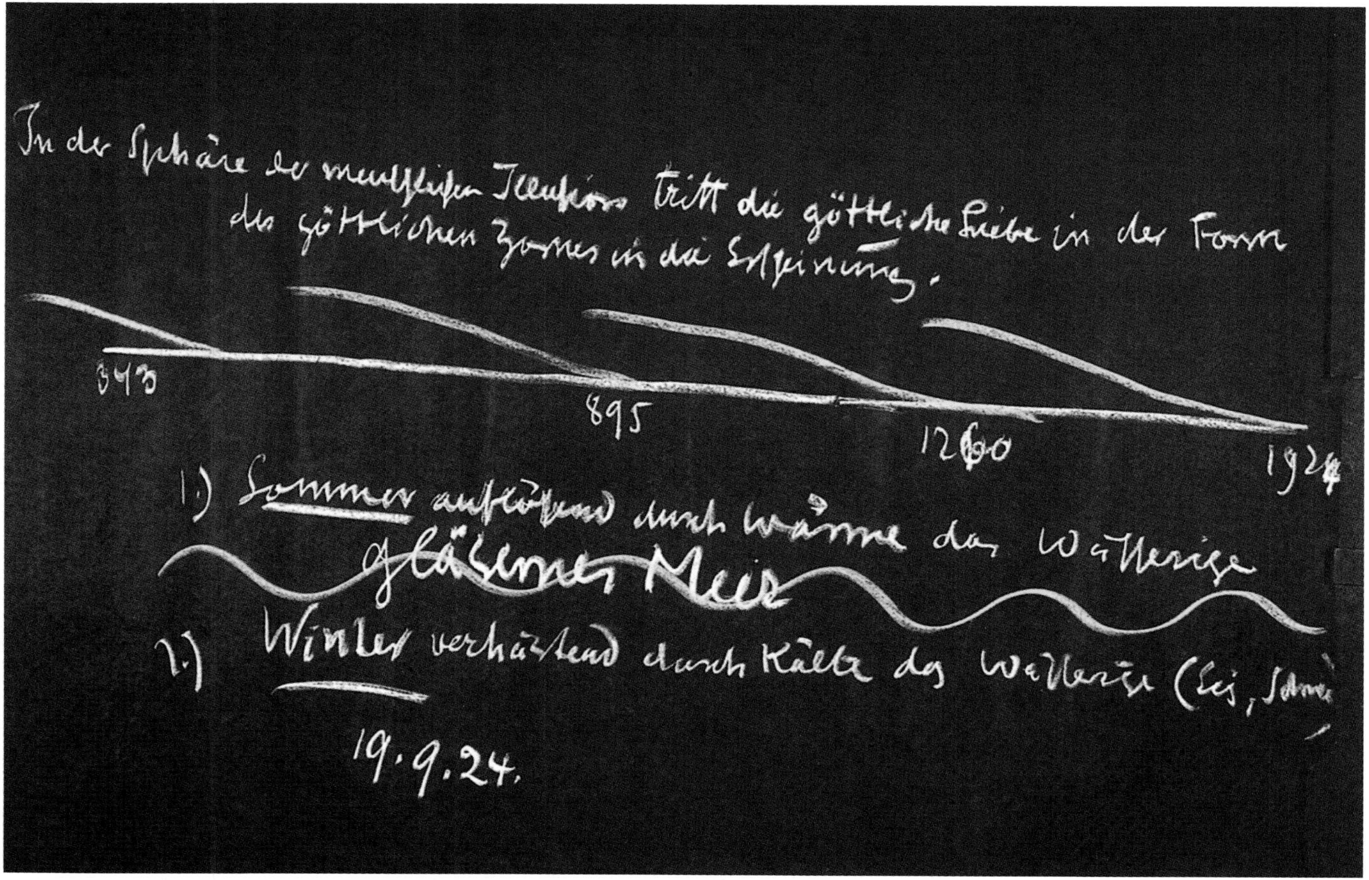

PLATE 5

Lecture 15, 19 September 1924

1933

20.9.24.

PLATE 6

Lecture 16, 20 September 1974

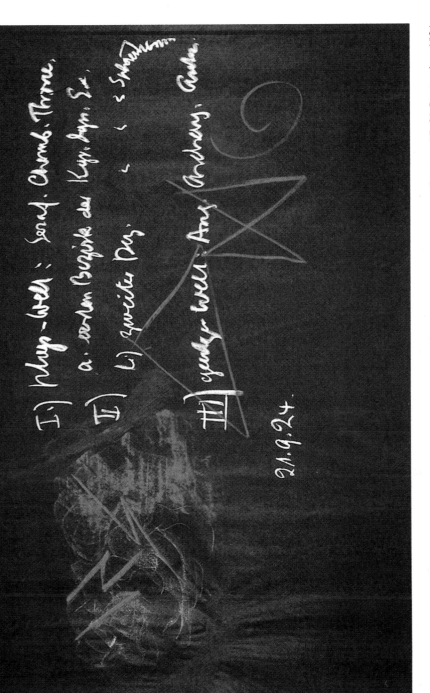

PLATE 7

Lecture 17, 21 September 1924

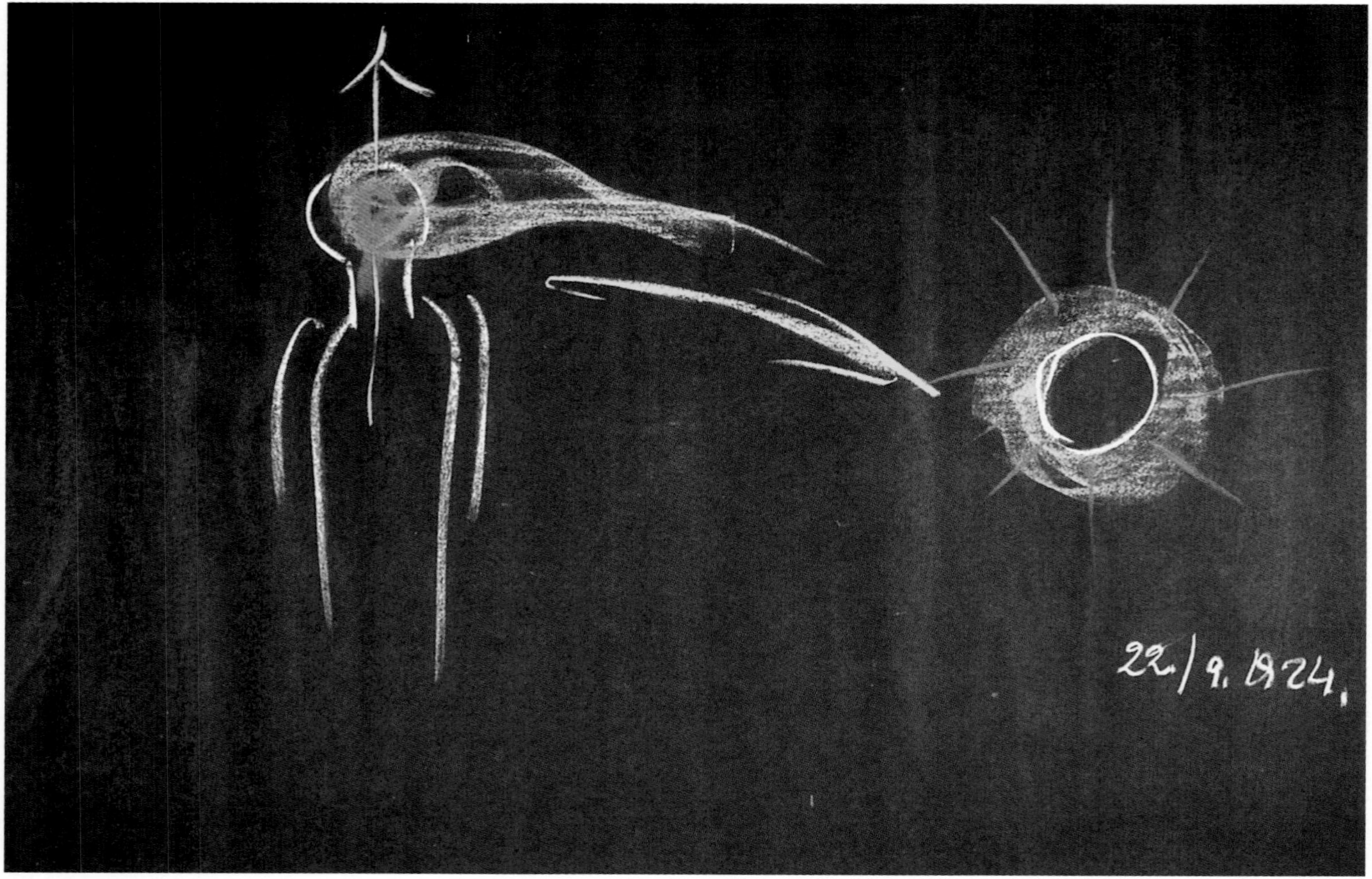

22/9. 1924.

PLATE 8

Lecture 18, 22 September 1924

discuss later. At present I simply want to look qualitatively at what is to come.

The second downfall is one in which not only human beings alone participate. Those actually affected by the fall of Babylon are human beings; it happens because of human error. In the fall of the Beast and of the False Prophet who represents the teachings of the Beast something supra-human, something spiritual falls, not something human. Something falls that is not within the human kingdom. The Beast who breaks in on human communities falls and the one who proclaims the teachings of the Beast, the False Prophet, falls. What falls is something that can make human beings possessed. Unlike in the case of the medium, it is not the weakness of human nature that is the cause of the fall but something supra-human that brings about the impulse for evil in human beings.

To make the picture even clearer we could say the following: All those who will be affected by the fall of Babylon will have been corrupted by having striven for things for which their organization is not strong enough, things in connection with which their organization will have grown weak, so that they will have become corrupted. So in the fall of Babylon it is a matter of the human organization acting out of weakness. When the Beast and the False Prophet fall it is not like a medium having become corrupted through having grown weak. It is as though the spirit who has laid claim to the medium's 'I' and astral body were to go—once the hypnosis has ceased—into the physical and etheric body and there make use of the human being's physical body in order to get up to mischief on the earth.

This is the exact picture given to us by the apocalyptist. A time will come—he wants to tell us—when we shall see human beings going about in the world who cannot tolerate what Christianity teaches, who take Christ into their souls but who cannot reach up to the exaltedness of Christ with their physical and etheric body and therefore succumb to other spirits—but not in full consciousness, so that they then fall into corruption. These are the first ones, those who are included in the fall of Babylon.

Others will also go about as human beings, but their lot will be that their human 'I' is not in them, so that one cannot address them as human beings because they are possessed by the Beast and by the False Prophet. This will come about after the fall of Babylon. After the fall of Babylon there will be people on the earth who will be like wandering demons; ahrimanic powers will act directly in them.

Enough preconditions already exist for these things today. The seeds for all this have already been sown. For example we have seen the frightful incident in which, through a human being, Ahriman has been among us as a writer—perhaps not in the whole human being but through a temporary weakness of that human being. Nietzsche was a brilliant, splendid writer, but during the periods when he was writing *The Antichrist* and *Ecce Homo* the Nietzsche individuality was not in him. I know the Nietzsche individuality, I even described him in my book *The Course of my Life*.[1] Directly through him Ahriman became an author, and Ahriman is a much more brilliant author than human beings.

The ahrimanic powers will interfere more and more, so that ahrimanic spirits will use human bodies for all kinds of actions. A time will come when Christians, on encountering some person or other, will seriously have to ask themselves: Is this a human being or is it a loose cloak for ahrimanic spirits? We shall have to add this to the distinctions we already make about people. So this will be the second downfall: the demonic Beast and his Prophet. They will themselves take possession of the bodies of human beings. But the Beast and his Prophet will be toppled. So first we have the fall of corrupted human beings and then the fall of certain corrupted spirits who are close to human beings. These spirits will fall as a result of the second downfall.

After this the Book of Revelation tells of a third downfall, the fall of Satan. Satan is an exalted being who, however, treads another path than those that can be trodden on the earth. The Beast and the False Prophet are powers who seduce human beings, who have the will to tempt humanity on to the wrong paths both morally and intellectually. The power, dear friends, whom we mean when we talk of the fall of Satan, this power has quite other plans. He not only wants to throw humanity off course but he also wants to do this to the earth as a whole. From the point of view of human beings and of the earth this power is a terrible adversary of God.

But, you see, we can say hypothetically—for only in this way can we do so without falling into intellectual sin or more especially into spiritual sin—we can say the following. We can ask: If we do not look at this from the point of view of human, earthly evolution, if we consider it from other, higher viewpoints—what, then, is the position of this power of Satan over against other spirits in the cosmos?

It is not surprising that Michael, whose standpoint differs from that of human beings, has quite a different view about Satan. Human beings remain in the abstract and think that Satan is an evil power. But Satan is also an exalted power, even though he is in error as regards the directions that are suitable for the earth. He is an exalted power. Michael, who has the degree of an archangel, does not have the rank of Satan, who has the degree of an archai. Michael is 'only' an archangel. From Michael's point of view Satan is not a power to be despised but a power to be immensely feared, for Michael sees this power who belongs to the hierarchy of the archai as being more exalted than himself. Michael, however, has chosen to go in the direction that is the same as that of earth evolution.

A very long time ago Michael decided to work in those planetary orbits that are preordained by the sun existence. Satan is a power who for ever lies in wait in the cosmos. There is something eerie about the way Satan lies in wait. We can perceive this, dear friends, in those moments when we see a comet shooting across our sky, a comet that follows quite a different orbit from that of the planets.

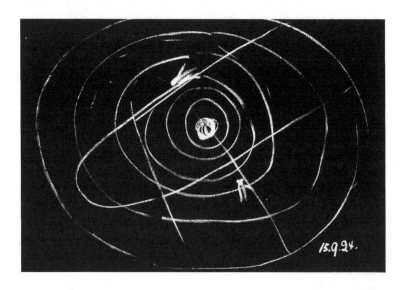

If we draw it how Copernicus saw it, which is not quite right astronomically, but that is not relevant here, we have Sun; then Mercury, Venus, Earth, Mars—these are the inner planets. The outer ones are Jupiter, Saturn, Uranus, Neptune. If we draw it like this we have to imagine how comets have entirely irregular orbits over against the regular ones of the planets. The idea that these comets describe elongated ellipses is nonsense, but we need not go into that just now. Anyway, the orbits of the comets, in so far as they come within our planetary system, bear no relation to the orbits of the planets.

Satan lies in wait for every comet that turns up. He wants to catch hold of it and use the direction of its momentum to disrupt the orbits of the planets and thus also of the earth. This really is going on in the universe: the satanic forces are lying in wait with the intention of changing the whole planetary system. If they were to succeed, the planetary system in whose orbits human beings are supposed to live would be taken away from those divine, spiritual powers and sent off in quite other cosmic evolutionary directions. Michael sees this intention as a terrible error, about which he has to say: It would be pointless for me even to harbour such an intention, since it would anyway be a hopeless project for a being in the hierarchy of the Archangeloi. Only beings in the hierarchy of the Archai would have sufficient strength to achieve such a thing. Among the orbits of the planets Michael works from the Sun and has become what occultism calls the archangel of the orbital periods, or the spirit of the planets. He decided long ago to continue with his work within the orbital periods. To remain with these orbital periods is an angelic decision.

At a specific time during the old Atlantean period it was possible to learn through the Mysteries into which the gods descended that the hosts of Archangeloi, which means such archangels as Oriphiel, Anael, Zachariel and so on, reached the decision to remain within the predetermined orbits of the planets. This happened at a particular time.

But the mighty cohorts led by Satan have to this day failed to reach this decision. They are still striving to use every comet's orbit to bring about a different configuration in the planetary system. We are here confronted with an adversary of Christ, one who wants not merely to corrupt single individuals, nor one who wants to corrupt a group of individuals, a human community, as do the Beast and the False Prophet. With Satan and his cohorts we are faced with endeavours to attack the earth in its context within the planetary system as a whole. That is the third downfall in the Book of Revelation. In connection with the first two downfalls we are told about the rejoicing of the luciferic spiritual beings.

We too must foresee these things about which the apocalyptist tells us. The first stage, the fall of Babylon, will bring with it human beings who have gone astray and who show this even in their physical constitution, so that there can be no prospect of these human bodies, over which the 'I' and astral body have lost control, ever becoming usable again in the future. These bodies must be given up for lost, although not the 'I' and the astral body belonging to them, for these carry on along the paths of karma in humanity. In a certain period we shall see human beings going about with their bodies, human beings who have fallen prey to the Babylonian temptation and whose bodies have therefore fallen away from evolution. That is the fall of Babylon.

In the second stage there will be people going about of whom one will have to say—and this will be visible: In these people live the ahrimanic powers. Here Ahriman is directly involved. This is the Beast, the fall of the Beast and of the False Prophet of the Beast who is not human but suprahuman.

In the third stage it will be noticed that something about the laws of nature becomes inexplicable. It will be the greatest and most significant experience through which human beings will have to go in the future when they have to recognize that something inexplicable is going on in the laws of nature, that phenomena are occurring that do not fit in with the laws of nature. This will happen to a high degree, and it will not be merely a matter of miscalculating the position of a planet, so that it does not arrive at the position one has calculated.

Satan will succeed in taking his initial steps towards bringing disorder into the planetary system. Humanity will have to develop a strong spirituality to counteract this. The disorder that will come about can only be counteracted by the strong spirituality of human beings.

These are things, you see, that we must foresee today when we call up before our souls the future stages of earthly and human evolution. These are things we must see when the apocalyptist speaks to us. You must strive, dear friends, to place yourselves into this concurrence between what can be won from Anthroposophy and what the apocalyptist reveals to us.

Based on existing revelations we can today already say about comets that Satan is lying in wait in the universe in order to use the orbits of comets and put them in place of the cosmos. If you take this in through your anthroposophical understanding and can rediscover it in the Book of Revelation, then this rediscovery brings about something important, namely a kind of meeting in soul with the Book of Revelation and thus with the apocalyptist himself—yes, with the apocalyptist himself: this is important. It will be extraordinarily important for a priest who lives towards the future increasingly to develop a longing—at any time, whether he is on the earth or not—to encounter the apocalyptist who saw into the future in this way after the Mystery of Golgotha.

The feeling must arise amongst the priests that the help that John, the creator of the Book of Revelation, can give those who want to work in a Christian way will be immensely important help, and it will be help that one needs. To walk in reality with John the apocalyptist will only be possible if we approach the Book of Revelation with the attitude of soul I have described. Then John will become our ally. He is, as we know, closely linked to Christ Jesus; he was initiated by Christ Jesus himself, he is an initiate of Christ Jesus. He is therefore an important ally, and to come to Christ through him is something immensely important.

A genuine understanding of the Book of Revelation leads deeply into the realm where one has the greatest conceivable prospect of encountering John and then the Christ himself. This is profoundly true, true in a way that we can only hope will work on in your soul and inmost heart. It is a truth that will draw the priest in a right way into the realm of the spirit. We shall continue from here tomorrow.

LECTURE TWELVE

Dornach, 16 September 1924

Let us be aware today of the propitious karmic circumstance that brings us together during this period when, two years ago, the first Act of Consecration of Man was celebrated here. The main developments of our spiritual life here have followed a remarkable sequence: the Act of Consecration of Man two years ago, the burning of the Goetheanum, one year after that the laying of the foundation stone of the Anthroposophical Society, and now, after the second year, here we are again, this time to contemplate the Book of Revelation as was your wish.

As I have been mentioning from the very beginning, there is a close connection between considering the Book of Revelation and what is encompassed by the Act of Consecration of Man, so that every day we spend considering the Book of Revelation is like a memorial celebration of what we made alive amongst us two years ago in order to bring into this life that which wanted to reveal itself out of the spiritual world as the present-day, modern cultus.

Taking the coincidence of events into account, it is perhaps fitting that today we should call up before us the point in the Book of Revelation that is most difficult of all to understand but which actually leads right into the heart of the Book and which is most intimately connected with the mystery of the Act of Consecration of Man because it is linked objectively with the Being of Christ. One can indeed only speak properly about this in connection with the Book of Revelation, for this Book bears so clearly the fundamental stamp of Christianity that we cannot possibly arrive at anything deviating from a

Christian consideration by looking at what is naturally connected with this Revelation. I can assure you that what I shall have to say about the point we want to consider today will emerge in quite an astonishing way from the visions of the apocalyptist.

Since the beginning of the fifteenth century, dear friends, we have been living in the fifth post-Atlantean age, and within this we are at the beginning of the renewed struggle that Michael will have to conduct in everything that will be happening in the near future. From here we look back to the fourth post-Atlantean age, the one that immediately preceded our own.

We know that the fourth post-Atlantean age began around about the year 747 before the Mystery of Golgotha, so that the Mystery of Golgotha took place during that fourth post-Atlantean age. Although not exactly, because it actually occurred more or less during the first half of the fourth post-Atlantean age, one can say that, give or take the displacements that always affect events in world evolution, it can be regarded as having taken place in the middle of that age. So we can make a diagram of our spiritual evolution like this (Plate 4): Here is the fifth post-Atlantean age. It was preceded by the fourth, third, second and first, right back to the Atlantean catastrophe which essentially gave the final formation to the surface of our earth, providing our earth with—you could say—a new face.

Let us now look at the fourth period, the Atlantean period. It was preceded by what I have often called the Lemurian period of earth evolution, and before that were those we call the second and the first period of earth evolution. The three periods leading up to the Atlantean period are recapitulations, the first of the Saturn condition, the second of the Sun condition, and the third of the Moon condition. Not until the fourth, the Atlantean period, does something new come about. The three periods that precede it are repetitions, recapitulations at a higher level.

The fourth, the Atlantean period, represents something new. What occurred during the Atlantean period occurred while the earth still had forms that were quite different from those that came later. Even in the middle of the Atlantean period the earth did not have a solid crust of the kind familiar to us now. The geological dating posited for these things today is an illusion. The time when the earth solidified out of a partially firm, partially fluid consistency lay in the Atlantean period. So the human race was quite different during the Atlantean period, for even in the middle of that period it did not have today's rigid skeleton. The substance of which human beings were formed in those times was more like that of the lower animals, although their form was most noble. The substance, however, resembled the consistency of the jelly-fish; it was soft, with some tendency to form cartilage.

We can state, therefore, that all physical conditions on the earth have changed since those times, and we now no longer have those radical metamorphoses, those radical transformations that were still possible in the middle of the Atlantean period. In those times we were able at any moment to metamorphose our shape—which was made of soft material—and grow larger or smaller, adopt this or that form, depending on our inner state of soul.[1] Every stirring of soul immediately impressed itself on our physical body. If someone in the middle of the Atlantean period wanted to take hold of an object that was situated at a distance, his will worked into his jelly-like organs in such a way that they were able to stretch the required distance. So the whole of physical life was different, physical processes followed quite different courses at any given moment. All physical processes, all transformations and metamorphoses provided a picture of actual spiritual happenings at any moment.

This is no longer the case today. Today we look out and no

longer see the spirit working in what happens out there, not even in the course of the seasons. Those rapid transformations that took place in old Atlantis left no room for doubt that this world contained the divine and the spiritual. Although the continent of Atlantis retained its shape in essence, it was nevertheless very mobile, and surrounded in every direction by weaving, viscous fluidity. You could not have called it semi-fluid, but it was viscous and was able to bear the bodies with their still very soft organs and also the plants that were at that time not yet anchored in the earth; the plants hovered or glided in the soft, mobile substance of the earth. So physical conditions were quite different then. You could say that sea and land were not yet separate in the way they became later, they still merged into one another. Those who were able to see these things clearly at that time spoke of the ocean—with its even greater capacity for expressing metamorphosis than the solid-fluid land adjacent to it—as being where the gods held sway. The gods were seen to hold sway all around the edge of Atlantis. There were no doubts about those gods who held sway, for spirit and soul were everywhere perceived as clearly as the physical. Human beings saw soul and spirit in the physical realm.

A characteristic possessed by the fourth post-Atlantean age was that people then were able to see the gods holding sway in the play of the air, although this was no longer so strong in the centuries leading up to the fifth post-Atlantean age, but in Grecian times it was entirely obvious. In old Atlantis human beings saw the gods hold sway in the solid-fluid element. In the fourth post-Atlantean age the gods were seen to hold sway in the fluid-airy element of the clouds, in the twilight formations and so on. The consciousness people had in the fourth post-Atlantean age was not yet very clear, so there are no descriptions defining this exactly, but nevertheless this is how it was. Surely any unprejudiced observation can only arrive at this interpretation of those wonderful paintings of clouds in early Renaissance pictures, an interpretation that points to the feeling of how something spiritual is born out of them, of how the working of the divine spirit is felt to be in the airy clouds, in the airy-watery being of the air.

Human beings at that time did not turn their attention very much to the physical aspects of cloud formations. They looked for what the clouds would reveal to them. The feeling this gave them was wonderful, but it is difficult to reconstruct it for today's consciousness. Even as late as the eighth or ninth post-Christian century, when people looked at the morning sky they saw before their soul the clouds shimmering in the dawn light and felt that there was something alive in the aurora, in the pink sky of morning; and the same was felt when the evening twilight came.

We can therefore say: In old Atlantis the spirit was seen physically. After Atlantis came the post-Atlantean period with its seven ages; and the recapitulation of what had happened in Atlantis, the recapitulation of what had happened physically in Atlantis, took place at the soul level in the fourth post-Atlantean age. The mighty upheavals I spoke about, the years AD 333 and 666, which are upheavals at the soul level in human evolution, these correspond to physical upheavals in old Atlantis. When they saw the revelations in the fluid-airy element, the seers of the Greco-Latin age felt that they were seeing in their soul something like a recapitulation of earlier conditions of earth that had once taken place in the physical realm. They were aware of this, although somewhat dimly, as befitted the consciousness of that time.

Everything that lived in schools like that at Chartres, which I have been mentioning in the anthroposophical lectures,[2] showed in its descriptions that the soul experiences of the Greco-Latin age were a recapitulation in soul of the more dense, physical experiences and events in Atlantis.

We are now in the era of the consciousness soul. Any direct soul experience of what happens in the airy-fluid element is extinguished. But through the kind of catastrophe with which the fifth, the post-Atlantean period began, the further development of the consciousness soul of humanity is beginning to be prepared. As regards external civilization we are still somewhat bogged down in the chaos of this development of the consciousness soul. However, the dawn of the Michael age should bring in some vision that will provide order for this chaos. This vision will be as follows: No longer physically as in Atlantean times, no longer in the soul as in Greco-Latin times, but entirely spiritually, pictures will arise like memories in the human being, pictures that are somewhat like a mirage of thoughts, and this will happen particularly after the appearance of the Etheric Christ. Something like an inner mirage in pictures of a visionary nature will arise in the thoughts of human beings, and in the era of the consciousness soul these pictures will come in full consciousness. Just as the heat in the desert air creates a mirage, so will the human thought be carried in a way that leads to an understanding of what the airy-fiery, the airy-warmth element is.

We can put it this way: In Atlantean times the human being perceived the divine in the solid-fluid element, which means more in external, physical matter; in the fourth post-Atlantean age, the Greco-Latin age, the human being perceived the spirit in the wonderful formations of the fluid-airy element; and now, in the fifth post-Atlantean age, when it will be the consciousness soul that does the perceiving, we shall experience how more and more there will appear in our consciousness what is airy-fiery, airy warmth. This will cause what the Greeks experienced in soul, and what the inhabitants of Atlantis experienced in body, to appear to human beings now in mighty spiritual pictures.

So a time is coming in human evolution when visions will appear that are as clear as thoughts, visions about primeval earth times and about the origin of the human being, and everything connected with these. Darwin's view that attributed a lowly ancestry to the human being based entirely on a single line of reasoning will be superseded by inner visions, by the development of wonderful Imaginations that will arise out of inner human warmth linked with the breathing process, like vivid, coloured visionary thoughts full of meaning. The human being will know what he once was through seeing something like a reflection of the Greco-Latin age, and then back beyond that of what was there in Atlantis.

You see, dear friends: This seeing concerns us very directly, for it will begin to happen in the next age of humanity. Because this seeing is so close to us we find ourselves looking into the heart of the apocalyptist. The seeing that is about to begin is what he describes in the picture of the woman clothed with the sun with the dragon beneath her feet, and giving birth to a male child.[3] (Rev. 12,1)

Through what is expressed in this picture many individuals will indeed become seers still in the course of this twentieth century. Much rays forth from this picture that will bring understanding to human beings. First of all it shines back into the Greco-Latin age, where at the soul level an understanding was prepared for the shape of this picture as it will appear in the near future. It has taken on all kinds of shapes: Isis with the child Horus, the mother of Christ with the Christ child; especially in the Greco-Latin age these things lived with wonderful profundity in many metamorphoses that are still preserved in tradition.

In the near future, human beings will look back to the kind of seeing that people had in the fourth post-Atlantean age when they saw this picture in the clouds, in the airy-fluid element. Looking back even further they will see what lived in the physical processes of Atlantis. This image of the woman clothed with the sun giving birth to a male child, and having the dragon beneath her feet, will be seen as though through a kind of spiritual telescope, a kind of ocular, pointing towards a long distant past in which the earthly, physical element was linked with the supra-earthly, cosmic element. In those times there was a far more intimate contact between the earth and the world of the planets and the world of the sun.

As we know, during the period of earth evolution when the ancient Saturn condition was being recapitulated there were many characteristics of Saturn in earthly existence, although in a denser form. During the second period of earth evolution that brought with it the recapitulation of the Old Sun condition, the sun, which had still been bound to the earth during Saturn, separated out from the earth, and with it went all the beings belonging to the sun. In the third period of earth evolution, the Lemurian period, the moon, too, departed from the earth, so that this triad of earth, sun and moon became the reality for the subsequent Earth period. You can see in my book *Occult Science*[4] how the planets came to be added as well. It is also necessary to look at all the processes I have described in connection with the return of human souls during the Atlantean period. These are earth processes seen from the earthly perspective.

There is also something else we should add. Since the Mystery of Golgotha, dear friends, initiates who have understood cosmic secrets have regarded Christ as a Sun Being who was connected with the sun prior to the Mystery of Golgotha. Mystery priests in pre-Christian times looked up to the sun when they wanted to be united with Christ. But since the Mystery of Golgotha, Christ has been the Spirit of the Earth. We must now look for Christ the Sun Being in earthly life and in earthly work, whereas those who wanted to see and have communion with him prior to the Mystery of Golgotha had to raise themselves up to the sun.

This Sun Spirit, who is rightly regarded as male in the way he came to the earth—and there have indeed also been similar events in earlier ages, which I have often mentioned—is brilliantly described in the apocalyptist's vision, that profound vision which appears with an immediacy almost tangible in the middle of the Atlantean period and stands there as a shining physical appearance. After that moment in time the wise scholars of the Mysteries saw, when they looked up to the sun, how Christ was developing and maturing there, up to the point when he became capable of going through the Mystery of Golgotha. What they saw when they looked towards that point in evolution during Atlantean times was a birth taking place out there in the cosmos inside the sun.

Before seeing the birth of Christ as a male being in the sun in the middle of the Atlantean period, the priests saw a female being in the sun. The important change that took place in the middle of the Atlantean period is that before the middle of that period the cosmic female was seen in the spiritual aura of the sun, 'the woman clothed with the sun'. Putting it this way corresponds exactly with what happened in the supra-earthly world, in the heavens: 'The woman clothed with the sun giving birth to a male child'. The apocalyptist rightly calls him a male child, and this is the same being who later went through the Mystery of Golgotha and who had earlier gone through other forms of existence. What took place during that Atlantean period was a kind of birth, which was actually a complicated kind of metamorphosis. One saw how the sun gave birth to what was male in it, to what was of the nature of a son. But what does this mean for the earth? In the middle of the Atlantean period there was of course quite a different feeling about what a sun existence is. Nowadays the sun is regarded as a conglomeration of craters and fiery masses; what today's physicists describe is an abomination. But in those times the initiates saw what I have just described. They really saw the woman clothed with the sun, with the dragon beneath her feet, and giving birth to a male child. Those who saw and understood such a thing said: For the heavens that is the birth of Christ, for us it is the birth of our 'I'. They said this although the 'I' only entered into the human being much later.

Since that moment in the middle of Atlantis, evolution has meant that human beings have become ever more aware of their 'I'. They were of course not as aware of it as we are today, but in a more elementary way they became ever more aware of it when the priests of the Mysteries showed them: The sun kindles the 'I' in the human being. Through the birth shown by the apocalyptist in that picture, the 'I' was continuously kindled from the outside through the way the sun worked, right up to the fourth post-Atlantean age when the 'I' had finally fully entered the human being. The human being, it was felt, belonged to the sun. This was a feeling that entered deeply into human nature.

Having become such weaklings in our soul life today, we cannot imagine how the soul experiences of human beings surged and stormed in bygone ages. As a result of receiving the 'I' out of the cosmos, human beings on the earth felt that everything in their earlier nature had become transformed. Earlier they had been dependent on their astral body, on what lived in the astral, and this worked in the soul-spirit in such a way that human beings in those times saw this picture: Here (Plate 4, left) is the human being, and above him is the sun; the 'I' has not yet arrived, and what works down from the sun is astral. The human being carried in him the astral body, which came from the sun, the astral body that is not as yet governed by the 'I' and so still has animal-like, though more refined, emotions. But now he is an entirely different human being, he has become 'I', whereas what bubbled through him earlier was the astral body. All this came from the sun.

Let us now imagine something that I shall draw like a diagram (Plate 4, bottom left): Here is a picture of the sun in oldest Atlantean times, filled with living, shining light bubbling and moving in the lower half of the sun being; out of this, something is born in the upper part; the hint of a face was sensed here. Down below in the being of the sun the human being felt the origin of all the emotions surging in his own astral body, but also of everything that gave him his soul and his spirit being. The next phase, showing how the sun was seen later, would have been like this (Plate 4, bottom middle): emerging more clearly, its face becoming more defined, and assuming the form of a woman. You see—not clearly yet—what is to be brought to the human being as the result of the 'I' taking charge. The space down below, writhing like an animal, grows smaller and smaller until finally the moment comes when the woman is in the sun and gives birth to the male child; and beneath the feet of the woman is that which was formerly here (Plate 4); the woman in the sun, giving birth to the 'I', showing the image of how the dragon may be controlled—the astral world of the earlier period that is now beneath her feet.

There in the sun, at that time, the struggle began between Michael and the dragon. The consequence of this was—and it was perfectly apparent physically—that all things in the sun gradually moved towards the earth and became earthly ingredients, earthly content which ruled the human being in his unconscious while into his consciousness the 'I' entered more and more.

What took place cosmically in this way in the Atlantean period found its mythological counter-image in the Greco-Latin age. In the next age immediately following ours, human beings will be able to experience retrospectively the earlier picture of Isis with the Horus child that then became the picture of the Virgin with the Jesus child. Human beings will see in this picture the woman clothed with the sun, and the dragon beneath her feet, the dragon that was thrown down to the earth by Michael that can no longer be found in the heavens. This picture, which will change, will appear at the time when the dragon will be unbound and when what I described yesterday will come about. It is a fact that humanity will be experiencing a deepened vision of earth's primeval times and of the origins of humanity, and at the same time also an etheric vision of the Christ-Being, for during the age of Michael those events will occur which the apocalyptist hints at when he speaks of Michael throwing the dragon creature down to the earth, where it works within the nature of the human being. Michael, however, will concern himself with that in human nature which he has thrown down as the dragon creature.

Dear friends, let us try to imagine vividly what this means. Let us look once again into the Atlantean period. The apocalyptist does so in advance of us. He has the vision of the woman clothed with the sun, giving birth to the Jesus boy and having the dragon beneath her feet. This picture grows weaker and weaker as Atlantean times advance. At the end of the Atlantean period the new continents rise up out of the ocean, the continents that contain the forces through which human beings have fallen into the various errors of the post-Atlantean period. Out of the ocean rises the Beast with the seven heads (Rev. 13,1), and sevenfold land rises up out of the ocean, dragging down the human being through the vapours that arise spiritually from the earth out of the human being's emotions.

The apocalyptist also sees the Atlantean catastrophe in the form of this seven-headed Beast rising up out of the ocean, and this will reappear in the future when what he is indicating will occur again in the Michael age. The apocalyptist is speaking of entirely real happenings which are very much our concern with regard to the spiritual life of humanity. The content of this picture in particular is connected with the Being of Christ.

We are approaching an age when we shall once again see how the spirit lives in the earthly realm; we shall see how the spiritual processes at work in the Transubstantiation will once again be able to appear before the souls of human beings. Especially in the Transubstantiation there will appear the earthly reflection of what has taken place in heavenly regions in such a way that what has happened since the middle of the Atlantean period is but a small section of everything that is connected with the Being of Christ. Then one will understand how a metamorphosis such as that taking place in the Transubstantiation becomes possible when one regards what is today physical and chemical as merely an episode, and when one relates the Transubstantiation to something entirely other than what is seemingly material.

In this way let us deepen our commemoration of the first Act of Consecration of Man two years ago, this commemoration of what truly descended from heaven, shone down from heaven from the Atlantean period, this commemoration of what appeared in the clouds of the Greco-Latin age, of the Christ who walks on earth and is grasped by human beings in their visions, of Christ who walks on the earth etherically in our time and can be grasped by human beings in Imaginations, in visions. The Christ is present in the Transubstantiation and he will be more and more present to human beings. The processes I have described today comprise the paths through which the Christ gradually entered into the happenings of earth evolution.

Let us take this in as a kind of festive inner picture in memory of the first Act of Consecration of Man celebrated in the Goetheanum two years ago.

LECTURE THIRTEEN

Dornach, 17 September 1924

From one specific point of view I have already shown how the Book of Revelation is built on the principle of numbers, which is one of the occult principles. In the considerations earlier today[1] about fundamental rhythmical numbers of the cosmos and of the human being you will perhaps have seen once again how profoundly numbers, in that they can reveal rhythms, are embedded in the cosmos.

With occult revelations given in the form of John's apocalyptic Book it is entirely a matter of course that they are structured in accordance with numbers. The vision about which the apocalyptist is speaking arises, in keeping with the modern initiation principle, when Inspiration speaks into the Imaginations one has before one. The vision then takes place in that the picture quality of the Imagination expands, whereupon the Inspiration speaks through the Imagination. Things then proceed according to the principle of numbers, so that this principle helps one follow what is going on. For occultists seven is always the most perfect number; it almost amounts to an occult rule: Seven is the most perfect number. But do not think that this number seven is so very important for the content; its immeasurable importance has to do with being able to hear the Inspirations. If one lives in the number seven oneself, one is able to understand the Inspirations in all kinds of ways. Let me give you an example. Suppose someone is sensing important spiritual backgrounds in connection with his own time. When the overall picture of the cosmos is taken into account it is of course more or less arbitrary to sense spiritual backgrounds for one's own time in particular;

humanly it is natural, but nevertheless it is rather arbitrary. If I am the observer in the year 1924, this means that the year being observed is solely 1924. Someone else is the observer in the year 1903, in which case the year 1903 is the year under observation.[2] If as an observer I am independent of when my observation is taking place and if I have proper insight into what I am observing, and also if I have the ability to go backwards over seven impressions regardless of where I begin to go back from, then, in accordance with the laws of the spiritual world, it is always the seventh impression that provides enlightenment about the first, and the fourteenth that gives enlightenment with regard to both. It is really a matter of method, to find one's way into what can provide enlightenment. If you know a language, you can understand a person speaking that language; similarly, what matters here is to be able to live in the number seven. This is how we must understand these things, for giving revelations in accordance with the number seven is exceedingly complicated. All kinds of things in the cosmos are ordered in accordance with the number seven, and to a lesser extent in accordance with the number twelve and also other numbers. It is possible to follow events from any point by using multiples of seven.

When I was endeavouring to interpret John's Book of Revelation in Nuremberg in 1908, that was of course quite a different period for the whole of the anthroposophical movement. My foremost intention at that time was to interpret Anthroposophy itself on the basis of the Book of Revelation. A great deal can be interpreted through this Book because world events, too, can be gleaned from it, and at that time it was important for these to be mentioned. But for you today, as I have already said many times, it is necessary to identify with the Book of Revelation in your 'I' and to look absolutely concretely at the real fact of how the Book of Revelation shows a whole range of events moving forward in accordance with the number seven. I have indicated the events connected with 'the woman clothed with the sun ... and with the dragon beneath her feet' from the point of view of the consciousness soul's experience. From the way I have done this you will deduce which period we are living in according to the Book of Revelation's calculations. As regards the consciousness soul, we are living in the age of the trumpets' sounding—not with regard to the development of the astral body nor with regard to the development of humanity in general, which was more what my lectures in 1908 were about. We are living in the age of the trumpets' sounding with regard to the development of the consciousness soul, which does not run parallel with the other developments but as it were edges its way into these.

We are at present still only in the beginning stages of the consciousness soul, so we can only perceive the sounding of the trumpets if the consciousness soul raises itself to supersensible vision. This is because human beings at the present time cannot find a supersensible interpretation for what goes on down here on the earth. The significant aspect is that people do not apply supersensible interpretations; instead they merely accept things with indifference. When talking of anthroposophical considerations I have often pointed to a definite moment in the nineteenth century, namely the beginning of the 1840s. I have said that seen spiritually the early 1840s represent an important and significant turning-point in the development of the civilized world. These years brought with them, so to speak, the culmination of materialism.

Everything about materialism had in fact already been decided by 1843/44. What followed was no more than consequences, and there will continue to be consequences. But with regard to what came upon the civilized humanity of Europe and its American appendage, the time of the early 1840s was indeed of infinite importance because that is when the onslaught of ahrimanic powers on human affairs was tremendously intense. You might want to maintain that even worse things happened after 1843/44, but this only appears to be so. Do not forget that Ahriman is cleverer than human beings, and Ahriman was the chief instigator in the year 1843/44. He arranged things in accordance with his kind of intelligence. That was the nadir, or perhaps one should say the culmination of the materialistic path. Thenceforward human beings carried on with the mess in their own way and although outwardly what they did may appear much more ugly, it is not all that frightful when seen in conjunction with human evolution as a whole; and seen from a spiritual vantage point it is merely a consequence of what Ahriman projected at the beginning of the 1840s.

The sixth angel began to sound his trumpet at the beginning of the 1840s, and he will continue to sound it until the events I spoke about yesterday take place at the end of the twentieth century, when the trumpet of the seventh angel will begin to sound. We are definitely already within the realm of the woes. In the realm of the consciousness soul as civilized human beings we are in the second woe. This was preceded for about 150 years by the fifth trumpet. If we follow the trumpets backwards in accordance with the number seven in the era of the consciousness soul we arrive at a somewhat earlier point in time. Here down below on earth the era of the consciousness soul begins in 1413. But things get somewhat displaced, so earlier times also have an effect. So with the sounding of the trumpets we go back to the time of the Crusades. In genuine Mystery centres the period from the Crusades up to our time now was always regarded as the age of the sounding of trumpets. You will be able to find the stages through what is described in the Book of Revelation. You will be able to find when materialism burst in on humanity, for example when Copernicanism approached, that one third of human beings were killed spiritually, which means that they ceased to develop full spirituality. (Rev.

9,15) And the plague of locusts described in the Book of Revelation is indeed truly horrible.

This brings us to a matter that one does not like to put into words but which is nevertheless one of the things that is definitely relevant to one's work as a priest. In theory the plague of locusts has in the broadest sense already begun if we look at it from the point of view of consciousness. We should not bring up such matters when we are talking to people, for there is always a possibility that healing might take place in situations of illness. But if one is to work as a priest one has to know what one is often dealing with in human beings.

On the whole people who call themselves liberal or democratic are immensely delighted at being able to quote again and again figures that prove tremendous population growth in certain parts of the world. Population growth is greatly longed for by people who are democratic liberals in the political sense and also by those who consider themselves to be free thinkers.

Well, first of all the facts are not quite what they seem because the statistics are based on errors; statistical comparisons never refer to the earth as a whole but only to parts, and one forgets that at other times different parts of the earth were more densely populated than they are today. So the details are not always quite correct, but taken as a whole it is correct to say that in our time certain supernumerary people are appearing who have no 'I' and are therefore not human beings in the full sense of the word. This is a terrible truth. They go about but are not incarnated 'I's; they take their place in physical heredity, receive an ether body and an astral body and in a sense become equipped inwardly with an ahrimanic consciousness. They appear to be human if you do not look too closely yet they are not human beings in the full sense of the word.[3]

This is a terrible truth and it is a fact. The apocalyptist is pointing directly at human beings themselves when he speaks about the plague of locusts in the age of the fifth trumpet. Once again we can recognize the apocalyptist by the manner of his vision. In their astral body such people appear just as the apocalyptist describes them: like etheric locusts with human faces. It is definitely necessary for us to think in this way about such supersensible matters and for priests to know these things. A priest is a shepherd of souls. He must be able to find words for everything that goes on in such a soul. These are not necessarily always evil souls; they may merely be souls that develop as far as the soul realm but lack an 'I'. One is sure to notice if one comes across such a person, and the priest must know about it, for it will have a bearing on the quality of community in his congregation. Above all, people who have healthy souls suffer as a consequence of those who go about as human locusts. So the question can arise, and indeed must arise, as to how one should behave towards such people.

This can be quite a difficult task, for such people often have deep feelings; they can have very deep feelings and yet one notices that there is no actual individuality in them. Of course the fact that there is no individuality in them must be carefully concealed from them for otherwise they would go mad. Despite having to conceal this from them one must ensure that such souls—for soul they are, even if not spirit— can make contact with other human beings and can develop in their wake, so that they can, as it were, tag along with the others. Such human beings fairly accurately demonstrate the nature and being of man up to the twentieth year, for it is not until the twentieth year that the mind soul or intellectual soul is born, which is what provides the possibility for the 'I' to live on the earth.

It is a great error to believe that one need not behave compassionately towards these 'I'-less, individuality-less human beings on the grounds that as they have no individuality they will have no future incarnation. Someone who believed that would equally have to believe that one need not behave compassionately towards children. In each case one has to discover what is present in such people. In some cases it might be a posthumous soul, posthumous in comparison with souls who came into being at a particular stage of evolution and have repeatedly been incarnated as human beings. Others might be retarded souls who have come back from another planet to which almost the whole of humanity once went at some specific time. This kind of soul, too, can enter such a human body. In full awareness of this we must bring up such human beings like eternal children.

All this is hidden in the Book of Revelation. The pictures that appear in it are sometimes quite heart-rending and it is terrible to read about all kinds of suffering coming upon humanity on earth. And when these pictures, which appear as Imaginations, are taken in this way one cannot help saying that a great deal of what they show is really present in our time—in its spiritual aspect, of course.

There are also other pictures in the Book of Revelation, pictures of wonderful gentleness like that of the angels coming down with the censer. (Rev. 8,3) Incense is mentioned, and our attention is turned towards much that occurred during the time of the Crusades. The first trumpets transport us to the Crusades; we go back to the period of the Crusades when we survey the development of the consciousness soul in humanity. We see that certain personalities appear in the age of the Crusades and the times connected with them, personalities who had immensely strong impressions of sharing in the life of the spiritual world. They are, I would like to say, the geniuses of piety. It is very important to be clear about the fact that we find geniuses of piety there.

Going back still further we find before our field of consciousness the time from the Mystery of Golgotha up to the Crusades and everything connected with these. We can regard this period of time as a smaller epoch of the opening of the seven seals. We can only understand this fully when we are clear about the following. Consider how many personalities there were during the age of the Crusades almost all of whom turned their religious feeling inwards towards the depths of their inner being, towards an intensity of feeling, an inner mystical experience. This began to happen in those times, whereas earlier on people had looked up into the universe when they wanted to see the divine world—or at least those in authority did, even though they continually had to struggle with the stream emanating from Rome. There had been an understanding of a god who lives and weaves and works in the sense-perceptible phenomenon to which one looked up. But then everything was turned more or less inwards, and the great geniuses of mysticism appeared. First there was a vision of the universe as a revelation of the divine; afterwards one had to feel one's way towards what the human heart sensed as the inner kindling of a light, so that the divine could be lit from within the human being.

These stages described in the Book of Revelation are also present in the spread of Christianity. First there is the quiet yet triumphant progress of Christianity through the victorious spirit, the victorious Word. You could describe Christianity as spreading through the subterranean passages of social life at that time. In the second stage the spread of Christianity involves robbing the earth of much of what we call peace. Christianity participated thoroughly in the conflicts of this second stage. Then we see a stage in which the inner impulse of Christianity gradually dies; Christianity becomes a state religion which amounts, of course, to the death of the genuine, original Christian impulse. Then comes the stage that must be seen as that of the fourth seal, when Mohammedanism arrives in the manner I have described. Seal after seal is opened in this way, and what happens under the influence of the Crusades is influenced by those important religious geniuses. You can observe this if you observe more accurately what happened. In this sense all written history amounts to a forgery.

Before the Crusades Christianity was disseminated in what I would term a good way. As Christianity spread up to the time of the Crusades, what happened again and again through countless members of the monastic orders, even things that were bad in the external sense, happened in Europe more or less in direct imitation of the Palestinian stories, although the Gospels were not read by lay people, for they were the concern of the priests. But what happened at that time was most certainly influenced by what the priests saw in the Gospels. The priests had the Gospels and the cultus. In the cultus the supersensible world was mirrored in a sense-perceptible way. The Mass, the celebration of the Mass, was what the priests saw as direct doors to the supersensible. That is why they gradually desisted from looking up to revelations of the divine spirit through the starry heavens and all those wonderful prophecies that had remained in what I termed astrosophy—as distinct from astronomy and astrology—this morning.[4] All this old wisdom had gradually grown almost entirely obscure by the time of the Crusades.

During the time of the Crusades we suddenly see individuals appearing everywhere moving from East to West, either those returning from the Crusades themselves or others who came somewhat later and in whom secrets of the Orient had taken root. A profusion of writings was brought to Europe from the East, but these were later lost because the watchers over written works were not as Argus-eyed as are those who watch over such things today. So hardly a great deal has remained of those writings. Instead far more about cosmic Christianity was disseminated by oral tradition, and this took root especially at the time of the Crusades.

Here a kind of seventh seal is opened. With regard to

respect for the written word, just consider the fuss that is being made because an Italian professor is said to have discovered Livy's manuscripts; what a fuss the Italian state is making today to get its hands on those manuscripts of Livy, even though nothing definite is known about them. We need only go back a little way to find a time when the state could not have cared less whether some manuscript or other had been found. This interest in preserving written texts is fairly recent.

I myself observed quite a successful little drama in this connection when I was working at the Goethe-Schiller Archive. We were sent a letter written by Goethe that looked very odd because it was so dirty and torn.[5] At that time such a thing was already regarded as a sin: this was not the way to treat Goethe's letters. So we tried to find out what had happened. The letter had once been in the possession of Kuno Fischer,[6] and he had simply sent Goethe's letter to the printer. Instead of sending a copy he had sent the original to the printer together with his notes and comments. So it was a miracle that the letter survived at all, since it was not usual at that time for printers to preserve manuscripts.

It is, then, not surprising that during the time when Christianity was coming into contact with Orientalism through the Crusades truths about Christianity were disseminated that we would term cabalistic today. There were perhaps a good many people alive at the time who knew more than Jakob Boehme did without causing any stir, whereas by the time Jakob Boehme came along the very fact of such a person's existence caused a stir.

The time of the Crusades is the time of transition from the age of the seals to the age of the trumpets. Saying this is not so much a reminder of external events documented in history books but rather an indication of what was going on in human consciousness. Individuals with more profound feelings have always tended to say about the period from the Crusades up to our time: Alas, such terrible things—I am looking at this from the supersensible point of view—have been going on in human souls under the sign of the sounding trumpets. But in fact human beings on earth do not listen to the trumpets as they sound.

Many people in our time ought to have this awareness about this age of the sixth trumpet in which we are now living; you know what its most essential characteristics and its most essential effects are. One third of humanity, so it is said, will be killed. (Rev. 9,15) This will of course happen gradually as time goes on. The word 'killed' refers to that absence of 'I' in those human beings who have already been prepared in advance by the locust form.

These are the things that make it imperative for priests to look more deeply into how what is going on is structured. Priests are directly concerned with the supersensible, and we are surrounded in every direction by the supersensible world. The part of human beings that can be observed through the fact of their having a physical body is only a section of their human life. As soon as we begin to make our way into the supersensible world we discover the real deeds of human beings, and we see how people are often entirely unaware of the consequences of these deeds. One can sometimes remain entirely ignorant of what one person does to another by passing him by without taking any notice of him, when according to his karma he should have behaved towards him in some specific manner. Later this karma will exert its influence more strongly, so a compensation will indeed come about in the end, but actually the compensation ought to have happened in *this* life. It is quite possible not to notice this in external physical life, and there is actually nothing reprehensible in what the person has done. From an external, civilized point of view he has done his duty, yet in terms of his connection with world evolution he may have inflicted a terribly deep wound. This is not a supra-earthly matter but a *supersensible* matter, for supersensible processes are constantly at work in earthly life.

To understand the Book of Revelation with this level of earnestness will be necessary to the degree that the one whom I have called the Etheric Christ will become visible amongst humanity. So it was out of a truly healthy sense of what is needed, coming from your deepest subconscious, that you, dear friends, chose the Book of Revelation as the subject of these considerations. Perhaps you imagined that what I am able to give about the Book of Revelation at this time would be somewhat different, but your wish to hear me speak about the Book of Revelation surely emerged from the mood of these times dwelling in your hearts. In fact it is quite possible to say that the way you as a group of priests who belong together formed the wish to understand the Book of Revelation shows that you are already in some degree related to John the apocalyptist. So this thing that you need above all else, this filling of yourselves with the spirit of the Book of Revelation, will in no way clash with the necessity to distinguish between certain epochs according to the principle of the number seven or with the fact that one can actually begin anywhere and from that point find out how things go. One will never find the interconnections in world evolution if one does not apply the principle of numbers as one's method of observation. So with this we have touched on that side of the Book of Revelation that is essential and fruitful especially for our time.

There are also other events to be found interspersed here and there in the Book of Revelation, usually at points where there is a transition between the number seven and other numbers. So this is something else that needs explaining. We are shown the following through numbers: At a specific time there is a particular number of human beings who bear the seal of God on their forehead; these are the lucky ones, the ones who will be saved or redeemed, or call it what you will.

(Rev. 7, 4–8) The others, however, cannot find redemption at all. Reading the Book of Revelation in this external way gives one a feeling of depression.

One must realize, however, that ancient texts everywhere differentiate between racial development and the development of individual human beings. One must realize that individuals in earlier times did not feel in the least depressed by being told that a certain number of a particular race would be saved while the others would perish. This was because, just like people who have the urge to insure their life, no one included himself amongst the ones who would perish.

The likely duration of one's life is calculated and, as you know, insurance companies do not accept people who are likely to die soon, for if they were to insure people likely to die soon their coffers would quickly be empty. They want to insure people who will live and pay their premiums for a long time. So by using a calculation based upon probability— which is quite an interesting type of calculation—they have to work out the likely life-span of a person by applying a variety of antecedents. I have never yet met anyone who felt obliged to die at the moment worked out by the insurance company—using that assuredly correct method of calculation—as the probable moment of death. There is no such thing as feeling obliged to die at that particular moment. This, too, is founded on a reality. Once you enter into the world of numbers you are not concerned with the level of spirituality occupied by the human individuality.

When one makes statements like this one is touching on a degree of mystery, an occult secret. It is based on the belief that if you count off one, two, three, four, five individuals and then apply this figure to something spiritual, then this counting will also have a meaning with regard to the spiritual world. But it does not have a meaning in the same way. The principle of numbers comes into play at the moment when the spiritual world breaks through and reveals itself, for example in the Platonic cosmic year, or in the number of breaths and so on. When you are ascending to spirit consciousness, you need the number at the border, at the threshold to the spiritual world. This is where you get stuck if you do not have the number or something resembling the number. But nothing fits at all if you try to use numbers once you have crossed the threshold into the spiritual world. So it is perfectly in order for someone like the apocalyptist who is writing an occult document to speak—when discussing the development of races on the earth—about a particular number who will be saved and another number who will perish. But individual human beings cannot feel that this applies to them because such numbers apply only to the development of races and not to that of individuals.

I shall say more next time about how this can be understood in detail.

PARTICIPANTS' QUESTIONS

The following questions were handed to Rudolf Steiner in written form on 18 September 1924 before the lecture.

In the handwriting of Johannes Werner Klein:
The source of certain difficulties we encounter from time to time in our circle is our lack of clarity regarding the spiritual tasks and the background of the Circle of Seven and, in connection with this, regarding the earthly leadership of our movement.

Specific questions that concern us at the moment about the continuation of all our work are:

1. Is it a good thing to continue placing the main emphasis on outreach or should we for the time being, in the interests of preparing ourselves rightly for our future tasks, concentrate more on intensive work for the deepening of our own personality? This question is brought to the fore by a deterioration of health in both body and soul of several members of our circle of priests since autumn 1922 which is causing us concern.
2. What measures should we undertake towards founding spiritual colonies in other countries?
3. How are we to handle the membership of our congregations and in connection with this the administration of the Communion? Hitherto most of us have been very free and easy about this. In some towns all those present at the regular Sunday Communion service for the congregation have been allowed to participate.

In order to recognize each other in all our karmic diversity and to discover the extent of the tasks facing the circle of priests as a whole, we have concerned ourselves a good deal over the past few weeks with the karmic situations that have led each of us to this circle of priests. The revelations you have given us in your lectures have once again brought us face to face with the question of the being and karmic structure of our circle of priests.

In this connection we need to ask about the karma of the traditional Christian churches and how this karma, through individuals, works into our circle of priests.

The apocalyptic part of the Gospels (Mark 13,20) contains the sentence: 'And if the Lord had not shortened the days, no human being would be saved; but for sake of the elect, whom he chose, he shortened the days'. What is the meaning of this sentence in view of coming events, perhaps the war of all against all?

These are the questions with which our whole circle of priests is concerned. However, because of some implications these questions have and also because of the matter of the towns and a few quite brief concerns, we would like to request a meeting with you for the Circle of Seven *Oberlenkers* and *Lenkers*.

For the circle of priests: Joh. Werner Klein

In the handwriting of Friedrich Doldinger:

1. In the Catholic Church it is the custom for the bishop <u>consecrating a church</u> to write the letters in the ash on the floor. Is a corresponding ritual necessary when we consecrate a church? Who (*Lenker?*) would do this? (The case in question is the inauguration of a room in Freiburg at Michaelmas which will be used solely for services.)

2. The use of <u>candles</u> for other cultic occasions. Can we use the seven-branched candlestick with lit candles for purposes other than the Act of Consecration of Man, e.g. when a baptism is taking place near the altar?

3. <u>The Breviary</u>.

There were many participants at the first course in Dornach, when the Breviary was given, who subsequently did not become priests. Since then, chiefly through these individuals but also initially as a result of a lack of clarity within our circle of priests, the Breviary has been given to people who have never even considered entering the priesthood, and even to some who are causing practical difficulties for our work. Some of those who had received the Breviary as a 'loving gift' without realizing that it contained meditations for priests returned their copies as soon as this was made known. The circle of priests would now like to approach all those who possess the Breviary without having made the vow with the request to return it. There is, however, a lack of clarity within our circle of priests as to whether this is possible in the case of all those who ought not to have it, e.g. some wives. However, almost all of us think that only radical measures allowing no exceptions can achieve the necessary orderliness in the matter, for the Breviary was quite clearly only intended for those directly involved in preparing themselves for the priesthood.

Many of us are worried by the incorrect distribution of the Breviary. In connection with the way the verses for the Class* are dealt with, the question has arisen as to whether the Breviary might have become ineffective through the way it has been distributed and whether even if the unauthorized copies are retrieved a desirable situation can be restored at all.

---

* The First Class of the School of Spiritual Science, Dornach.

LECTURE FOURTEEN

Dornach, 18 September 1924

I shall endeavour to answer the questions that have been handed to me alongside the other things I have to say. However, there are some questions amongst them which I should like to answer within the Circle of the *Oberlenkers*, even if they were asked by someone outside that circle. This can be done in the next day or two, and the answers can then be passed on.

Today I want to draw your attention to a picture in the Book of Revelation, an Imagination of the apocalyptist that has been represented in many paintings depicting the Book. Not all the pictorial representations of the Book of Revelation are as successful, but with this picture—the realization of which falls exactly in our time, as was pointed out yesterday—it was hardly possible to misunderstand the different parts because the way they are described for us in the Book captures their characteristics exactly. In order to grasp this picture fully, we need to mention a parallel matter that is important for our time and has already been touched on in connection with Anthroposophy; the point we have reached in our present discussion of the Book of Revelation will illumine it especially.

When the human being makes the transition in consciousness from the physical, sense-perceptible world to seeing the spiritual world he becomes, in a way, a being in three parts, in the way I have described in the chapters about the Guardian of the Threshold in my book *Knowledge of the Higher Worlds*.[1] In the form of his physical nature the human being possesses a combination of a trinity and a unity, and this combination is perfectly plain to see. It is clarified by following the description found in Anthroposophy of how he is structured. Take spirit, soul and body. The way in which this structure corresponds to the other one given by Anthroposophy is quite clear.

In the spirit possessed by the human being today live thoughts, thoughts such as I have described, for example, in my book *The Philosophy of Spiritual Activity*, thoughts not drenched in sensual perceptions but freely created, pure thoughts within human consciousness.[2] In quality, these thoughts are only an appearance, their reality is so small that they have no inner strength. We can partly, though not totally, compare them with mirror images. An image in a mirror has no strength in the direction its lines follow; it is entirely passive. Human thoughts do have strength as they unfold, so we can, as I described yesterday in the esoteric lesson, take hold of this and steep it in will.[3] But to the cosmos in all the full content of its existence these thoughts that the human being has during life are as mirror images; so although we carry spirit in our human being it is spirit in a mirror image.

Dear friends, what we bear within us in this way stems from the world that I call the spirit land in my book *Theosophy*,[4] and when we think on earth we bring down to the earth the ingredients of the spirit land as an appearance, as a reflection. When we think, we bring what theosophy calls devachan down to the realm of earth, although only in a weak reflection. On earth we carry these contents in us; an appearance of heaven in a weak reflection.

Moving on now to the soul realm, we find that feeling is what chiefly lives there. When we are awake it is feeling, and when we sleep it is the pictorial nature of dreams. The only distinction between dreams and feelings is that feelings are the content of our soul when we are awake while dreams are the content of our soul when we sleep. What we carry in our feelings as earthly human beings between birth and death stems from a different world, from the soul world that I described in that book *Theosophy*, the soul world through which we live in its true guise after death. Our feeling world, which we only dream, for we only dream this soul world in our feelings, relates to that true guise of the soul world that then confronts us not like a mirror image but like an image held in our soul by creative elemental powers—I have described this from a particular angle in *Theosophy*. Reality is not yet in it.

What our body develops through our existence as earthly human beings is not a consciousness of archetypal images; our body carries in it the strongest realities of existence. We are really active in our body, but only in the physical, earthly world.

So the three parts of our human being belong to different worlds. And you, dear friends, since you intend to work on the being of man, will have to have in your feeling some indication of what lies in the being of man. You must develop a right view of these things.

One misunderstanding after another has been presented to me by people who are quite good philosophers, mis-understanding after misunderstanding showing just how difficult it is even for people in the present time who are quite capable of thinking clearly to find the right way into Anthroposophy. In a discussion about the threefold human being, one such philosopher interpreted this to mean an arbitrary division of the human being intellectually worked out and signifying a merely formalistic approach. You can of course look at a table as consisting of the table top, the legs and so on, but the whole table is made of wood; or you could look at it as being structured from left to right. Arbitrary structuring of this kind is not what is meant in connection with the threefold being of man. Another way of putting it would be to say that hydrogen is something that exists in the real world and oxygen also exists in the real world. Together they yield water; they are real things, not artificial constructs. In the same way the parts of man's being are not arbitrarily distinguishable. They have merged so thoroughly to make the real nature of the human being that one can say: The spirit stems from the spirit land, the soul from the soul world and the physical body from the physical world; these components of the human being stem from three different worlds yet are joined together in man.

And when the human being takes his consciousness away with him out of the physical world, his inner being splits; out of one he becomes three.

Through the development of its various races and peoples, what happens with individual human beings is also happening to the whole of humanity—without the human being as an individual having to play a part in it. Evolving humanity lives in the subconscious of every individual human being but this does not rise up into ordinary consciousness; evolving humanity is going through stages of development that are similar to those gone through by each individual. Just now in our time humanity is going through a phase in its evolution that involves a kind of crossing of the threshold with the accompanying split into three. If the individual human being is to go past the Guardian of the Threshold in this era of the consciousness soul—he must work at this himself if he wants to accomplish it. Humanity as a whole, however, is going past the Guardian of the Threshold without individuals in our time realizing this is happening. Humanity as a whole is crossing the threshold. Until the end of the eighteenth century the physical, bodily nature was still able to give the human being something on earth through the elemental beings dwelling in it. In future, however, the human being will have to derive everything in himself that is inwardly productive, including his virtues, from the spiritual world, not as an individual but as humanity. A crossing of the threshold is to happen in the evolution of humanity as a whole, and this appears to the apocalyptist prior to the vision of the woman clothed with the sun and with the dragon beneath her feet because in time it also happens prior to that. This prior vision is clearly represented in what the apocalyptist says: The time is coming when the whole of civilized humanity will have to cross the threshold, when a threefoldness will appear as the cosmic Imagination of what humanity is undergoing. Beside the feeling that can arise when something healthy borders on something pathological, more and more individuals will have another feeling as well: My thoughts are trying to run away from me, my feet are being pulled downwards by gravity. There are very many human beings today who feel very strongly that their thoughts are flying away from them while their feet are being excessively drawn to the earth. But in our civilization people are persuaded not to take such things seriously, just as children who experience visions of things that have a real foundation are persuaded that such things are meaningless.

This thing that is so strongly alive in our time appeared before the clairvoyant eyes of the apocalyptist as the figure who materializes from a cloud, has a sunlike countenance that merges into a rainbow, and fiery feet one of which is planted on the sea and the other on the land. (Rev. 10,1–2) One could call this the most significant appearance that present-day humanity ought to be contemplating. In the countenance up above, born of the clouds, lie the thoughts that belong to the spirit land; in the rainbow lies the human soul's world of feeling that belongs to the soul world; in the fiery feet that have received their strength from the ocean-covered earth lies what is contained in the human being's body which belongs together with the physical world.

This points out to us the fundamental secret of today's culture. It is not that human beings immediately appear as though split into three parts. What we see—and this is really tangible in our time—are cloud people who can only think while the other two parts, the rainbow and the fiery feet, have become stunted. Then we have rainbow people in whom the feelings are more developed than anything else, those, for example, who can only grasp Anthroposophy with their feelings and not with their understanding. Such people exist in the world outside as well as in the Anthroposophical Society, of course. They can only grasp the world with their feelings; while their thinking and will have become stunted their feelings are strongly developed. Finally there are those whose will has hypertrophied. In them thinking and feeling have become stunted; they behave like bulls, merely reacting to stimuli from outside. These are the people with the fiery feet.

John's vision depicts these three types of human being whom we meet in real life. We must make ourselves familiar with this secret of our present civilization so that we can assess human beings properly. And, by the way, this also shows when we consider world events.

Look at what is happening in Russia just now. There we have the influence of the cloud people, those who mainly think, while their feelings and will are stunted. They want to hand the will over to social mechanisms; and feelings are taken over by ahrimanic powers because human beings do not take them in hand themselves. They are thinkers, but because earthly human beings also have ahrimanic and luciferic forms they have a specific kind of thinking. Let me use a picture that will be obvious to those who are familiar with spiritual science but will shock anyone who still needs to find his way into such things. If you take the thoughts of Lenin and the others and see them as a picture, what does the confluence of thoughts from Lenin, Trotski, Lunacharski and so on look like? If you imagine a world consisting of these thoughts you will arrive at what physics calls a system of forces. If one were a gigantic elemental being one could take these forces and form clouds to cover a vast area, generating thunder and lightning. This is what these forces are like when seen as belonging to the region of clouds. They do not belong on the earth. This picture might surprise you, but anyone who can look into the occult background of existence has to say this. In the heads of the leading Russians the same forces are at work that exist in lightning, forces that are formed in the clouds above our heads and send lightning down to earth, and let the thunder roll. This is where such forces belong; they are out of place in the way they work in the leading Bolsheviks.

Thus there is much that exists in our time that is entirely clear in the apocalyptist's prophetic vision. He knew that an epoch such as this, a period representing a specific time, can be indicated through numbers. I myself, dear friends, have indicated an approximate number of years for the period during which something like the consciousness soul, or the mind or intellectual soul, develops. I have said that its duration is one twelfth of 25,920 years.

For a long time I was extremely puzzled as to how one might understand the passage in the Book of Revelation about which I am speaking now, for in his prophecy the apocalyptist mentions 1,260 days. Days are often mentioned when years are meant. But what did the apocalyptist mean by the figure 1,260? I had to do a considerable amount of research before I discovered that these 1,260 days (Rev. 12,6) are an actual 'printer's error' that must have arisen in the handing down of the Book of Revelation (please excuse this common or garden expression). '2,160 days' is what the passage ought to say, and then it corresponds with what can be seen today. It is quite possible for this lack of clarity to have arisen in some school or other where the text was being handed down, especially as in visionary sight many numbers are seen as mirror images. However, this is less important as one looks more deeply into the Book of Revelation.

Beside those whose way of belonging to their race is that of cloud people, we also have rainbow people. Their thinking has become stunted, so that they prefer conservative thoughts, and they are rather shy of approaching the spiritual world through thought. Very many people especially in Central Europe show themselves to be rainbow people.

The further westwards we go, the more are thinking and feeling stunted, so we come to pathological developments of the people with fiery feet. There are many such people with fiery feet in Western Europe and presumably also in America. In this sense we can now structure the earth as follows: In the East there are many cloud people, in the middle many rainbow people, and in the West many people with fiery feet. As regards the coming into being of races, one might say that looking at the earth spiritually from outside we would see spread across it something like a picture in exactly the shape presented to us here by the apocalyptist. If we were to rise up from the earth—spiritually of course, not in a hot-air balloon or an airship—if we were to rise up spiritually from a point somewhere, let us say, in Westphalia, and then look down at the earth, we would see Asia taking on a cloud-like, sun-shaped countenance. We would see the colours of the rainbow spread out over Europe, and further westwards there would be fiery feet of which one would be planted in the Pacific Ocean and the other on the Andes in South America. The earth itself would be beneath this picture.

Dear friends, these for our time most far-reaching prophecies of the apocalyptist are extremely important for the work of the priest, for they make up the great riddle of our time that has emerged since Napoleon. It was the influence of Napoleonism, of the first Napoleon, that initially brought out clearly this tendency of human beings to strive for races, for nations. In today's Wilsonism this is finding expression again in a most injudicious manner. It is truly terrible to see human beings striving to belong to races and peoples and on the whole burying any kind of cosmopolitanism. It is happening because this passage through the place of the threshold is going on. Just as the individual becomes split through his development towards the realm of the spirit, so is humanity as a whole splitting into regions of which individual human beings remain unconscious, the region of the cloud people, the region of the rainbow people, and the region of the people with feet of fire. The splitting of the human being into three in the way I described for single individuals in *Knowledge of the Higher Worlds* has now taken place for humanity as a whole on the earth; it is now in place. The tremendous picture drawn by the apocalyptist is now in place in Asia, in Europe, in America. People can as yet find no harmony among the three parts; instead of the harmony of unification they are seeking fragmentation, and in individual situations the result is most peculiar.

In this entirely outward way of thinking that humanity is taking on you can see, for example, that people do not find their togetherness through an inner understanding but instead get together for external reasons. Look at the region between the Bohemian Forest and the Fichtelgebirge, from the Erzberg in the Politz-Adersbach sandstone hills down to the March and to what used to be Pressburg. You can see, if you take the Mannhartsberg as the southern boundary, how the Czechs there are eminently cloud people who have developed only their thinking and how without any inner understanding they have been welded together with the Slovaks, who are quite different and in whom thinking hardly exists because they are rainbow people in the exact sense of the words. On the other hand we see how a different relationship that had been formed shortly beforehand is being dissolved again quite externally. There is no spirit at work in such things any longer but only earthly human beings acting in a way that wants to exclude the spirit. What we see is the whole of Slovakia being separated off from Bohemia, Moravia and Silesia, which is the region I mentioned just now. We see how the whole of Slovakia was formerly united with the country of the Magyars, the genuine Magyars. (You have to distinguish between the genuine Magyars and the immigrant Magyars whom you can recognize by their names. The genuine Magyars have names no one in the West can pronounce, especially if they are already old; but they are called Hirschfeld if they are one of the especially loud-mouthed agitators of today. So you must go back to the genuine Magyars.) The genuine Magyars are eminently fire-footed people who were briefly welded to the rainbow people of Slovakia. This is the game of chance being played by the lack of spirituality in the world, so that the Slovaks who were formerly joined to the Magyars are now lumped together with the Czechs. This is the game of chance being played today. It also finds expression in more profound symptoms such as that a truly great man like Masaryk who heads the Republic of Czechoslovakia is a Slovak and not a Czech.[5] If you know Masaryk you know that he is a rainbow person who is quite incapable of thinking. Read his books and you will see: in his books it is time that thinks. He is a rainbow person, a true Slovak.

You have to be able to see human beings today in the light of these categories if you want to understand the game of chance that is going on at the moment, though of course this, too, has its origin in world karma. We must look at an age, our own time, that is penetrating further and further into human consciousness, into the consciousness soul. Previously people saw the content of ancient tradition and wisdom written in the stellar script, they saw it all outside themselves. The human being, split into three, now bears what is written in ancient books like a memory within him. Looking at various centres we see this figure spread out over Asia, Europe, America. Everything that was proclaimed in the Mystery-rich places of Macedonia, Greece, Asia Minor, everything that was proclaimed about the world in Ephesus,

Samothrace, Delphi and elsewhere, all this is the Book that has been preserved from ancient times; it is in the hand of that angel who makes his countenance of the clouds, his breast of the rainbow and his feet of fire and who stands there powerfully planted. But for the human being with the consciousness of today all this can only be kept vivid and alive if we seek out the source within ourselves through which we can learn to see the spirit. We must 'eat up' the book that was previously available from the outside, we must take it into ourselves. At first this book containing the secrets of the universe is sweet in the mouth for some. People are very partial to what spiritual vision wants to give them; they find it tastes like honey. But when they get down to the truly profound requirements of life that are part and parcel of a spiritual understanding of the world, then, especially when this comes to today's materialistically-minded human beings, what the apocalyptist described as being sweet as honey becomes an ache in the belly, for it is painful to digest the spiritual food of which human beings are so very much in need.

Seeing all this we have to admit: With all these games of chance, with all this confused muddle, it will be essential to receive—from the spiritual power that shows us the threefold human being—the strength with which to measure everything anew. A reed is given from heaven, actually a yardstick with which to measure everything anew. (Rev. 11,1) Look at our own time, dear friends. Is it not necessary to make new measurements? Must we not add to that abstract construct of today's map of the world something like Asia as a figure of cloud, Europe coloured like the rainbow, America with feet of fire? Must we not measure everything anew from the viewpoint of spiritual life? Are we not in the very midst of seeing put into practice what the Book of Revelation has to show us?

If we can grasp with our full consciousness what we must

enter into, we shall move on from that layman's realm that has to accomplish so much in the subconscious, and enter an entirely non-rationalistic understanding of the tasks that need doing today through what shall become a new priesthood. This, dear friends, is what needed to be said with reference to the chapters of the Book of Revelation with which we have dealt today. Everything fits, down to the smallest detail. When we go into these things again tomorrow it will be easier to say what still needs to be said about the development of races and of individuals.

LECTURE FIFTEEN

Dornach, 19 September 1924

We shall now, dear friends, look at how in our time mighty revolutions of the future are already visible in seed form—although in one way this of course also points back to earlier earth experiences. We can imagine how what the Book of Revelation has to say about the woes and so on already plays a part especially in our time and how the consciousness soul can be caught up in this. (Rev. 8,13; 9,12; 11,14)

We must make it clear to ourselves that the things I described in the interpretations I gave yesterday exercise an important influence on the whole formation of human evolution. We must take into consideration that these things which go on in what might be called the spiritual field are not much taken into account, or perhaps hardly at all, by our contemporaries; yet these things, even if they are today regarded as purely spiritual events, do have an immeasurably powerful effect that stretches far beyond human awareness. Yesterday, for example, I mentioned the way certain leading personalities in today's Eastern Europe bear within them thoughts that actually represent powers which ought to be at work in the cloud formations. In other words, what is going on in the heads of today's Russian leaders will—when the seeds have germinated and begun to sprout—one day come to represent something that will manifest as cloud events. So today's revolutionary upheavals in Russia will one day manifest as mighty, thunderous revolutions taking place above the heads of human beings.

We have now reached something that likewise belongs to the secrets of apocalyptic vision and which can clarify another passage in the Book of Revelation. We are coming closer to an actual interpretation of the mighty visions of the Book of Revelation and we are approaching what we ought to be quite clear about in our present human experience. When we look at the short span of time in which we are accustomed to observe life today without embarking on any ambitious, and mostly foolish, hypotheses about the beginning or ending of the earth, when we survey this span of time without calling on any spiritual vision to help us, we can say: Out there, nature runs its course. We see smaller natural events taking place throughout the seasons, and we see greater natural events such as earthquakes, floods, volcanic eruptions, and so on. Side by side with these—and because of the brevity of the time span we are able to survey, we do not feel pressed to construct any connection between the two— side by side with these we have the course of history, events such as the Thirty Years' War, Louis XIV and so on. Such events might follow one another or they might take place simultaneously, but no one feels the urge to construct a connection between the two sequences, the events in nature and the parallel events in history.

If we look at a longer span of time, however, we shall immediately see how misleading is this idea of events being merely parallel. When you look back from your present incarnation to an earlier one—although this remains theoretical today until it can be comprehended properly in the Imaginations given by a spiritual researcher—when you make repeated earth lives a reality and really experience this, then, when you look at a meadow or a wood you immediately get the impression of how different these are from what they were in your former incarnation. You notice this even if you are now in quite a different region, for everything on the earth is constantly changing, and wherever you were, the plant world, the animal world will have taken on quite a different character now. Initially you feel this the moment you sense something of a former incarnation and then look with an open mind at the natural world around you; you feel quite bewildered, even perplexed by this. You get a kind of inner feeling: What I see around me now has not arisen out of what was there at the time of the earlier incarnation, for the essence of what is here has come from quite somewhere else.

It is like this: The ordinary scientific view considers the natural world to be proceeding in a straight line. (See below and Plate 5) Here is the year 1924.

343   895   1260   1924

People imagine that what is growing in the meadow today has come into being out of the seeds of what grew there earlier on. They go back to 1260, to 895 and so on and imagine a straight line of seeds growing out of seeds growing out of seeds. But this was not so. I have often pointed out that the body you are wearing today is not the one you were wearing seven or eight years ago, except for a few enclosures. Some portions harden as life goes on—as I described in the other course[1]—but when you were a three-year-old child your body certainly contained nothing of what it contains now. The whole of its physical matter has been exchanged. In the same way nothing is left now of all the flowers that were once in the meadow. You must imagine it like this: What is meadow today has come down from spiritual worlds; what used to be meadow had also come down from spiritual worlds, and so on; and what was meadow centuries ago has passed away completely. There is the heredity of physical seeds, but there is also the fact that spiritual seeds from higher realms constantly take the place of what was there before.

You must grasp the fact that the meadow today was not the meadow in, say, the thirteenth century, for then another meadow was there, which has meanwhile died away. When you have grasped this you will be able to imagine the mission of snow, you will gain an idea of how snow is the bearer of what is continually dying away. Snow renews itself each year, and so does ice. And as nature constantly dies off in this entirely elementary form that lies in the dynamic of snow and ice formation, so is it constantly renewed again from above.

This is how it is in our time. But this, too, is a condition that is not entirely permanent. We shall speak about it in a moment, but first I still want to say the following: Once you discover this in looking out at the meadow—it is irrelevant whether you were incarnated in the same district before—and notice how it arises via snow and ice out of supra-earthly regions, you know that between the time of your last incarnation and today you yourself have played a part in making this meadow; you know that you yourself have played a part in creating what you have around you in your present incarnation, including the natural environment. First you notice this, and later you also notice that this, too, is a transitional condition. When they make a discovery about something going on in nature, scientists always assume it to be something that will last. But this is nonsense. In reality nothing remains. In reality everything changes, even the laws of nature. That is why even scientists in our time have come to regard only the most abstract laws as permanent. 'There is a cause for every effect'. 'Matter is constant'. Generalizations like this, which actually mean nothing, then come to be regarded as eternal laws of nature.

Today's condition showing us the earth as it changes—the burgeoning of summer that dissolves moisture into warmth, the wilting of winter that hardens moisture into ice and snow—is in its turn something that has not always existed and that will not always exist. Things will come into being that do not yet exist. Today we have the alternating condition, and I want you to establish this quite firmly and also to understand it firmly; we have the alternating condition: (Plate 5)

1. Summer, dissolving moisture through warmth,
2. Winter, hardening moisture to ice and snow through coldness.

Oscillating between these two we have autumn and spring. Gradually this will even out. There will not be such a pronounced summer when moisture is entirely dissolved, nor will there be such a pronounced winter when moisture is hardened to ice and snow; an in-between condition will arise when moisture will have a different consistency, a rather more gelatinous one than in summer, but it will not entirely change into something else; it will remain the same. Ice and snow will then not look like they do today; they will look like a reflecting mass that is transparent, a transparent, reflecting mass that remains in summer and winter. This is the sea of glass, the advent of which is described by the apocalyptist in the Book of Revelation. (Rev. 15,2)

It is a natural phenomenon that we comprehend through observing events in nature, and we have placed this in a temporal context. So now that we know that what is all around us actually stems from us, now that we know ourselves to be its co-creators, just as we work at creating the meadow into which our karma places us in this present incarnation—now that we know this, we must learn to extend it to include the great transformation of the earth as a whole. It is quite true. Through what they experience by way of intellectuality in the era of the consciousness soul human beings will contribute more and more through their inner dynamic to the creation of the sea of glass. Thus do human beings participate in the great events of the future. This is no mere parallelism, for it is a collaboration between what takes place in the human being and what takes place out there in nature.

You will now be in a position to understand something else, namely the following, about which we must be clear: When we enter into that divine condition which is in a state of balance, a state of ever-repeated balance between the luciferic and the ahrimanic, and when we grasp this in its deepest essence, we then realize—if we look correctly—that wherever the influence of Lucifer is not and wherever the influence of Ahriman is not, that is where there exists what comes from the progressive divine spirituality which is linked to the evolution of humanity. If, in the realms into which the luciferic constantly streams and into which the ahrimanic constantly streams, we look towards the divine that holds the balance, we find there pure love as the fundamental force of everything that streams continuously, forming the human being outwardly, and giving him soul and spirit inwardly. This fundamental force is pure love. In its substance and in its being, and in so far as it is the cosmos of the human being, the universe consists of pure love, it is nothing other than pure love. In the part of the divine that is associated with the human being we find nothing except pure love. This love is something inward; souls can experience it inwardly. It would never achieve an outward appearance if it did not first build itself a body out of the etheric element of light. When we observe the world in a genuinely occult manner we cannot help but say to ourselves: The ground of the world is the being of inward love appearing outwardly as light.

This is not something merely believed by those who can discern such things; it is knowledge objectively won: The universe, in so far as the human being is rooted in it, is the being of inward love appearing outwardly through light. It is being because it is to do with all the beings of the higher hierarchies who are carried by this love and who inwardly experience this love which, however, if we want to employ an abstract idea, appears as light. The outer appearance of beings is love, and the outer appearance of love is light. This has been emphasized over and over again in all the Mysteries; it is not mere belief, it is the truly won knowledge of every genuine occultist.

The fact is, however, that this is *one* stream in the universe, one stream which is, though, our particular concern as human beings, but nevertheless it is *one* stream. We can well imagine the age of materialism since the fifteenth, sixteenth, seventeenth century, and also the culmination of materialism during the 1840s; we can well imagine the further ramifications of materialism after that with all that has been in human thought and action, with all those terribly destructive forces that have been raging in humanity since the middle of the nineteenth century, even though many still hardly notice it at all. Over all this weaves divine love unfolding in the light.

Dear friends, take some absolutely pure water, some crystal-clear water, and then take a dirty sponge, a sponge that has dirt in it. Put the sponge into the crystal-clear, crystal-pure water, dip it into the water and then squeeze it to let the water flow out again: now the water is dirty, muddied. You have let the dirty sponge absorb the crystal-clear water, you have squeezed it and the water has become dirty. How can the pure, crystal-clear water help flowing out dirty when the sponge is squeezed? How can the divine love springing up in the pure light help being taken up into the age of materialism like the clear water into the sponge filled with dirt? How can it then help becoming something different when it next appears? Here is the picture: Crystal-clear water, sucked up by the dirty sponge, becomes muddied, undrinkable water. Divine love appearing in the light, sucked up in the era of consciousness soul development by all those ingredients of evil that rage in humanity either latently or manifestly during this era of consciousness soul development, becomes divine wrath.

The secret of the next age is that divine love will appear in the form of divine wrath because of what happens within humanity. It will appear in the form of the divine wrath which will give protection from all material constructs that will arise as the result of the materialistic consciousness soul era; by causing those constructs to perish it will give protection against further damaging effects. Speaking of what appears to him, the apocalyptist tells of the pouring out of the phials of wrath in the next age. (Rev. 16,1) This is what was spoken in the Mysteries in a sentence that was terribly shocking to the neophyte: In the sphere of illusion in human beings divine love will appear in the form of divine wrath.

There is a saying many thousands of years old that runs through the Mysteries; it lives prophetically in John's visions in the way the Book of Revelation describes first how the divine love is muddied and then what will have to take place as the necessary fulfilment of this having happened. That fulfilment will be the pouring out of the divine wrath in the age when—far more so than in ours—what human beings do will influence what happens in nature. For the parallelism that gives human beings the illusion that nature on the one hand and the human spirit and the human soul on the other go along side by side—this parallelism only exists in the middle ages of evolution, thus giving rise to that illusion. Even in the earlier and latter stages of a smaller period of evolution, for example the one lasting from the Atlantean catastrophe to the war of all against all, what goes on in human beings always exercises much influence on natural events. So it is no idle chatter to say that when, in the final stages of the Atlantean period, a large proportion of humanity was occupied with black magic, the consequences of human beings' misdeeds in black magic led on to the natural disasters of the Atlantean catastrophe.

In the same way, many things that are happening at the moment will find their fulfilment in natural phenomena. One of these happenings will be that the Russian revolution—which also had many occult causes—will pour down on to the heads of human beings in storms of thunder and lightning that will last for whole summers. Other things that are accumulating as a cosmic element muddying the divine love will also appear in natural phenomena that we shall be able to interpret in no other way than as the transformation of divine love into divine wrath through the illusions human beings cherish.

What I have just said is how the saying I mentioned is formulated. Yet what the divine wrath pours out on to human beings is in truth still a revelation of divine love. For if at this time the divine love were seemingly to have mercy on the weakness of human beings, this would in reality be no true mercy. It would amount to turning a blind eye to all the consequences so richly deserved by human thoughts and deeds, which would be the most loveless act of all, since then humanity would truly perish. Only the pouring out of the divine wrath, which is nothing other than a metamorphosis of the divine love, can bring about the removal of all the damaging things humanity has created, which would other-wise remain unutterably damaging for its onward evolution. The saying written in the scriptures is so ancient that in Europe it is still very often spoken in its oriental form: In the realm of *maya* divine love appears as divine wrath.

Herewith we have seen another example showing how thoroughly the Book of Revelation is derived from the essential ingredients at work in the cosmos. The more we penetrate into it the more do we find everything in it that shows in the truest sense how much we can rely on it—if I may use an everyday expression. Basically it can be regarded as giving the priest knowledge of what happens in the course of human life in the world. Originally it was given to priests as the esoteric content of Christianity, side by side with the other things, which were exoteric.

*Discussion of the questions handed in on
18 September 1924:*

Rudolf Steiner: Regarding the Breviary, I did not give it to anyone personally, but only to the course itself. We must distinguish between the gatherings we still had in the Goetheanum and the later ones. One of them took place in the autumn of 1921 in the Great Hall of the Goetheanum and was attended by a large number of people of whom it could have been thought that they were interested in the movement for Christian renewal. Then, in September 1922, we had the more intimate gatherings to which you said that you would come after having prepared yourselves thoroughly and which then led to the actual inauguration of the movement when the first Act of Consecration was celebrated. These are two stages. There was no one at the second gathering who subsequently left; at that gathering all the participants received the vestments and were declared ordained priests. There were none who left this gathering, which was in the strictest sense the inaugural point of your work as priests. However, there were persons present at the first gathering who not only did not become priests but who, you say, are now actually hostile, genuinely hostile?

Friedrich Rittelmeyer: For example Bruno Meyer, the chaplain for youth.

(*Werner Klein spoke about the distribution of the Breviary saying that there was no proper control over where copies had ended up.*)

Rudolf Steiner: Is there no way of finding out who was here in autumn 1921?

A participant: Yes, there is.

Rudolf Steiner: Surely no one else was given the Breviary?

Friedrich Doldinger: But the others passed copies on.

(*The participants asked whether they might be given a preliminary meditation.*)

Rudolf Steiner: A preliminary meditation would be the last resort. Before saying any more about this I want to touch on the other question you asked, which I think is important in connection with this one. The question is [reading from the note from Johannes Werner Klein] whether it is a good thing to continue placing the main emphasis on outreach or would it be preferable, in the interests of making better preparation for future tasks, to concentrate more on intensive work for the deepening of one's own personality? The connection between the two questions is not obvious, but it is there.

At all events in the present stage of your work as priests you should look for ways of not curtailing the outreach activity, as you call it. Your need for inner deepening is all too understandable, and the worries a number of you in the circle of priests have had since autumn 1922 in connection with 'a deterioration of health in both body and soul' are also understandable. All this is understandable. But please do not forget, dear friends, that things which can be done in all seriousness out of the spiritual world must be done up to a specific point also in connection with the outreach work. Until we have arrived at this point we have no right to withdraw into ourselves.

We have experienced terrible blows with a number of people in our movement, as you know; I have had to put up with a good deal of this kind of thing over the last few years. When the movement for university students was established I said to the founders who set it on its way: If you do such a thing, you must know that one is only permitted to do such a thing if one has enough strength to persevere regardless of whether one is successful or unsuccessful; it is necessary to persevere in treading the straight path up to a specific point.

But this did not happen. Hence the serious set-back we are experiencing particularly as a result of the movement for students, for few things have caused us as much damage as that movement which has collapsed in on itself, or rather on the souls of its members. It has petered out completely. Its place has been taken by a kind of introspection of young souls, and this is the situation now. The movement for students as such has split entirely.

Of course this is not something that bears comparison with your movement, but this one aspect is valid here too: If we inaugurate a movement that draws its original impulse directly from the spiritual world, we must totally disregard success or failure, we must totally disregard what becomes of our efforts and not out of ourselves decide on a change of course.

A good many things are still likely to become very difficult. Regarding the deterioration of physical health, this is of course a matter of searching for ways and means of helping to replenish our physical forces. Those amongst you, however, who speak of a deterioration in the health of your soul must first ask yourselves very seriously: To what extent can that which flows from the living source of this religious movement filled with the Christ-Impulse help me, to what extent can this help my soul forces retain their strength at every moment?

Dear friends, one's soul forces must be maintained through what flows through the cultus and the teaching. As far as one's physical forces are concerned one must look for physical ways of maintaining them. But as to one's soul forces—it has to be said that finding out whether one is capable of deriving from this movement that which can maintain one's soul forces, however much one's physical forces have deteriorated, is almost like a test with which this priestly movement is being faced. We must not lose our courage, our inner intensity with regard to our concrete work, our clear pursuit of the priestly aims, and connected with this our firm footing on divine and human ground that bears up the soul firmly in the universe. If we did, this would prove that the part of us which should be the strongest is not strong enough. In fact, to put it like this is in itself incorrect, for it *is* strong enough. The deterioration of soul forces is therefore something that is connected to some kind of illusion, chiefly causes of depression coming from quite other quarters that dim the bright rays which emanate from this religious movement and which prevent any kind of deterioration of soul forces. Look about you and you will everywhere find these soul forces, even if you thought that they had deteriorated. They deteriorate because of some kind of influence playing in from outside, something to which one accords too much credit with regard to these soul forces and against which one does not sufficiently call up the springs of the spirit in defence. But this can change if one becomes fully aware of the lofty mission of this priestly profession.

In saying this I also mean to suggest that it is a prerequisite for being able even to think about doing something to restore the Breviary, which is endangered, to its original effectiveness. These two things, dear friends, must be seen together if, and this could happen by tomorrow, it turns out that you can achieve clarity about how to free the matter of the soul forces from all illusion—and I mean the soul forces, for the physical forces can be dealt with by our clinical-therapeutical institutions—so that the movement can retain the momentum it had from the beginning. Once this is settled, even if it proves impossible to retrieve all the copies of the Breviary, we can then turn our attention to doing something to restore what is damaged in it. More about this tomorrow.

PRELIMINARY TALK

Dornach, 20 September 1924

Rudolf Steiner: You have asked for something to be discussed before the lecture.

(*Johannes Werner Klein spoke.*) [Not recorded]

Rudolf Steiner: Well you see, I wanted to formulate my answer to your question to fit in with the way the question was asked, and there was certainly an intimate connection with what you wrote about the deterioration of physical and soul forces which you seemed to be tying in with whether you should do more on the outreach work or work more extensively with the inner aspect. It would have been difficult for me to reach a conclusion other than that your awareness of the deterioration of forces was leading—in the way you put the question—to the suggestion that you might work less with outreach this winter and instead withdraw into more inward work. I had understood the question to be suggesting the choice between whether the outreach work should continue as inaugurated or whether, in consideration of the physical and soul forces, the work should continue for a while amongst the priests themselves. Perhaps I misunderstood the question?

(*Johannes Werner Klein spoke about this.*) [Not recorded]

Rudolf Steiner: Well, you will have gathered from my reply that the outreach work is necessary for the present. But this does not mean that, if things are as you say, we cannot also speak about the deterioration of soul forces. The deterioration of physical forces is a medical matter, but the deterioration of soul forces is of course something that should be discussed in the way in which it is understood. Before we continue, would anyone else like to speak about it?

(*Emil Bock asked about karmic connections. Then Friedrich Doldinger spoke.*[1]) [Neither contribution was recorded]

Rudolf Steiner: The only problem for me personally is that you are speaking at all about difficulties at the soul level. One does not speak about difficulties at the soul level if one is convinced that they do not exist. There is one thing that we must include in our considerations, and that is this: The way in which the movement for religious renewal has been developing since the first Act of Consecration of Man two years ago should surely fill everyone with satisfaction—taking into account all the factors that have a bearing on this development. Naturally there are always failures or else inhibitions coming from outside, or perhaps arising from the fact that not everyone is immediately equal to his task in an absolutely ideal way. But if we leave these details out of account—most of which can anyway be overcome if the development of the work continues, and which the main direction in the development of the movement for religious renewal certainly promises will be overcome—and consider the broader picture, then we have to say: The inhibitions at the soul level, if they are regarded as inhibitions of the movement itself, are something of an illusion, for within the movement these inhibitions do not manifest as such. The movement is developing quite well, to put it plainly. So the existing inhibitions are, in fact, more or less the private concern of individuals. At least this is how they appear. It is not as though anything in the movement itself might be influenced by them. However, there are some points within the movement itself which might perhaps still be regarded as inhibiting factors, and these should probably be discussed.

The question is how to shape this discussion. Perhaps it will be possible for me to speak about some points, one in particular, with the *Lenkers* first before embarking on a general discussion. Or perhaps it is not feasible to extend the discussion beyond the *Lenkers'* circle; in that case it would be up to them ... to decide how to share it with the circle of priests. These are questions that simply lie along the way of development. But if there are psychological inhibitions that are taken to be inhibitions of the movement itself, there is really no need to regard them as such if you look at the whole way in which The Christian Community has been developing. Or, put differently, there is no need to regard them as a reality, for a certain amount of illusion is playing a part in the matter.

I must say that the point in your question about working inwardly or with outreach is not important just now. In many ways, what your question contains simply does not exist, especially if you look at the facts, for what is essential for the movement is the intensity in its substance, indeed the very fact that the movement exists. I must say that with regard to the intensity in its substance I consider the movement to be essentially oriented in the right direction and I also think that at present it has the characteristic of going with the spiritual. I could give you various external examples for this that I found when looking through the recent issue of your journal, where you discussed certain points in the Book of Revelation showing how it can be applied to today.[2] It is not a matter of whether this is correct or not, but the very fact that the question is brought up and dealt with in the way it is—basing what is written on substance that can be linked to the spiritual—shows that the movement really is moving in the right direction.

There are many successes that could be mentioned, and I mean genuine, intensely inward successes. Let me put it like this: Surely it can be counted as a success that you are indeed able to discuss these points—with the seriousness that obviously emanates from this community—especially when you know that your journal already has a circulation of 6,000. You must include positive things in your reckoning, and surely this is a very positive outcome. When I look at all the things that go in this direction I cannot help telling myself how remarkable it is that so much has become possible in religion in a way that is so different from what was there before. Where, until now, has it been possible to speak to 6,000 people about such things through a journal? And of course there are more readers than that. It was possible in sects, large or small ones, which no one actually takes seriously; and if the most modern theology did so, the subject was treated in a very unbelieving, rationalizing sense. The very tone in which the Book of Revelation is discussed in your journal is an achievement when you consider that it has a circulation of 6,000. These are things that must be included on the positive side of your reckoning. The value I accord them is entirely objective. In the light of these things you cannot talk of the movement having any inhibitions worthy of that name. You must also consider how immensely powerfully the cultus works whenever it takes place. If progress continues as hitherto, then in ten years' time the movement will truly be what it is intended to be for humanity. So if you are asking whether the direction you have followed hitherto should be maintained—and I cannot interpret your question to mean anything else—then all I can say is: There is not the slightest reason to consider doing things in a different way. This is what I think as regards the movement for religious renewal.

It is true, though, that in some respects some individuals have not been functioning at the level of the movement as a whole. Please forgive me for putting this so bluntly. But this should be a reason for considerable satisfaction, not dissatisfaction, since it offers the guarantee that individuals will increasingly grow into the movement that is so filled with spiritual substance. These are things that strengthen souls. And there is another positive thing worth mentioning, which is the way various aspects of the Book of Revelation are now being unveiled together with you here. I am afraid there is a good deal of illusion involved in the way private inhibitions that exist are being transferred on to the movement. These things that are being transferred on to the movement are personal, and they will quite definitely be removed again by and by. This is how I see it, but I am not sure whether it fits the direction of your question.

You must also not recoil from asking yourselves how you can remove from your soul any remnants of Protestant theology that may still be lurking there. This must be rooted out, for it represents one extreme, just as Catholic practice is another extreme in the opposite direction. The Catholic church says: We need not concern ourselves with the individual priest; the individual priest is entirely insignificant, for what matters is the substance represented by the church. As soon as he wears the stole the individual priest is regarded as a representative of the church, and I have never known anyone in authority to be upset by depressions assailing individual priests, let alone by quite other things than depressions. They never mind these things because they count on the spiritual leadership which—although it is rather questionable these days—does after all point towards the spirit. Protestantism, on the other hand, having put the whole emphasis on the personality, has separated itself off from the spirit almost entirely. That was the opposite extreme, and this is what must be removed from your hearts and souls. You really must look towards the reality of spiritual life, for this reality exists. Whatever might be the matter with the individual, whatever might be churning about in his own soul, he must realize that spiritual life proceeds in objective reality. If you take into account that certain Protestant attitudes might well still remain in some souls in consequence of their university studies or their education and so on, then you will be able to heal yourselves of difficulties you may be having in connection with the movement. I am not referring to individual souls with their own private feelings, for this belongs elsewhere. This is the same in the Catholic church, for of course someone in trouble can always go to a colleague for advice and so on. But towards the lay congregation and believers the church presents a united front. The added factor with the Catholic church is that it has gradually succumbed to a spiritual leadership that is ahrimanic. It can be proved that this is so.

At the beginning of this century the Pope at the time published an Encyclical against modernism.[3] You know that these things are always couched in phrases such as: We prohibit, or we forbid such and such. And then the positive assertions are made. This is the way the Syllabus of the 1860s is written, and so is the Bull on modernism.[4] I have made some investigations about this and discovered that the papal Encyclical was in fact a spiritual revelation, only when the revelation was put into writing every positive assertion in the spiritual original was turned into a negative assertion, so that the Bull said the exact opposite of what had been spiritually revealed. This shows that the Catholic church receives its spiritual revelations falsified by Ahriman. Nevertheless, this does not mean that there is nothing spiritual about it. This spiritual element is present in The Christian Community in the most appropriate way for the stage of evolution humanity has reached today. The Christian Community is established on spiritual soil by spiritual beings in reality. When this is accepted in full seriousness it will heal every faintness of soul. We now have several other things to speak about.

LECTURE SIXTEEN

Dornach, 20 September 1924

I shall begin by returning to something mentioned earlier, which we shall then use as our point of departure. I drew your attention to the notable fact that in people's subconscious longings there is a strong need for spirituality and also that what happens superficially in experiences of the physical plane is something fundamentally different from what is actually going on in human souls today. There is an astonishing fact that goes to prove this. A few days ago I mentioned the remarkable way in which the content of my lectures to the Goetheanum workmen takes shape through the questions asked by the workers themselves.[1] This reveals something of the longings that are developing. I also pointed out how one can speak to people out of the spirit of the Book of Revelation if only one finds the right tone. Without mentioning the Book of Revelation as such one can speak in the spirit of this Book precisely as we are doing amongst ourselves now.

I had decided on the subject of today's talk to you out of the whole context we have been discussing. Then, astonishingly, this morning in my lecture to the workmen a question was asked that made it necessary for me to explain the very same scientific matters to them that I was intending to talk to you about. You see what effects are going on beneath the surface; something truly spiritual is going on in that the lectures I am giving here call forth longings in that other group of people, longings which otherwise they would not have. I would never have been called on to give that lecture there if I were not speaking here about the Book of

Revelation. Yet I gave that lecture in answer to a question that was asked but which I did not know about outwardly. Such a thing shows how our time is being touched by a spiritual life that is chiefly going on below the surface of consciousness, a spiritual life that is most strongly the concern of the priest who has to try and find out the degree to which souls are inclined to enter into spiritual matters.

Our considerations here will be carried out in a way that allows them to be guided by the spirit of the Book of Revelation. This is the given situation here, but this morning I had to touch on the same matter from quite another angle in answer to a question. Such things must be taken very seriously, for they are significant. We must now ask ourselves, dear friends, in which way the terminology of the apocalyptist is even more intimate. If you look at everything I have said, you will understand that when the apocalyptist is speaking about how the human being stands in the midst of the whole universe he has before him a oneness of the stellar world and the earthly world, so that he links the essence of the human being as much with the stellar world as with the earthly world. We must also point realistically to what he means when he speaks of beasts, of the seven-headed and the two-horned beast. (Rev. 13) So far we have only been speaking about what the human being can experience inwardly. You will find, however, that wherever the apocalyptist speaks of fixed stars he is speaking of the divine spirit in the way this was still spoken of throughout the Middle Ages. When he speaks of planets he is speaking of angelic Intelligences, of Intelligences that are angelic or hierarchical in character. And when he speaks of beasts he means something equally specific. In our inmost being he lets us participate both in the crystal heavens and in the heavens of the fixed stars and planets, but also in what is founded on the animal character in the whole way it has evolved, on these beasts that keep playing a part in the Book of Revelation.

What are these when it comes to the external, physical reality of the world?

Wherever the apocalyptist is speaking of the beast he is actually referring to the powers and effects of comets. Only when you are familiar with this terminology will you also understand what the apocalyptist knew about the nature of comets, knowledge which subsequently became completely buried. So let us now look at the nature of comets in the light of what the Book of Revelation tells us. Take the Copernican system as it is taught in schools nowadays: Sun, Mercury, Venus, Earth, Mars, then Jupiter and Saturn, and you might as well add Uranus and Neptune. (Plate 6) The movements of all these are calculable so long as you avoid making big mistakes and if you take into account the adjustments that have always been necessary. You only have to point your telescope at the spot you have calculated and there you will find the planet. These are the calculable things. But within this planetary system we also have the paths of the comets. Many cometary paths are also calculable, and these calculations lead to quite remarkable results, which can give rise to a lot of excitement if they are simply taken in the way they appear according to today's astronomical calculations. I will use just one of these as my starting point.

In Paris in 1773 it was announced that Lalande, the famous astronomer, was to lecture on comets at the Academy.[2] Rumour had it that he was going to prove the imminence of a collision between a comet and the earth in that very year, for calculations of the comet's path were said to show that it would cross the earth's orbit and so cause the collision.[3] Imagine the mood in the population at that time. The rumour caused the whole of Paris to panic, especially when it was announced that the police, who always act correctly, had had nothing better to do than forbid the lecture on account of it being dangerous. There were large numbers of miscarriages and premature births, seriously ill people died, and Catholic priests did a roaring trade selling absolutions because everyone rushed to confession and wanted to receive the sacraments before the end of the world! Since the lecture did not take place, quite a while passed before people found out what Lalande had actually intended to say. Lalande's calculations were quite correct and did indeed show that a certain comet would cross the earth's orbit, and if it were to collide with the earth this would most certainly cause great masses of ocean water from the equator to flood the land masses that lie between the North and the South Pole. This terrible thing did not happen, yet the calculation was correct.

We can find out what was at the root of all this, dear friends, by looking at the situation with another comet, the famous Biela's comet. In 1832 people quite rightly paid close attention to the path of Biela's comet and everything that could be mathematically foreseen as resulting from that path. When the comet appeared it behaved exactly as the calculations had foretold. It came so close to the earth that people said: It is getting closer to the earth every time it appears, so a time will come when this will be dangerous. Since Biela's comet approaches the earth's orbit every six to seven years, a huge amount of attention was focussed on it in the 1840s when calculations showed that it would come so close to the earth's orbit as to be thirteen times closer to it than the moon. Things were looking grim indeed! As the comet continued to come closer and closer to the earth's orbit, astronomers noticed that it was growing dimmer the closer it came. When it came dangerously close to the earth again in 1846 they observed that it was not only dimmer but had split into two. In the 1860s conditions were unfavourable for observation, so people became very curious indeed about its next appearance due in 1872. If the calculations were as correct as Lalande's had been for the comet in 1773, it was thought that disaster would be likely. I was only a small boy in 1872, but I clearly remember leaflets being distributed where I lived, and of course they were distributed elsewhere as well, stating: The world is going to end. Everyone was talking and writing about it. There was a lot of anxiety, although in this instance I cannot give you any statistics about miscarriages, deaths or absolutions! I well remember the excited anticipation as the day approached; but what happened? The comet failed to appear. Instead there was the most wonderful, beautiful meteor shower, as though a fire were falling to the earth from the night sky in myriads of tiny fading sparks. Having split into two, the comet then proceeded to disintegrate into nothing but tiny splinters that the earth's atmosphere was able to absorb and which became united with the being of the earth. It chose the path of becoming absorbed by the earth.

In 1832 a well-known astronomer, Littrow, published a treatise that was very interesting.[4] I can still recommend studying it, even today; it is most interesting and its complicated calculations are entirely correct. Here was someone who knew what he was talking about. He made a calculation that took every possibility into account. He worked out that in 1832 there could not yet have been a calamity caused by a collision, but he said that if everything remained as it had been when the comet's course was plotted when it was still a single body and not yet split, then a calamity would definitely occur in 1933; 1933 is what he said. So if the comet had remained as it was, then there would definitely be a catastrophe in 1933 in which all the oceans would spread over the earth in huge floods, making life on earth die out. Instead, the comet has disintegrated; in tiny particles it has been absorbed by the earth, the earth has nourished itself on this cosmic substance. So instead of a collision in 1933—that year is not far off now—what the earth has absorbed is spiritualized by other substances, and the spiritual rises up. The earth digests the comet and something spiritual rises up. Dear friends, spiritualized cometary substance does indeed rise up in the earth in this way from time to time.

Let me tell you the purpose of this, for there is a profound cosmic purpose. I have often mentioned some rather grotesque things that happened when railways were first built. One of these was that when the building of a railway was mooted, the minister for post in Berlin[5] retorted that he sent off two mail coaches each week and there were no passengers in them, so what would be the point in building a railway. Another thing that happened was that when asked for an expert opinion about the building of a railway from Nuremberg to Fürth, a panel of physicians at Nuremberg recommended desisting from doing such a thing since people's nerves would suffer dreadfully in consequence; they ought not to be exposed to it for they would be damaged in body and soul; but if it was felt necessary to give in to this foolish urge, then it would be advisable at least to build high plank walls on either side of the railway to prevent the farmers from getting concussion.[6] This was the scientific opinion given by the panel of physicians in Nuremberg. Today we deride the small-mindedness of such people. But as I have often said, I cannot quite laugh in the same way because they were right according to the scientific knowledge of their day. According to what was known at that time you had to say that people would ruin their nerves if they travelled by train, and to a certain degree this is indeed the case. If you compare people's nerves today with the nerves of those living some time ago you will discover a small clue that exonerates the physicians of Nuremberg to some extent. What science was saying was, in effect, that human beings would not be able to tolerate the demands made on their physical body via the astral body if the astral body, the animal part of the human being, did not constantly receive a correction, a therapy, through that which rays back up to the surface of the earth from the absorbed cometary substances, exercising a balancing effect on human capacities.

So here we have the human being placed into the universe

in a remarkable way. Here is Biela's comet in 1872. Fire falls from the sky; the earth absorbs it in such a way that someone with spiritual vision can see how it returns and influences the human astral body either favourably or unfavourably. There are comets that influence human beings in the way I have described by therapeutically balancing their nervousness, and there are others that let loose wild astral forces when they make their way up to the earth's surface again after having been absorbed. This is how the apocalyptist regards the cometary appearances. When he describes the beasts he also describes the cometary appearances, he places them side by side because they can be seen as parallel phenomena; he draws a parallel with the seven-headed beast because at that time such things were much more closely linked with the whole physical world and because there was a comet then that had split into seven pieces, thus expressing in a heavenly way something that was happening on the earth. Similarly the two-horned beast I mentioned is linked with a comet, a comet with two tails.

Dear friends, wild superstitions have become attached to comets and these have prevented their significance from being considered in the right light; their paths have merely been plotted and people have been irritated by their whimsical behaviour. At least once in a while some intelligent thinker such as Hegel has condescended to draw attention to different types of link between the nature of comets and the nature of the earth.[7] Hegel, who was not averse to the occasional glass of sparkling wine, made the entirely correct observation that good and bad years for wine are connected with comets.

Let us now look at this whole matter on a cosmic scale, dear friends. The earth imbibes cometary substance and subsequently gives it off again in a spiritualized form; this then unites with the astral bodies of human beings either in a good or in a bad way. When we see a comet in the sky at a certain time, where is it after that time? In a lecture I gave in Paris in 1906 I drew attention to the fact that cometary substance contains cyanide, compounds of carbon and nitrogen.[8] It was a good while before external science began to mention this, but later it was proved by spectral analysis. The fact that there is cyanide in comets is most important, for distributed over the earth in tiny amounts this substance is needed for the purification of astral bodies. There is an immensely great cosmic physician at work in the cosmos who is more or less constantly busy administering therapies like this. Just think: What we see above us as a comet in the sky in one period then becomes atomized as I have described; it comes down from the sky in showers of fire; later it is in the soil and still later it moves from the soil into the plants, into their roots, stems, leaves and flowers. We eat the cometary deposit, the cometary leaven that is given to the earth by the cosmos, we eat it with our very bread. When the apocalyptist contemplates this phenomenon he sees favourable effects from one comet and unfavourable effects from another rising up before his spiritual vision. The Beast will be let loose from its imprisonment in the earth; that is what the comet is in the cosmic sense. That the Beast will be let loose is significant for the development of human beings. Such things are exceedingly powerful realities, great and significant points in the evolution of humanity and of the earth.

In 1933, dear friends, there would be a possibility for the earth and everything living on it to perish if there did not exist also that other wise arrangement that cannot be calculated. Once comets have taken on other forms calculations can no longer be accurate. What needs to be said in the sense meant by the apocalyptist is: Before the Etheric Christ can be comprehended by human beings in the right way, humanity must first cope with encountering the Beast who will rise up in 1933. This is what the apocalyptic language tells us. Here a view of the spirit unites with a view of nature. What is there in the cosmos becomes clear to us in its fundamental spiritual character. Take the way the peasants described what they saw in 1872 as they stood and watched the shower of light, and add to it what the spirit tells us as I have described it, and compare this with many of the descriptions in the Book of Revelation, and you will see that even the very words used match one another. You will see that the Book of Revelation is speaking of actual natural events.

These are things that justify calling the Book of Revelation a book with seven seals. They have to be unsealed in this way in order to discover what is actually meant. When people ask why the apocalyptist gives us a book that is sealed I do not find this question any more intelligent than when someone asks why we seal our letters when we send them off in closed envelopes. We seal them so that they will not be read by those for whom they are not intended. The same goes for the apocalyptist. He wanted the Book of Revelation to be read only by those called upon to do so. No one will know how to open the seal who has not first, you might say, received the appropriate paperknife from the spiritual powers.

Dear friends, in 1872, when that comet was supposed to be returning, there was a shower of light instead. This means that everything was already much more spiritual than when this comet made its earlier appearances. This comet will now only appear in the form of a shower of rays of light falling to earth. What happened at the end of the 1870s was that the regency of Michael came down to the earth in that shower of golden light.

Thus we have natural events that are actual spiritual events, and spiritual events that have the power to be natural events. Only when you can penetrate into the world with an intensity that makes all natural events into spiritual events and that gives all spiritual events the intensity of natural events will you truly gain insight into the formation of the world. Then the moral and the natural will join in a single evolution, and the inclination will arise to take knowledge as the content of religious life. Then there will no longer be any need to fall back on the excuse that only faith, but not knowledge, should provide the content of religious life.

This is what you can gain through a deeper approach to the Book of Revelation. I hope we shall be able to finish these considerations tomorrow or the day after.

LECTURE SEVENTEEN

Dornach, 21 September 1924

In addition to the content about which we have been speaking, the Book of Revelation also has an aspect that makes it a book of initiation. This is the way in which it describes evolution in time, the sequence of stages that it will become possible for those to experience who have ears to hear and eyes to see, whereas it will of course pass by those who are earless and eyeless. These various stages are introduced to us through the inner nature of the content which shows us that the Book of Revelation is indeed a book of initiation.

We must realize that as we enter consciously into the world—as our vision expands more and more—those things will disappear which are at present the content of our soul life and which are actually a kind of mirror image of external nature. The physical, sense-perceptible world disappears as we move forward with inner vision, and then gradually, as though emerging out of the background, the spiritual world comes into view from the other side. The apocalyptist shows quite clearly that he has a very intense, correct understanding of how to enter into a relationship with the spiritual world, and this is what has enabled him to discover so appropriately what he has been able to discover in his imaginative visions. There are, dear friends, two ways of seeing the spiritual aspect of the world. The one is simply to dwell upon the physical, sense-perceptible aspects, getting to know them from all angles with a kind of loving devotion. Through this you learn to recognize it as the work of the gods. You have before you what we mean by 'nature' in the widest sense when you look at the physical world not only externally and mechanically but also inwardly and spiritually. We can also imagine, however—and we would be right to do so—that it would be possible to arrive at the same world content in a purely spiritual way, from the inside through one's own soul. You can then go so far as to say that someone with sufficient inner strength might—even if he had nothing historical to go on—see something at a specific point in world events, something that manifested as a natural phenomenon. It is perfectly possible to begin with an inside view and arrive at the outward conclusion: In such and such a year, when a certain event occurred for humanity, there were earthquakes and so on. Many people have the feeling—whether they are aware of it or not—that it is possible for the human being to get to know the concrete details of the world by beginning from within, and this feeling is perfectly correct. But what is actually happening when a human being enters the spiritual world on the path of Imagination?

We can discuss this in connection with the Book of Revelation, for in this Book we find described the sequence of different stages in which the apocalyptist sees things, and these lead further and further into the spiritual world. First he introduces us to letters, then to seals; then he moves on to something that in human language can only be expressed by something audible, namely the trumpets; and from there he reaches what I described the day before yesterday as the divine love with its counterpart, the divine wrath. When we understand him rightly, we know he is telling us that what he gives us through the content of the Book of Revelation by means of the letters he has received through Inspiration relates to the physical world. When he moves on to the seals and opens them, this relates to the astral world, the world of Imagination, what can be called the soul world. With the sounding trumpets we enter spiritland. And when we experience the divine love and the divine wrath in accordance with the content of the Book of Revelation, we are entering the inner realm of spiritland. We must realize that while he is treading this path of Imagination the human being is in the world with his experience, so that his experience is world experience. But he does not notice this in the initial stages. The more his initiation progresses, the more he experiences how whatever takes place with him, through him, in him, is also taking place cosmically. He feels himself more and more to be poured out into the objective content of the cosmos. The apocalyptist hints at this very clearly. We can say, then, that the content of the letters refers to the physical world.

Let us look at the physical world as it appears before us. This physical world only seems to be what we see before us. This physical world would not present all those myriad nuances of colour, nuances of heat and cold, and all the other nuances that flow towards the human being from all directions, if we were to think in all that appears to us in the present age only of its physical content and fail to notice that what appears to be physical is actually spiritual. Looking into the soul of a human being such as the apocalyptist, we must learn his soul language, and this soul language must grow so familiar for our own personal spiritual use that we can feel it in our bones, to use an everyday expression.

I should therefore like to introduce you to those parts of the inner soul language of the initiate which he does not always use externally, but which provide the means by which he can inwardly form his inner pictures, his own personal sharing in the spiritual world. Here is an example: Subdue the lightnings and you will grasp colour. That is the language of initiates. What does it mean? The initiate sees how the lightning appears, he sees it flaring up out of the cosmos, he regards it as the spirit glimmering in the universe, and he imagines this lightning becoming more and more suppressed and subdued, milder and milder, so that what he then has is the damping down, the gentle shaping of colour. The light-ning spreads out, in a way, and becomes a coloured surface. This is what an initiate has as an inner picture. Or perhaps he says: Quieten the thunder, let the thunder grow ever quieter and listen to it modulating, and music will arise. This is how the initiate sees the spreading tapestry of the sense-perceptible as a revelation in one direction, and for him it is entirely realistic to think: Here is the content of the universe in all its coloured manifoldness. What I am drawing here in colour might just as well be musical sound. (Plate 7, left) The way in which the content of the universe approaches our senses is like a sense-perceptible, physical veil spread out in the form of our sense-perceptible world into which we first of all weave our abstract, apparent thoughts. If you imagine the blackboard (Plate 7, far left) to be a tapestry spread out in every direction representing the world of sound, the world of colour, the world of heat and cold, then it is behind this tapestry that the initiate sees the lightnings striking. They are behind, and what you occasionally see as actual lightning is breaking through this tapestry of the senses from behind, out of the spiritual world. The spiritual world is shining in towards us in every manifestation of lightning. And if we look at this lightning made mild and suppressed until it becomes the even spread of colour over the earth, then we have before us the earth in its manifestation of colour.

Looking up to the sky and the stars, what we see as the starry points—which likewise appear to be emerging out of the spiritual world—is another manifestation of lightning, only here it lives as a permanent phenomenon. The initiate sees all this as an external revelation of what is behind it, so he says: What I should be seeing—and he does see it, when his soul becomes ever more active—is the red rose. It begins to splash its redness upwards and downwards like gentle lightnings, and as the foreground grows dim, the red reaches backwards into the sphere of the Seraphim, just as all musical

sound reaches into the sphere of the Cherubim, and everything we touch into the sphere of the Thrones. When we see
nature all around us, what we are actually seeing is everything in the physical world as an illusion, for all of it is, in
truth, the works of Seraphim, Cherubim and Thrones subdued and hushed. Look, dear friends, at how the world of
colours appears to us; it is merely the lightning work of the
Seraphim evenly subdued. This is what in ancient times was
called the *maya* character of the sense-perceptible, physical
world; it was this not-knowing that in reality Seraphim,
Cherubim and Thrones are everywhere.

Let us now take another step in initiation. Let us move on
to the passage where the apocalyptist places the main
emphasis on the opening of the seals. What is happening
here? It is that the colours in the world are being peeled
away, the heat and cold are being peeled away, so that more
and more effects arise that are spiritual and that are beginning to resemble the true forms of lightning taking shape. In
place of the zig-zag irruption of the lightnings, we now see, as
we penetrate through the sensory tapestry, the spiritual
world behind it; we see lightnings that move gently. We know
the beings living in these to be the servants of the Seraphim,
Cherubim and Thrones. And it is similar with musical sounds,
with heat and cold, with what we can grasp and touch. To the
degree that what we see as the earthly tapestry of sense fades
away so that behind it this world of lightning-like formations
appears, shaping self-contained figures out of the astral fire,
expanding more and more—in the same degree do the stars
begin to shine down. Like threads of light they can be
followed, and star threads, star rays, lights mingle with the
things of the elemental world. The earthly unites with the
heavenly, and we know that we are entering into the first
condition of the second world, where everything is still
shining as in nature, where we only guess that behind it there
are beings. We perceive at most the elemental beings, we see

them to some extent as the functioning organs of mighty, great and lofty beings. We are entering, you could say, the first region of the Kyriotetes, Dynamis, Exusiai. They are, as it were, still in the background, but they enter into these beings, and as we progress along the path of initiation we gradually reach the point where these Kyriotetes, Dynamis, Exusiai more and more reveal their own essential being. This is bound up with the way the harmony of the spheres begins to play in cosmic sounds. The single notes that sound and only form harmonies and melodies over long periods, that only combine to form melodies in time when time becomes a unity[1]—these are what the apocalyptist calls trumpet soundings. In the soundings of the trumpets we have the pure life of the second hierarchy, whereas the first hierarchy in its mighty greatness is the foundation of sense experience.

Moving on from this world in which all the phenomena of sense have become flowing and grand and majestic and are thus no longer only spread out over the things and processes of the physical world but also are the actual expression of the elemental beings at work in the second hierarchy—moving on from this world, we enter more and more into a third region where we no longer perceive anything belonging to nature, not even nature dissolved in elemental beings, but where anything we want to perceive must be perceived spiritually. We enter a region of the spiritual world of which we have to say: Having gone through the sense perceptions of earth that are dissolving and yet at the same time forming themselves into shapes and that are seized hold of by our expanding sense perception of the stars, we have now learnt to recognize—as though in last residues of sense perception—everything that works in the cosmos in the Kyriotetes, Exusiai and Dynamis in a way that shows them to be inwardly bound to the true substantiality of the stars. The stellar world has transformed itself for us into the beings of the hierarchies. Instead of looking up to the stars through the senses' illusion we are now living in the world of the hierarchies. Here the hierarchies are still steeped in what I should like to call the dispersed, dissolved knowledge given by the senses. Now we are entering the third region, where we no longer perceive all the things of the earth with our senses, where we must perceive the supersensible soul element without any hint of sense-perceptibility. We are entering the region of the actual spiritual world where we first of all get to know it in Angeloi, Archangeloi, Archai. We can recognize these beings in their spirituality, and when a painter or other artist gives them shape he must know that they only have this sense-perceptible shape because they are woven into the soul-spiritual elements, into the beings of the higher hierarchies. If we paint wings on them, for example, we must know that these wings come from the beings of the second hierarchy who lend them their substantiality, and that they receive their head from the first hierarchy who lend them this shape together with its content. We must be absolutely sure of the fact that the only thing we can see in spirit is what belongs to the third hierarchy—Angeloi, Archangeloi, Archai.

What I am telling you now, dear friends, is of the greatest possible historical importance, for if you take on ancient texts that treat intimately of these spiritual worlds, you will be utterly incapable of reading them unless you know that when we enter into the spiritual world it is the lowest hierarchy that we first perceive spiritually, whereas we still perceive the higher hierarchies with ingredients of the sense-perceptible world. You must know that the ancient initiation wisdom, which described these things quite correctly in the way I have been doing, gradually fell into all kinds of errors in times when spiritual matters became decadent. Thus the more worldly initiates of the Middle Ages always described the Seraphim, Cherubim and Thrones as being the lowest hierarchy closest to the earth, so that one ascended via

Dynamis, Kyriotetes and Exusiai to the angels, archangels and archai. Look at illustrated medieval books. You will not know what they mean and will ask why the angels are seated above the Seraphim. This came about because people no longer understood these matters intimately and could not imagine them quite organically enough. This error arose in particular when the once pure teaching became contaminated by the symbols of the Babylonians during the Jewish captivity in Babylon in pre-Christian times through the contact of the Jews with the Babylonians. This error about the ranks of the spiritual hierarchies then spread further via the Cabala, via medieval Jewish mysticism. If one wants to understand how ideas about the spirit in human evolution have developed, one must know about such things, and in connection with our work on understanding the Book of Revelation this is the right place for such things to be discussed.

So, we go out into the spiritual world. The first beings who come to meet us in the purely spiritual realm are the beings of the third hierarchy. The apocalyptist shows how intimately familiar he is with all this, for in everything he describes he shows angels as being the messengers. The interesting thing is that earthly realms can mirror something of what the angels, as the messengers of the higher hierarchies, bring in. With the angel appearances in particular we enter the realm in which we see how the divine love reigns as the real ingredient of the world to which we human beings belong. First of all we see how the normal Angeloi, Archangeloi and Archai are in a way embodiments of the higher hierarchies. When we look at the hands, arms, feet, legs and the rest of the human body we have the feeling: This is the body of the soul-spiritual element. In the same way, when we ascend into the world of the third hierarchy we have the impression: These are angels, but they are like limbs, they are like the bodily nature of the higher, divine spirits; they are bodies made of soul and spirit.

We feel, dear friends, that we are in pure spirituality, and with this spirituality in the body of God. It is to this that we ascend.

We must also concern ourselves with another inner picture. Everyone who truly wants to become familiar with the occultism on which spiritual life is founded must do this. Look at a human being with his physical body on the earth, dear friends. You cannot possibly think of this body as living solely in constructive processes, sprouting and burgeoning processes that build the human being. You must also think of the destructive processes in the organism, those leading to secretions. The destructive element that shows the body to be in a constant process of demolition is there for a purpose, which is that the destruction in the physical body enables the spirit to enter and live in these processes of physical demolition.[2] The spirit in the human organism does not live in the constructive processes. When the child is growing, when the physical processes are in the ascendancy, the spiritual element is suppressed, not promoted. Materialists make the perfectly ridiculous assumption that thinking comes about when the human being purifies the sprouting, burgeoning life in his brain and refines and transforms the other life processes. If such a thing were to happen in the brain, this would merely mean a continuation of digestive processes, and the result would be a dim, plant-like inner experience. The spirit is able to enter the brain only because the brain is constantly destroyed, because it constantly disintegrates, because it is, as it were, constantly being riddled with holes by physical processes. Along the path of destruction the spirit finds ways through which it can play a part creatively in the physical. So the physical accepts the processes of destruction. Growth is provided with inbuilt hindrances and impediments.

It is immensely interesting to observe this in detail. For example you can watch how the Fichte individuality came down to incarnate in a poverty-stricken village.[3] You can observe this individuality establishing itself in the physical body and watch the young boy grow. You see how bit by bit hindrances interfered with his growth just a little more strongly than usual, not much, in fact very little, but this is what happened. The boy Fichte grew and grew, but perhaps he would have grown a little more quickly if there had not been a tiny something constantly restraining his growth. It was this restraint exercised on his growth—he did indeed remain small in stature—that allowed the particular nuance of his philosophical gift to develop. Thus does the spirit become effective in the physical. So we must entertain not only antipathy but also sympathy towards the destructive forces; we must be assured that they are acceptable, that we can regard them with love, for in addition to growing, sprouting life there must also be something that exercises restraint.

We must become aware of how the whole world of Angeloi, Archangeloi and Archai is actually the bodily aspect of the divine spirit, we must see in this weaving, living, blossoming and working of the Angeloi, Archangeloi and Archai how the world is woven, how the individual human being is cared for in his soul by his Angelos, how different groups of human beings are moved by the Archangeloi and how various streams of universal happenings are pushed along from age to age by the Archai. When we see the whole weaving of this wonderful garment as it is woven—which is so beautifully expressed in the Greek myth of Proserpina or Persephone—when we look at this whole garment of the world, we see the divine love flooding and flowing in it like the red blood in the body. Added to this as a necessary adjunct is the stream of the divine wrath that is formed from all the hindrances in world events brought about by beings with a sense of morality, beings with genuinely moral feelings who can only be in harmony with the progress of the world through their morality.

In the divine love we see the divine body in its sprouting and burgeoning. And in connection with weak creatures who nevertheless indicate the way in which the gods want to lead the world, we see something that emanates from the weak creatures; we see the spirit body of the divine spirit interspersed with something resembling products of secretion in the human physical body; something that in human beings is secreted in glands, something that separates itself off.[4] These centres of secretion appear as the phials of divine wrath, woven into the onward progress of the world.

Within these three worlds we recognize the connection between divine love and divine wrath, and inwardly we receive a picture that fills us with reverence: What is it that happens when the phials of wrath are poured out? It is the divine, spiritual beings who are considering how they can take forward the continuing progress of the world despite the misdeeds of the weak creatures and against the hindrances— how they can transform the hindrances into vehicles of forward-urging, spirit-filled happening, so that the human being in his destructive processes can seize the opportunity not simply to vegetate physically but to press forward in his physical body in a spirit-soul way. The way the apocalyptist shows all this is entirely in accord with initiation. In the Book of Revelation he enters marvellously into the progress of the world, penetrating right down to concrete, physical events— as we saw yesterday and before that as well. At the same time he enters wonderfully into the paths of initiation.

When we contemplate the Book of Revelation thus, it in some ways opens our eyes to the progress of the world, so that we are looking into what we need from the future and can take it into our inner pictures. Further than this, it also becomes a meditation book; it can be used as a book for meditation in a wonderful way; in fact it is marvellous in this respect. When you come to a passage in the Book of Revelation depicting something that seems paradoxical to you, you should stop reading and begin to meditate. Such passages are the places where you can grow in spirituality by absorbing and working inwardly on something that you cannot comprehend with your intellect. For example when you come to a passage that speaks of a grievous sore (Rev. 16,2), then as an intellectual you will of course say: Only human beings and animals can have sores; what is this supposed to mean; it must be a poetic image. So you read past it. But this is not what it is. The apocalyptist uses the word 'sore' because he knows that what is real in the microcosm can also justifiably be imagined in the macrocosm. You will surely discover how what has to do with glands, which produce secretions, leads on to the functions of the divine wrath. In this way the seeming paradoxes in the Book of Revelation are the very thing that helps us make the transition from the merely intellectual processes of soul life—to which people are so accustomed—into spiritual processes.

This brings us to the point where it is so necessary to see things clearly and accurately, especially in connection with the work of the priest. People feel that in today's times the soul is becoming entirely intellectualized. In reaction to this they want inner heart and feeling and long for it in every realm. Look at the way the religious denominations are objecting to today's general intellectualism. They no longer want the truths of salvation preached in intellectual terms; they want them to be given form out of the feeling life, out of what is irrational. This longing is surely justified, but if things were to develop solely along these lines, then the result of wanting to have religion merely through the feelings would be the loss of religion altogether.

The same applies to education; this has taken a very peculiar path, which you as priests would do well to note. Education originated in the life of instincts. It worked best where people did not think educationally but did what instinct told them to do. In days gone by people did not teach pedagogically but did what instinct inspired them to do. Only since we have forgotten how to educate instinctively have we begun to talk so much about pedagogy, and all our talk about it proves that we are the worst teachers there have ever been. People usually begin to talk most about something when they no longer have it. In the same sense they began to talk about the Transubstantiation when they no longer understood it or its secret. The often first-rate intellectual discussions in a particular age ought to make us ask what the people in that age are lacking. When the labour question was being most ardently discussed it meant that people actually understood very little about it. This was even more so in the age when human beings invented writing, and when the use of writing turned more and more to the use of printing. It was the age when human beings understood less and less of the divine script speaking out of the stars, out of sun and wind.

When the members of Arthur's round table were still able to read what was being told to them by the sea splashing up, by the spray of the waves pounding on the cliffs and mingling with the waves of air steeped in light, in that time, when they could read all this like a clear handwriting, there was not the least need to seek the help of some kind of replicable script. What one must do, basically, is to take the sheen of what is visible and deduce from it the fading invisible world of the spirit. Then, when the spirit rises particularly strongly to the surface, one perceives how the sense-perceptible, physical outer symbols recede.

This is what makes us aware that our rejection of intellectualism should not take the form of a shadowy, nebulous feeling life in the soul, but that we can enhance our feeling life in the soul by allowing what is intellectual to metamorphose more and more into something spiritual. Then we shall find that our feeling life in the soul can truly be ennobled through the spiritual content of the revelations that are then objective and no longer subjective.

LECTURE EIGHTEEN

Dornach, 22 September 1924

We have considered the inner spirit of the Book of Revelation, and we have considered the Book of Revelation in relation to your work as priests. Of course it would still be possible to say all kinds of other things in connection with it, for example one could go deeply into the way it is structured. But it seems to me that this gathering here at Dornach will receive the best content of all if what has been said so far now continues to make its appearance in truly practical ways in your work as priests.

There is one more subject we must touch on. We must consider that we are living in the era of the consciousness soul, that stage of overall human evolution in which the human being has to grasp hold of intellectuality and integrate it into his own individuality. This is, of course, what you might call the first stage, the stage as yet confined to the spirit of the human being, the stage in which the integration of intellectuality will take place in human contemplation and thinking. Another stage will come in which deeper forces of the human soul will also be seized by what at present is taking place more in the realm of thoughts and aspirations and thinking.

At present human beings are still capable of having ideas about how they might make use of the intellectuality that is breaking into their own individuality. But this era of consciousness soul development will not pass before souls, too, will be seized by intellectuality in their deepest emotions, in their feelings and passions. When this has happened, what the Middle Ages still sought in the stars and termed the angelic Intelligences of the stars will have entered even more deeply and thoroughly into human beings. All this will be deposited in the human being. Later still, when the Jupiter condition comes, even the body will be seized by intellectuality. In our present time, while the situation is still such that human beings can put into thoughts and words what this is all about, while the soul has not yet been seized in its inmost being by intellectuality, it is still possible, for priests especially, so to direct their work that the cosmic purposes, the cosmic goals can really be achieved.

Although it is part of cosmic wisdom that the human being should grasp the intellectuality in the cosmos for himself, nevertheless there remains the possibility that while he is doing this he might—in those unguarded moments that always exist—allow those ahrimanic powers known as Satan in Christian tradition to snatch this intellectuality from him. Satan should not be confused with the ordinary devil who lacks Satan's characteristics and is merely a more lowly power. Satan has the rank of an Archai, and it was he who seized hold of this intellectuality during the course of cosmic evolution, long before it approached the human being in the manner described. At present Satan is what you might call the most comprehensive owner of intellectuality, and he is striving to bind human intellectuality firmly to his own, an occurrence that could cause the human being to drop away from his proper evolution. In other words, the ahrimanic power is striving to make the Mystery of Golgotha ineffective.

This ahrimanic power known as Satan in Christian tradition is not strong enough to have any effect in the various levels of the cosmos that are above the human being. It is inconceivable, for example, that the intelligence of, say, an Angelos could be directly seized by this satanic power. Such a thing can only happen in certain exceptional cases. Knowledge of the possibility that, in the future, moments can arise in which the satanic power will be strong enough to bind to itself not only human beings via their intellectuality but also beings from the realm of the Angeloi, particularly Arch-angeloi—this knowledge still belongs at present to the higher secrets of occultism about which for the present one must not speak and which can only be revealed under certain cir-cumstances. So just now we can only hint at the fact that in future the temptation and seduction even of beings from the hierarchy of the Angeloi and especially the Archangeloi might be possible. What we have to reckon with today is that the power called Satan in the Christian tradition has the ability to attach itself to something in the human being that exists in him as independently as does the intellect. Once the intellectuality in the human being has been taken hold of by the ahrimanic power, then the human being can be torn away from his evolution and taken to quite other paths simply by having his being dragged along by his intellect to which Satan has the power to attach himself. This would not be possible in the case of any other force of soul or spirit, nor in the case of any bodily force in the human being. It is possible only in the case of the intellect, for the intellect is situated in the human being in a way that makes it the most independent of all aspects. Every other aspect is attached in one way or another to certain divine powers. So if Satan wanted to seize hold of feeling, for example, or of desires and wishes in the human being, he would find himself up against the supra-human forces hidden in these soul capacities. The intellectuality is the first aspect with which the human being can detach himself from the beings who bring about his personal evolution. It is the first aspect in which the human being must attach himself through total freedom to those powers who from the beginning have been present in his evolution.

The human being will have to learn that he must identify of his own free will with those ultimate aims in the Book of Revelation that are hinted at by the apocalyptist; he will have to learn that a power will appear who is the Alpha and

Omega of the continuous creative powers, the continuous creative being of evolution; and he will have to learn that he must attach himself out of his own resolve to that being who had been guiding him while he still lacked maturity for the cosmos.

Satan, however, can make use of this great moment in the evolution of humanity to draw the human being across into his own realm through the intellect. Already now we can observe how the satanic power is endeavouring to draw the human being across into *its* evolution. The method used is to combine human beings into groups the seeds of which are visible everywhere today—groups in which the old group souls cease to exist and in which a new kind of group soul nature can begin. What is happening over in the East of Europe just now is so terribly satanic because its whole aim is to force human beings together in ways that make it necessary for there to be group souls. Once the most intelligent have been dragged across into the lower realm of Ahriman, then will the groups being formed be allotted to the ahrimanic powers. If this were to happen, the way would be open for the satanic powers to drag humanity away from earth evolution and take it across to some other planetary evolution. The introduction of this group soul nature will only succeed if the element of intellect can be completely detached from its links in a specific way. Some most cunning beginnings are in progress over in the East today towards the achievement of this. You ought to understand this in your work as priests, for although these beginnings are most noticeable in the East, the same is happening all over Central and Western Europe as well.

We should therefore also mention something which may appear to be relatively harmless at the moment, but which must be regarded in all seriousness in exoteric life, and that is the way psychology, the science of the soul, is being allowed to become a kind of experimental observation. This is one of the ways leading to a situation in which the soul forces no longer work from human being to human being in the sense required by the old divine powers. Instead they are determined quantitatively from the outside through an intellect that has become detached, or in some other external manner. These things are still relatively harmless in Central Europe, but you should not ignore the fact that in the West, especially through William James[1] but also through others, a way of looking at things statistically is coming to the fore, an intellectualistic way of looking at things, a way that is detached from the life of soul, and that this is being applied even to inner transformations in human beings, to what one might call the inner, religious finding of oneself that occurs today in many cases round about the twentieth year. Round about their twentieth year many people these days experience a moment of inner conversion, a conversion that comes about entirely from within. They are taken hold of by something that is like a kind of whirling up of divinity out of their own soul. In America statistics are compiled about what percentage of the population goes through this kind of inner conversion. This matter is treated statistically. What is satanic about this is the way it is treated statistically, the way things are lumped together by the detached intellect. These conversions are something that happens as a result of karma, and therefore each case should be looked at on its own.

In science today statistics are praised to the skies. If you follow scientific matters you keep coming across tremendous acclaim for statistics. People are no longer capable of getting close to inner aspects, so instead they seek to find laws through statistics. Opposing this is most difficult of all in the field of medicine where it has gained ground frightfully, and where clinical methods all culminate in statistics that tell us which medicines have worked positively or negatively and so on. This is where the statistical element has crept in, and this is also where it is entirely useless; to know how many cases had this outcome and how many had that outcome is meaningless. The important thing is to understand each individual case thoroughly, regardless of the outcome. Only after all the different methods have been applied to studying the individual case with all its idiosyncracies is it acceptable to employ statistics. (As you know, statistics has played a huge role in social considerations where social democracy is in the forefront.) In reality statistics is only acceptable as the final stage, after everything else has been looked at individually. Then it is permissible to say how many cases had a favourable and how many an unfavourable outcome.

Statistics of suicide or madness are equally nonsensical. People work out what percentage in certain professions commit suicide or go mad. Yet for a true understanding there is no value in knowing this. What is essential is to know why the individual person commits suicide or what makes the individual person go mad.

This statistical way of looking at things, that is regarded as so important these days wherever scientists write about their theory of knowledge, this preoccupation with statistics really does make it look as though Satan has broken loose. It is truly terrible. This way of looking at things, which has revealed the machinations of the satanic power in Central Europe and in the East, has become a philosophy with Avenarius and Mach, and their ideas in turn have been studied by the leading Bolshevik philosophers who then took this philosophy to Russia.[2] Even those who good-naturedly want to regard humanity as progressing in an evolutionary way—there is not much you can do about what happens! they say—even such people tend to think that the seeds of Bolshevism were sown decades ago in Central Europe and then merely transferred to Russia, just as though a seed can be transplanted and expected to germinate anywhere.

So the satanic power is at work everywhere already, appealing to the detached intellect that regards things as having no inner connection with one another; it is at work in matters of soul and in matters of spirit, in inner conversions and so on. If Satan should succeed in making things happen in the way he wants them to happen by a certain point in time, then things would come about that would damage human evolution. The events of which the apocalyptist speaks are coming, but the question is what their outcome will be. There are in fact really only two possibilities for the future. One is that things will turn out to be in harmony with the evolution planned by the gods for humanity, and the other is the opposite.

Intellectuality, then, is breaking in on us, and human beings are becoming more and more intelligent not through Inspiration but by their own efforts. This is happening. Yet on the other hand influences coming from the luciferic direction are also there, and they have kept humanity in a weakened state. So groupings will form, despite the fact that in the age of individuality—in what is actually the Christian age—everything that is individual is what would be salutary for humanity. Groups will form, but these groups must be removed from the danger in which they will find themselves.

A time will come when the satanic power will have made great efforts to win over humanity's powers of intelligence and when this satanic power will have grown so great that it will approach all the groups that have formed; so the situation will really arise in which Satan's power will work into all the four corners of the world. These groups—smaller ones: Gog, and larger ones: Magog—will be exposed to temptation and seduction by the satanic power. The outcome of this will be decided by whether those who have meanwhile taken spirituality in hand will have generated such a degree of intensity that human intellectuality can be led, with the help of Michael's strength, to where it belongs, which is to the originating powers that were there when human evolution began and that want to take forward in collaboration with human freedom what human beings have since become. An immense amount will depend on whether human beings will succeed in thoroughly understanding genuine spirituality with its own inner order.

This whole matter of humanity must be taken into consideration when one works as a priest, for only if we succeed in guiding everything in this direction will the great act of seduction that Satan is planning in connection with Gog and Magog end in a way that will be beneficial for human evolution.

Otherwise the only outcome will be that at some time in the future everything human beings have experienced since about the seventh century, since the year 666, will be snatched from them, everything they will already have experienced under the influence of the developing individuality. Darkness would obscure all the earlier incarnations of humanity, and a new world evolution would replace earthly evolution. We can see the beginnings of this today and we can also see the great danger already threatening humanity. All human weaknesses are being used—for the ahrimanic powers have the greatest conceivable intellectuality—all human weaknesses will be used, especially people's vanity and their lack of truthfulness, to get human beings on to the wrong side. The power that was at work at the beginning of the World War was something terrible. It was terrible how people's vanity was used by the satanic powers to bring about—within a few days, once a monstrous sleep-like consciousness had been induced—a whirlwind that set off a terrible frenzy, so that even today it is not clear what actually happened then.

Yet that is merely *one* phase. Far worse phases are at present taking place in a preliminary way in the purely intellectual so-called cultural battles of our time. Where, tell me, does truth still exist? Everywhere you can see how things are being arranged in a way that makes people less and less inclined to take truthfulness into account. Think of the ever increasing efforts that are being made to make cultural life conform with state requirements. How much of our cultural life is already dominated by the state! All such things pose a great threat to humanity, but people are not at all inclined to engender a genuine understanding of them. You saw what happened when the movement for a threefolding of the social order first began to work against the seduction of Gog and Magog so that future events might be guided in a direction that would be favourable to the further evolution of humanity. The way in which the idea of a threefold society was received, the way this idea that was intended to lead humanity across this present threshold of its evolution was received, shows the immense dangers threatening humanity in connection with these things. That is why it is necessary for priests, too, to take these things absolutely seriously.

There was once an individuality who lived on the earth in the early centuries of Christian development and experienced the year 666. With a degree of clairvoyance this individuality saw what was taking place and what it meant that the satanic power was preparing such a mission even then. This individuality, who lived in the very place where the real struggle of the church was taking place, in Rome, and who then prepared the way for Christianity in Europe, recognized this with spiritual clarity. Later on—as happened to so many—this individuality mistook the satanic power, whom even Michael recognizes as superior to himself, for the devil of the Middle Ages; he spoke of the devil, but in such a way that it is obvious that it is the satanic power which is meant. This individuality was reincarnated in Berlin during the first half of the nineteenth century. His name was Trahndorff, and he was an ordinary grammar-school teacher.[3] Yes, he defended the existence of the devil, or rather Satan. He wrote a book *Ist der Teufel ein Hirngespinst?* ('Is the devil a chimera?'), and not only that; he also wrote a book on aesthetics.[4] Read that book!

There is no point talking to theologians about him because he has been ignored by them; the leading clergy in Berlin were his enemies.

All these things culminate in the question: Will the priests be capable of representing the spiritual world in its full reality rather than in the sentimental manner that has come into fashion over the last few centuries, so that as soon as one talks of the spirit one feels disinclined to include the power of evil? The question is whether their energy will be sufficient to represent the reality of the spirit. This, dear friends, is absolutely the main thing. The main point is that we need the same attitude of soul for contemplating things such as the knowledge of karma, honestly contemplating earlier lives on earth, as we do for contemplating the Transubstantiation when it is celebrated during the Act of Consecration of Man. Such inner pictures must become real again for humanity. Only if they become real will it be possible, dear friends, to present what the apocalyptist was so deeply concerned about as a prospect for humanity so that all these things may be guided in the right direction. The things we have been talking about here in connection with the Book of Revelation are truths that one ought not to receive without uniting one's whole humanity with them, that one ought not to receive without regarding them as a kind of Communion.

One can truly say: A genuine *ecclesia* comprises the congregation as its outer reality, while the priests must regard themselves as that group of beings within the *ecclesia* through whose work the spirit flows into humanity. For this, one does need, with the right understanding, the small tabernacle with the consecrated Host wherein the mystery of the Transubstantiation is contained. Imagine you have the chalice in which the Transubstantiation is accomplished. Through the Transubstantiation human beings seek the path to the Father, to that primeval creator-power who has his being in it in all reality, and who cannot be found if you look onesidedly for spirit alone or onesidedly for matter alone, but who is only found when you directly discover the oneness of spirit with matter. Genuine understanding of the world is only present today when the Transubstantiation is celebrated on the altar. Then indeed that holy event happens in which the Father is sought, and the Son shows the human being the way to the Father, the Son who is the one who mediates the path to the Spirit.

So when he sees what is represented everywhere by the physical world, the human being can find in the Transubstantiation the wholly hidden spirit in the physical, the work of Seraphim, Cherubim and Thrones whose hidden work appears as physical substance. If one wants to have this as spirit, one must tread the path to the Father. The path to the Father is shown by the Son, who then brings it about that the spirit appears out of the physical.

The bread—to speak only of the bread, but the same can be shown also for the wine—the bread is bread, but the Father can be sought in it. Christ shows the way. Through the Transubstantiation the bread surrounds itself with the aura. In the aura the human being experiences the spirit. The wine merely represents an amplification of what is in the bread. (Plate 8)

We can therefore say: One's yearning for the Father lives in seeing the sense-perceptible in which Seraphim, Cherubim and Thrones are hidden. Christ leads the human being to the path, so that before him Kyriotetes, Dynamis and Exusiai begin to work in the manner described yesterday, and he ascends to that realm where today he can only observe the spiritual world in its spirituality, where the Holy Spirit is right in the middle: Angeloi, Archangeloi, Archai.

This, dear friends, is told in the Book of Revelation. To understand this, to conclude that it must be understood today—what does this mean? It means that someone who understands it will find his own understanding already set out in the Book of Revelation. It is therefore possible to say: It is entirely up to you, dear friends, whether or not it is you about whom the Book of Revelation has been speaking. If you take the impulses of the Book of Revelation into your work as priests in a truly spiritual sense, then you are the ones, dear friends, about whom the Book of Revelation has been speaking as being the ones who come to turn aside the might of the Beast, of the False Prophet, of Satan. Then, wherever the chalice for the Transubstantiation stands, you will always imagine beneath it the apocalyptic Book. You will think to yourself: The chalice is standing upon the apocalyptic book. And as you think this you will be able to say: Therein lies my calling, and what we do above this is the enactment of my calling.

Dear friends, I did not want to start a theoretical discussion during this conference. Since you had the justifiable wish to hear something about the Book of Revelation, I wanted to give you what I have given you, thus placing for you the Book of Revelation beneath the chalice. It is to this that our considerations were intended to lead. Whatever the circumstances, you will succeed in achieving what it is possible to achieve, dear friends, if you extend the ideals of your work as firmly as they can be extended, especially when you make our earnest considerations of the Book of Revelation into the inmost impulse of your own work.

This, dear friends, is what I wanted to bring to you in conclusion of our considerations here. You will surely believe that the most intensive thoughts regarding your intensive, urgent work, worthy of a great task, will accompany all that you will now do in following up these considerations.

(*Friedrich Rittelmeyer expressed the gratitude of the participants.*) [His words were not recorded.]

Rudolf Steiner: These words do not refer to anything external. What they express is an inner heartfelt vow, and if we can learn to place this into the light of rightly comprehended grace, then what is to happen will indeed happen, which is that the paths of gods and men must merge in our time. Michael will be the great mediator between the paths of gods and the paths of human beings. Let us pay heed to his work! Let us learn from the beginnings of his work in the past what is to be achieved in the future! Then shall we be permitted to look to the future not merely with well-meaning enthusiasm but with courageous enthusiasm, then shall we find our will conjoined more and more with the divine will that has guided humanity from the beginning, then shall we feel our freedom join forces with the freedom of the gods. This is what we must feel. If we do, we shall be permitted to say each day when we have finished our daily work, hoping not for smaller but for greater things for the following day: Perhaps the gods are looking down upon us and saying: Yea, so be it.

APPENDIX

In the Newsletter for Members of the Anthroposophical Society *Was in der Anthroposophischen Gesellschaft vorgeht* of 5 October 1924, Rudolf Steiner wrote:

To the Members

Regarding the lectures on the Book of Revelation
given at the Goetheanum in September
I wish to say the following:

Among the courses of lectures given here at the Goetheanum between 4 and 23 September there was one for priests of The Christian Community. Attendance was strictly limited and apart from the priests the only other participants were the members of the Executive at the Goetheanum.

Sometime prior to this the priests had expressed the wish that the content of the course should be based on the Book of Revelation.

A course of lectures given by me in 1908 to members of the then Theosophical Society in Nuremberg had been printed for members of the Anthroposophical Society under the title 'Theosophy in relation to the Apocalypse'.[1]

It was not possible to tie up what was said on that occasion with the substance presented this time. On that occasion our dear friends from among the membership had been full of expectations with regard to hearing about the knowledge one can have, through being able to see into the supersensible world, concerning the evolution of humanity on earth and of the earth as a part of the stellar system. That is the kind of theme that fits in well with the Book of Revelation, of which the content is puzzling for all those who read the Bible, in which it is the final book. It contains information of a prophetic kind relating to the evolution of earth and humanity. In the Nuremberg lectures I was able to show how in the picture language of the apocalyptist one can often rediscover what can be said through anthroposophical research (which goes further into the spiritual realm but is nevertheless conducted with strict scientific conscientiousness) about the development of humanity and the earth within the solar system. As a result of this it was also possible for me to show in the right light how the esoteric truths of Christianity relate to Anthroposophy. I was able to help my audience understand how eternal truths that deeply move the human soul can be heard from two sides, from the side of vision attained in esoteric Christianity and from the side of knowledge attained in spiritual science. I was able to show that the same is heard from these two sides if only one listens properly.

This time, however, my task was different. Although I do *not* intend to report on what by its very nature can only be intended for the circle of priests, I do feel an obligation to explain what anthroposophists ought to know about a process that is taking place within the Anthroposophical Society.

The spiritual substance streaming through the circle of priests of The Christian Community was bestowed on it through my mediation two years ago in the Goetheanum which since then has been burnt to the ground. This bestowal was such that The Christian Community remains entirely *independent* of the Anthroposophical Society. It would have been impossible to strive for anything other than such independence, for this movement for Christian renewal has *not* grown up out of Anthroposophy. It originated with persons who were seeking for a new religious path out of their own experience with Christianity, not out of their experience in Anthroposophy. They felt the urge to discover the connection of the human soul with the eternal world of its being, through finding a living way of taking hold of the supersensible content of Christianity, and they firmly believed that there must be a way of doing this. They felt, however, that the paths at present available to them for attaining the office of priesthood could *not* enable them to take hold of the content in the way they envisaged. So these pupils of an honest and spiritually appropriate priesthood placed their confidence in me. They had come to know Anthroposophy. They were convinced that Anthroposophy would be able to provide what they were looking for. They were looking not for the anthroposophical path but for a specifically religious one.

I pointed out to them that the cultus and the teachings on which the cultus is based could certainly be bestowed on them through Anthroposophy, even though the anthro-posophical movement had to regard its own task as lying in the cultivation of spiritual life from other angles.

It then became possible to approach Dr Rittelmeyer[2] about the quest of these pupils of a spiritually oriented Christian priesthood. His was a personality in which Chris-tian priest *as well as* anthroposophist were present in the truest sense of the word. To a great extent, although without the actual cultus, he had in his person lived Christian renewal in all his work. If something was to be bestowed out of the Anthroposophical Society that would serve Christian renewal, the practical question naturally arose: How will Rittelmeyer receive that which is being bestowed? What will be his stance with regard to realizing the desired outcome? The anthroposophical movement could not help seeing in Rittelmeyer the prototype of a personality who had combined Christianity and Anthroposophy both within the inner harmony of his heart and in the external harmony of all his work.

Rittelmeyer said 'Yes' with all the strength of his heart.

Thus a firm point of departure for the independent movement for Christian renewal had been won. What then had to take place was able to be inaugurated here in the Goetheanum two years ago.

Since then, the community of priests for Christian renewal has followed its path with the greatest of energy. It is developing a beneficial and healing way of working.

Two years on from that moment—the anniversary of the actual founding fell within the period of this course of lectures—these priests felt the need to achieve a closer relationship with the Book of Revelation.

I believed I would be able to contribute to such a closer relationship. The spiritual paths I follow had enabled me to trace the apocalyptist's footsteps.

So I felt that with this course of lectures I would be able to achieve a depiction that would convey this 'priestly book' in its true sense as a spiritual guide for the 'priest'. The Act of Consecration of Man is central to the work of the priest. From it there flows what comes to the world of human beings out of the spirit through the route of a cultus. The Book of Revelation can occupy the central place in the soul of the priest. From it can stream into all the priest's thinking and all the priest's feeling whatever the human soul conducting the offering is to receive through grace from the spirit world.

These were my thoughts as to the purpose of this course of lectures for priests when I was requested to give it. And this is the sense in which I gave it.

A NOTE FROM THE EDITORS OF THE GERMAN EDITION

Regarding the quality of the original German text (from which this translation is made)

There is no authentic record of these lectures in the sense of a literal rendering of Rudolf Steiner's wording; no stenographer was present.

The [German] edition is based on a compilation made from participants' notes which was put together as follows: At the end of the course, the notes taken by a number of the participants were collected and given to a group who were to work through and then duplicate them. In the 'Priests Newsletter' No. 38 of 30 October 1924 Wolfgang Schickler reported on this. Although Schickler's main argument is about the technical difficulties of the duplication, his description also reveals that at least six people worked on deciphering the various notes, as well as compiling, dictating and typing them up. The names mentioned are: Käthe Wolf-Gumpold, Walter Gradenwitz, Johannes Thielemann, Arnold Göbel, Hermann Beckh. Because of the virtual illegibility of some of the notes, Schickler playfully referred to them as the 'Pali texts'.

The rough text created in this way was immediately duplicated without having been critically inspected or worked on by a competent person from among the circle who had heard the lectures. Nothing is known about what became of the original notes.

This compilation of the notes—the only documentation on which this edition of the lectures is based—is therefore *not* a word-for-word record of Rudolf Steiner's lectures. *Neither* is it a report on the content of the lectures vouched for by any one individual. The compilation might best be described as a kind of memorandum for those who had participated. The general gist of the lectures and the main trains of thought appear to be well recorded, but when looked at in detail the text has a great many deficiencies and unclarities, of which the chief ones are:

— lacking or unclear sentence structure
— non sequiturs
— sentences of which the meaning is unclear
— obvious gaps, in most cases recognizable due to the fact that the train of thought is interrupted
— use of 'he', 'she', 'it' with no clarity about what is referred to
— repetiton of a noun in a wrong context, which entirely distorts the meaning of a whole sentence
— use of wrong tenses, e.g. present instead of subjunctive, or imperfect instead of future, which likewise distorts the meaning
— repetition of the same content with only slightly changed wording, whereby it is unclear whether Rudolf Steiner was repeating a thought or sentence, or whether the notes of several participants have simply been placed one after the other
— unclear wording of quotations
— etc.

Because of the obvious deficiencies of the notes the editors had no option but to edit the [German] texts; the following guidelines were applied:

— clear sentences have been constructed
— punctuation and spelling have been corrected
— quotations have been properly referenced and quoted correctly

— incomplete sentences have been completed
— in doubtful cases, variations have been included in the Notes and/or explained
— in the case of unclear passages, parallel passages have been sought in Rudolf Steiner's works and used to construct meaningful sense. The following is an example:

Unclear text
'On a number of occasions here and in various places I have described how this Michaelity was introduced in the spiritual sense. Part of this I mentioned the other day in a lecture where I pointed out that in the year 869 under Michael's regency the individualities of Alexander and Aristotle introduced a truly Christian impulsation. This was carried further. At the beginning of the new age, in which the consciousness soul is taking hold—I have described this—we have a wonderful insight. If we look up to spiritual events that belong to earthly humanity and which go on parallel with physical events, we find a supersensible school with Michael as the teacher.'

Edited version, using the lecture mentioned (10 September 1924 [in GA 238], which was taken down word for word in shorthand)
'As time has gone on I have spoken here and in various other places about how Christianity has been introduced spiritually through Michael. I mentioned one aspect of this two days ago when I spoke in a lecture about Michael's regency in the time of Aristotle and Alexander, during which a genuinely Christian impulse was already introduced, and when I also pointed to the year 869 in which a kind of supersensible Council took place. This continued further. And at the beginning of the new era, when the consciousness soul is beginning to take effect, we now have—if we look up to

spiritual events belonging to earthly humanity and running parallel with earthly events—the wonderful sight of a supersensible school with Michael as its teacher.'

The aim of the editorial work has been to create a comprehensible text in so far as this is possible on the basis of the inadequate documentation available. Obviously any such editing cannot help remaining unsatisfactory. It can never replace a word-for-word record taken down in shorthand.

NOTES

GA = *Gesamtausgabe*, the collected works of Rudolf Steiner in the original German, published by Rudolf Steiner Verlag, Dornach, Switzerland.

Publisher's Foreword

1. See Appendix; also for the following quotations in this paragraph.
2. Friedrich Rittelmeyer (1872–1938). When Rittelmeyer met Rudolf Steiner in 1911 his followers numbered thousands when Steiner's numbered barely hundreds, yet he recognized Steiner's unique spiritual stature. In 1917 Rittelmeyer was called to Berlin to one of the most influential pulpits in Germany and would have been offered the highest position in the Lutheran Church had he not chosen to support The Christian Community in its process of coming into being, and subsequently become its first *Erzoberlenker*.
3. For an overview of The Christian Community, see James H. Hindes *Renewing Christianity*, Edinburgh, Floris Books 1995.

Introduction

1. This Introduction first appeared in a slightly longer version in the Newsletter of the Anthroposophical Society in America, Spring 1998.
2. 1904: unpublished; 1907 and 1909: *Reading the Pictures of the Apocalypse* (GA 104a). Tr. J. H. Hindes, New York: Anthroposophic Press 1993; 1908: *The Apocalypse of St. John. Lectures on the Book of Revelation* (GA 104). Tr. rev. J. Collis. London: Rudolf Steiner Press 1977.
3. R. Steiner *The Gospel of St John and its Relation to the Other Gospels* (GA 112). Tr. rev. M. St Goar. New York: Anthroposophic Press 1982.

4. For more on the 666-year rhythm and Sorat see R. Steiner *The Apocalypse of St John*, op. cit., and R. Steiner *Three Streams in Human Evolution* (GA 184). Tr. C. Davy. London: Rudolf Steiner Press 1965.

Greeting by Johannes Werner Klein

1. Johannes Werner Klein (1898–1984), an *Oberlenker* of The Christian Community at the time.
2. In a letter dated 31 August 1924, Emil Bock (an *Oberlenker* of The Christian Community at the time) had told Rudolf Steiner that the circle of priests felt membership of the First Class of the School of Spiritual Science to be profoundly important for their lives. Seventeen applications for membership of the First Class were enclosed with the letter. Twenty-four priests had already become members; fifteen others had applied but not yet received an answer.
3. Since the founding of The Christian Community in September 1922, the following persons had also been ordained: Harald Brock, Robert Goebel, Johannes Hemleben, Hermann Heisler, Josef Kral, Karl Ludwig, Karl Luttenberger, Rudolf Meyer, Ernst Moll, Hermann von Skerst, Gustav Spiegel, Johannes Thielemann, Käthe Wolf-Gumpold. It is not known whether they all participated in this course of lectures.

Lecture One

1. The fire that destroyed the first Goetheanum on New Year's Night 1922/23 was first noticed in the 'White Hall' where the meetings of the founders of The Christian Community had taken place in September 1922.
2. At this point the internal record of The Christian Community contains the following sentences, which have evidently been inadequately recorded:

   'Then the substances were mixed in a way that had still been taught to, say, Alexander by Aristotle in olden times, so that the holy Imagination signifying the path to the gods emerged from the sacrificial smoke. Then this Transubstantiation, the priestly action, was a proper one. The act of consecration of man had indeed been achieved. The celebrant and the one who received it knew: This is the organ for perceiving knowledge, for when that which flows upwards to the gods lights up in the sacrificial smoke and in the prayer that is ceremonially shaped in magical sequences of words, then, as a gift of grace from above, there comes down the revelation, the apocalyptic revelation.'

The content only hinted at here is described in R. Steiner *Mystery Knowledge and Mystery Centres* (GA 232). Tr. rev. P. Wehrle. London: Rudolf Steiner Press 1997, lecture of 22 December 1922.

Lecture Two

1. In the internal record of The Christian Community this passage is as follows:

   'Becoming anointed takes place when one feels how the content of the Book of Revelation came into being in John; as soon as one feels: These human beings of today want to become priests through creating within themselves the experience of the 'I' itself in the Revelation. If the 'I' becomes apocalyptic, then it becomes priestly.

Lecture Three

1. Steiner was using Martin Luther's translation of the Bible. The English quoted here is from the Authorized Version.

Lecture Four

1. The Archbishop of Salzburg, Johannes Baptist Katschthaler (1832–1914), in a pastoral letter of 2 February 1905 on 'The respect due to a Catholic priest' published in Carl Mirbt *Quellen zur Geschichte des Papsttums und des Römischen Katholizismus*, No.4, Tübingen 1924, pp.497–499.
2. Rudolf Steiner went to Tintagel (on the westward facing cliffs of North Cornwall) on 17 August 1924. He spoke about this excursion in Torquay on 21 August and in London on 27 August

1924, see R. Steiner *Karmic Relationships, Vol 8* (in GA 240).
Tr. D. S. Osmond. London: Rudolf Steiner Press 1975; and in
Dornach on 10 September 1924, see R. Steiner *Karmic Rela-
tionships, Vol 4* (in GA 238). Tr. G. Adams, rev. D. S. Osmond,
C. Davy. London: Rudolf Steiner Press 1997.

Lecture Five

1. R. Steiner *Knowledge of the Higher Worlds* (GA 10). Tr. D.
   Osmond & C. Davy. London: Rudolf Steiner Press 1985; also
   published as: *How to Know Higher Worlds. A Modern Path of
   Initiation* (GA 10). Tr. C. Bamford. Spring Valley, New York:
   Anthroposophic Press 1994.
2. R. Steiner *Karmic Relationships, Vol 4*, op. cit., lecture of 7
   September 1924.
3. R. Steiner *The Evolution of the Earth and Man and the Influ-
   ence of the Stars* (GA 354). Tr. G. Hahn. London: Rudolf
   Steiner Press 1987, lecture of 9 August 1924.
4. Ibid., lecture of 9 September 1924.
5. Rudolf Steiner spoke about the karma of Ignatius of Loyola and
   Emanuel Swedenborg a number of times, but especially in R.
   Steiner *Karmic Relationships, Vol 6* (in GA 240). Tr. D. S.
   Osmond. London: Rudolf Steiner Press 1989, lecture of 24
   August 1924.

Lecture Six

1. R. Steiner *Speech and Drama* (GA 282). Tr. M. Adams. New
   York: Anthroposphic Press 1986.
2. Rudolf Steiner spoke a number of times, in esoteric lessons,
   about the periods in which the archangels ruled, using the
   chronology of Johannes Trithemius of Sponheim: R. Steiner
   Aus den Inhalten der esoterischen Schule (GA 266), Dornach
   1995. See also the lectures of 5 December 1907 in *Beiträge zur
   Rudolf Steiner Gesamtausgabe*, No.67/68; of 19 July 1924 in R.
   Steiner *Karmic Relationships, Vol 6*, op. cit.; of 8 August 1924 in
   R. Steiner *Karmic Relationships, Vol 3* (GA 237). Tr. G.
   Adams, rev. D. S. Osmond. London: Rudolf Steiner Press 1977;

and of 18 August 1924 in R. Steiner *True and False Paths in Spiritual Investigation* (GA 243). Tr. A. Parker. London: Rudolf Steiner Press 1986.

3. After Plutarch *Quaestiones conviviales*, VIII, 2.

4. From Homer's *Odyssey*, XI, 488–491.

5. The Eighth Council of Constantinople in 869 determined that the human being should be regarded as consisting of body and soul and that the soul 'has a number of spiritual characteristics'.

6. Joachim of Floris (d.1202) wrote *Evangelium aeternum* (an interpretation of Biblical prophecies). Alanus de Insulis (Alain de Lille) (c.1120–1202), scholastic philosopher, last of the great teachers of Chartres, wrote the *Anticlaudianus*.

7. Rudolf Steiner spoke in detail about the meaning of numbers in R. Steiner *Occult Signs and Symbols* (in GA 101). Tr. S. Kurland. Anthroposophic Press, New York 1972, lecture of 15 September 1907.

Lecture Seven

1. Fourth century controversy about the nature of Father God and Son God. Arius (d. 336), a town priest of Alexandria, taught that Christ was not identical with the Father God and had been created in time. Athanasius (295–373), Bishop of Alexandria, disputed this and taught that Father God and Son God were 'of the same substance'. The Council of Nicaea (325) decided in favour of Athanasius.

2. See Lecture Six, Note 5.

3. Constantine the Great (Emperor from 306 to 337).

4. Adolf Harnack (1851–1930), Protestant theologian, wrote *Das Wesen des Christentums* (published in 1900), English translation *What is Christianity?* (published in 1901). See also Lecture Nine, Note 1.

5. Julian (331–363), commonly called Julian the Apostate, Roman emperor.

Lecture Eight

1. The Hebrew characters with their numerical equivalents are

shown here in the traditional sequence. (See R. Steiner *The Apocalypse of St. John. Lectures on the Book of Revelation* (GA 104). Tr. rev. J. Collis. London: Rudolf Steiner Press 1977. See the special note on p.263 of R. Steiner *Die Apokalypse des Johannes* (GA 104), Dornach 1985. It is not known why Rudolf Steiner used the spelling 'Soradt' (Notebook entry, Archive No. 498). Another representation of the number 666 is to be found in Agrippa von Nettesheim's *De occulta philosophia*, Part II, Chapter 22:

Magic Square of the Sun

in

Numbers.   Hebrew Characters.

6	32	3	34	35	1
7	11	27	28	8	30
19	14	16	15	23	24
18	20	22	21	17	13
25	29	10	9	26	12
36	5	33	4	2	31

ו	לב	ג	לד	לה	א
ז	יא	כז	כח	ח	ל
יט	יד	יו	יה	כג	כד
יח	כ	כב	כא	יז	יג
כה	כט	י	ט	כו	יב
לו	ה	לג	ד	ב	לא

'... The fourth magic square, that of the sun, consists of the square of six and contains thirty-six numbers, six in each row, and diagonally from corner to corner, each row having the sum of one hundred and eleven. The sum of all the numbers is six hundred and sixty-six.'

Regarding Sorat and the number 666, see also the lecture of 27 April 1907 in R. Steiner *Ursprungsimpulse der Geisteswissenschaft* (GA 96), Dornach 1989, and of 11 October 1918 in R. Steiner *Three Streams in Human Evolution* (in GA 184). London: Rudolf Steiner Press 1965.

2. Regarding the Templars, see lecture of 25 September 1916 in R. Steiner *Inner Impulses of Human Evolution. The Mexican Mysteries and the Knights Templar* (in GA 171). Tr. G. Church, F. Kozlik, S. C. Easton. New York: Anthroposophic Press 1984.

3. Jacques de Molay (d.1413), last grand master of the Knights Templar.

4. On 10 September 1924 in R. Steiner *Karmic Relationships, Vol 4*, op. cit.

Lecture Nine

1. This statement by Adolf Harnack appears in the 8th lecture of his book *What is Christianity?*
2. In the internal record of The Christian Community this passage also contains the following notes by another participant: 'In so far as you are worthy of it, you will take on the New Jerusalem not merely as a picture such as that put forward by modern exegetists but also as something that hangs down from above as really as did the Old Jerusalem stand on its feet from below upwards.'

Lecture Ten

1. Iesus Christus: I CH.
2. For the 'wrong' translation Rudolf Steiner was quoting Luther. I have used the Authorized Version. (Tr.)
3. Johann Christian Friedrich Hölderlin (1770–1843) in *Hyperion*, Book Two.

Lecture Eleven

1. See R. Steiner *The Course of my Life* (GA 28). Tr. O. D. Wannamaker. New York: Anthroposophic Press 1970, Chapter XVIII. There are similar descriptions in the lectures of 8 August 1924 in R. Steiner *Karmic Relationships, Vol 3*, op. cit; and 20 July 1924 in R. Steiner *Karmic Relationships, Vol 6*, op. cit.

Lecture Twelve

1. Rudolf Steiner spoke in greater detail concerning this in the lecture of 7 November 1915 in R. Steiner *The Occult Movement in the 19th Century* (GA 254). Tr. D. Osmond. London: Rudolf Steiner Press 1973.
2. See lectures especially in R. Steiner *Karmic Relationships, Vol 4*, op. cit.

3. More about this image may be found in R. Steiner's article on the theosophical congress in Munich in *Luzifer-Gnosis*, No. 34 (Summer 1907) and the lecture of 21 May 1907. These items are contained in *Bilder Okkulter Siegel und Säulen. Der Münchener Kongress Pfingsten 1907 und seine Auswirkungen* (GA 284), Dornach 1993. See also *Occult Signs and Symbols*, op. cit., lecture of 16 September 1907.

4. R. Steiner *Occult Science: an Outline* (GA 13). Tr. G. & M. Adams. London: Rudolf Steiner Press 1984, chapter 'Man and the Evolution of the World'; also published as *An Outline of Esoteric Science*, Hudson N.Y: Anthroposophic Press 1997.

Lecture Thirteen

1. See R. Steiner *Pastoral Medicine* (GA 318). Tr. G. Hahn. New York: Anthroposophic Press 1987, lecture of 17 September 1924.

2. The notes recording the rest of this paragraph give no clear indication of what Rudolf Steiner actually said at this point. It is not possible to edit the text to fit in with what he said in Lecture Six, as he may in fact have brought in quite other angles. It remains for the reader to reach an understanding, perhaps with the help of the following: R. Steiner *Occult Signs and Symbols*, op. cit., lecture of 15 September 1907; R. Steiner *The Being of Man and his Future Evolution* (in GA 107). Tr. P. Wehrle. London: Rudolf Steiner Press 1981, lecture of 21 December 1908; R. Steiner *The East in the Light of the West* (GA 113). Blauvelt: Garber Communications Inc. 1986, lecture of 31 August 1909; R. Steiner *Occult Reading and Occult Hearing* (in GA 156). Tr. D. Osmond. London: Rudolf Steiner Press 1975, lecture of 6 October 1914. Also 12 lectures on planetary evolution in *Beiträge zur Rudolf Steiner Gesamtausgabe*, Nos. 67/68, 69/70, 71/72, and 78.

3. See also R. Steiner *Conferences with the Teachers of the Waldorf School in Stuttgart*, Vol. 4 (GA 300c). Tr. P. Wehrle. Forest Row: Steiner Schools Fellowship 1986–89, meeting of 3 July 1923; R. Steiner *The New Spirituality and the Christ Experience of the 20th Century* (GA 200). Tr. P. King, London & New York:

Rudolf Steiner Press & Anthroposophic Press 1988, lecture of 22 October 1920. H. P. Blavatsky spoke of 'soulless men' and 'death of soul' in *Isis Unveiled*, Vol. II and in *The Secret Doctrine*, Vol.III.

4. R. Steiner *Pastoral Medicine*, op. cit., lecture of 17 September 1924.
5. Goethe's letter to the physicist Thomas Johann Seebeck.
6. Kuno Fischer (1824–1907), professor of philosophy at Jena and Heidelberg, published a paper *Erinnerungen an Moritz Seebeck, nebst Anhange: Goethe und Thomas Seebeck* in Heidelberg in 1886. See also the essay Rudolf Steiner wrote in the same year 'Das Verhalten Thomas Seebecks zu Goethes Farbenlehre' in *Methodische Grundlagen der Anthroposophie* (GA 30), Dornach 1989.

Lecture Fourteen

1. R. Steiner *Knowledge of the Higher Worlds*, op. cit.
2. R. Steiner *The Philosophy of Spiritual Activity: A Philosophy of Freedom* (GA 4). Tr. rev. R. Stebbing. Forest Row, Sussex: Rudolf Steiner Press 1992.
3. In the sixth recapitulation lesson on 17 September 1924 in *Esoteric Lessons for the First Class of the School of Spiritual Science at the Goetheanum* (GA 270 I–IV). Tr. G. Adams, rev. M. Wilson, ed. J. Collis. London: Anthroposophical Society in Great Britain 1994, private printing.
4. R. Steiner *Theosophy* (GA 9). Tr. M. Cotterell, A.P. Shepherd. London: Rudolf Steiner Press 1970; also published as: *Theosophy* (GA 9). Tr. H. Monges, G. Church. New York: Anthroposophic Press 1971.
5. Thomas Garrigue Masaryk (1850–1937), professor of philosophy and sociology in Prague. From 1918–1935 President of Czechoslovakia.

Lecture Fifteen

1. R. Steiner *Pastoral Medicine*, op. cit.

Preliminary Talk

1. Emil Bock (1895–1959), an *Oberlenker* of The Christian Community at the time. Friedrich Doldinger (1897–1973), a *Lenker* of The Christian Community.
2. In the journal *Die Christengemeinschaft*, 1/6 (6 September 1924), Emil Bock had published an article 'Die Gegenwart als Weltenstunde. Die sieben Sendschreiben der Offenbarung Johannis' (The present time as a cosmic hour. The seven letters in the Book of Revelation).
3. In 1907 Pius X had declared modernism to be a 'pool of all heresies'. All its errors were rejected in his Decree *'Lamentabili sane exitu'* and in the Encyclical *'Pascendi dominici gregis'*. From 1910 onwards all the clergy had to take the so-called 'antimodernism' oath, an obligation that was not annulled until 1967. See R. Steiner *Heilfaktoren für den sozialen Organismus* (GA 198), lectures of 30 May, 3 and 6 June 1920, and R. Steiner *Vorträge und Kurse über christlich-religiöses Wirken* (GA 343), Dornach 1993, lecture of 26 September 1921.
4. Pope Pius IX's Encyclical *'Quanta cura'* of 8 December 1864 included a 'Syllabus' containing a list of 80 clauses stating the modern 'errors' of thought not compatible with Roman Catholicism.

Lecture Sixteen

1. See Lecture Five, p.77.
2. Joseph Jérome de Lalande (1732–1807), lawyer and astronomer, became professor of astronomy at the Collège de France in 1761 and director of the Paris Observatory in 1768. Main works: *Traité d'astronomie*, Paris 1764, and *Bibliographie astronomique*, Paris 1803.
3. R. Wolf *Handbuch der Astronomie, ihrer Geschichte und Litteratur*, Zurich 1892 (Book III, Section 578) contains the following description.

   'Great excitement was caused in the spring of 1773 by an announcement that Lalande of the Academy would be lecturing about "Comets which might come close to the earth". Owing to an excessive number of other lecturers in that sitting, Lalande's talk had to be cancelled. In consequence—it is not known whether through stupidity or evil intent—the rumour spread that he had intended to announce the end of the world for 12 May due to the earth's collision with a comet, but had been prevented from doing so by the police. The rumour alone sufficed to spread such panic and dread that as the whole of Paris bewailed the approaching day babies were born prematurely and people died from shock, while unscrupulous clergy plied a roaring trade selling absolutions for exorbitant sums. The hurried publication of Lalande's lecture and various attempts, both humorous and serious, to rectify the misapprehension did little to calm the situation. Not until the terrible day passed without incident of any kind did people return to their normal frame of mind.'

4. Johann Joseph von Littrow (1781–1840), professor of astronomy at Cracow and from 1819 at Vienna where he was also director of the Observatory. In his treatise *Über den gefürchteten Kometen des gegenwärtigen Jahres 1832 und über Kometen überhaupt*, Vienna 1832, he stated the following about Biela's comet:

'This year (1832) the comet will touch a point only $2\frac{1}{3}$ of the earth's diameter distant from the earth's orbit, though not from the earth itself, on 29 October. For that to happen, the earth itself would have to be at this point on its orbit on 29 October. However, on that date the earth will be far away from the point on its orbit that would bring it so close to the comet as to be a cause for concern ... It would be different if the comet, which will be closest to the sun on 27 November, were not to come closest to the sun until 28 December. If this were to be the case, the comet would indeed come as close to the earth as stated above ... This is not due to occur for the whole duration of this century. Not until 1933 will the comet's closest approach to the sun fall on the last ... of December if, that is, it continues on its present orbit of $6\frac{3}{4}$ years' duration. However, the distortions of its orbit that will be caused by the planets, in particular Jupiter, over this long period will bring about so many changes in its orbit that it is by then hardly or in fact no longer likely to pose any danger at all to the earth.'

5. Karl Ferdinand Friedrich von Nagler (1770–1846), General Postmaster of Berlin.

6 See R. Hagen *Die erste deutsche Eisenbahn*, 1885, and M. Kemmerich *Kulturkuriosa*, Munich 1909.

7 In Georg Wilhelm Friedrich Hegel (1770–1831) *Encyklopädie der philosophischen Wissenschaften im Grundrisse*, ed. C. Michelet, Berlin 1847, Part 2.

8 Rudolf Steiner lectured in Paris from 25 May to 14 June 1906. Edouard Schuré's summaries of these lectures are included in the volume *Kosmogonie*, Dornach 1987. However, Schuré did not record what Rudolf Steiner said on this point. The fact that spectral analysis shows cyanide to be present in the substance of comets became public knowledge around the year 1910 in connection with an appearance of Halley's Comet. Astronomers had been aware of this by the end of the nineteenth century.

Lecture Seventeen

1. See also R. Steiner *Turning Points in Spiritual History*, (in GA 60). Tr. W. F. Knox. London: Rudolf Steiner Publishing Co. 1934, lecture of 19 January 1911.

2. See R. Steiner, I. Wegman. *Extending Practical Medicine. Fundamental Principles based on the Science of the Spirit* (GA 27). Tr. A. R. Meuss. London: Rudolf Steiner Press 1996, Chapter I.

3. Johann Gottlieb Fichte (1762–1814). German philosopher.

4. This picture of glands (Drüsen) that secrete something leads two paragraphs further on to Rev. 16,2, in which English translations of the Bible speak of a 'grievous sore' and some German translations of a 'Geschwür' (a boil or abscess). Steiner, however, used Luther's word 'Drüse' (gland). For the purposes of this translation I have used the familiar 'sore', since a sore, like a 'temporary gland' also secretes matter. (Tr.)

Lecture Eighteen

1. William James (1842–1910), American philosopher.
2. Richard Heinrich Ludwig Avenarius (1843–1896), German philosopher. Ernst Mach (1838–1916), Austrian physicist and philosopher.
3. Karl Friedrich Eusebius Trahndorff (1782-1863), lived in Berlin. He wrote *Der Teufel—kein dogmatisches Hirngespinst— Offenes Sendschreiben an den Herrn Dr Sydow, Prediger an der Neuen Kirche zu Berlin* (The Devil—not a dogmatic chimera), Berlin 1853. Rudolf Steiner mentioned this also in *Necessity and Freedom* (GA 166). Tr. P. Wehrle. New York: Anthroposophic Press 1988, lecture of 25 January 1916.
4. K. F. E. Trahndorff *Ästhetik oder Lehre von Weltanschauung und Kunst*, Berlin 1827.

Appendix

1. R. Steiner *The Apocalypse of St. John. Lectures on the Book of Revelation*, op. cit.
2. Friedrich Rittelmeyer, see Publisher's Foreword, Note 2.

INDEX OF NAMES (* not mentioned by name.)

Alanus de Insulis 93, 272
Alexander the Great 60, 115
Aristotle 115
Arius 97, 99, 105, 272
Arthur, King 62–63, 246
Athanasius 97–99, 105, 272
Avenarius 252, 280

Bock, Emil 219, 269, 276, 277
Boehme, Jakob 185
Buddha 61

Constantine the Great 98–99, 272

Darwin, Charles 104, 168
Doldinger, Friedrich 191, 215, 219, 277

Fichte, Johann Gottlieb 242, 279
Fischer, Kuno 185, 276

Goethe, Johann Wolfgang von 185

Harnack, Adolf 104, 123*, 272, 274
Hegel, Georg Wilhelm Friedrich 230, 279
Hölderlin, Friedrich 144, 274
Homer 90*, 272

Ignatius of Loyola 81, 271

James, William 251, 279
Joachim of Floris 93, 272
Julian the Apostate 107, 272

Kant, Immanuel 43, 48
Katschthaler, Johannes 54*, 270
Klein, Johannes Werner 9, 190, 214, 219, 269

Lalande, Joseph Jérome de 226, 277
Lenin 198
Littrow, Joseph Johann von 228*, 278
Livy 185
Louis XIV 206
Lunacharski, Anatoli Vasilevic 198
Luther, Martin 270, 274

Mach, Ernst 252, 280
Masaryk, Thomas Garrigue 202, 276
Molay, Jacques de 114,
Moses 64

Nagler, Karl Ferdinand Friedrich von 229*, 279
Napoleon 200
Nietzsche, Friedrich 156

Plato 87

Rittelmeyer, Friedrich 3, 9, 214,
    258, 262, 268

Seebeck, Thomas Johann 185*,
    276
Steiner, Rudolf *(Works)*
  The Philosophy of Freedom
    194, 276
  Theosophy 194, 195, 276
  *Knowledge of the Higher
    Worlds* 72, 138, 193, 201,
    271

Occult Science 170, 275
The Course of my Life 156,
    274

Swedenborg, Emanuel 81, 271

Tagore, Rabindranath 49
Trahndorff, Karl Friedrich
    Eusebius 255, 280
Trotski, Lev Davydovich 198

Wilson, Woodrow 200